# THE ELEMENT ILLUSTRATED
# ENCYCLOPEDIA
## OF
# MIND
# BODY·SPIRIT
# & EARTH

# THE ELEMENT ILLUSTRATED
# ENCYCLOPEDIA
## OF
# MIND
# BODY·SPIRIT
# & EARTH

~ JOANNA CROSSE ~

# ELEMENT
## CHILDREN'S BOOKS

SHAFTESBURY, DORSET · BOSTON, MASSACHUSETTS · MELBOURNE, VICTORIA

First published in Great Britain in 1998 by ELEMENT CHILDREN'S BOOKS, Shaftesbury, Dorset, SP7 8BP

Published in the U.S.A. in 1998 by ELEMENT BOOKS INC., 160 North Washington Street, Boston, M.A. 02114

Published in Australia in 1998 by ELEMENT BOOKS and distributed by Penguin Books Australia Limited, 487 Maroondah Highway, Ringwood, Victoria 3134

Produced for ELEMENT CHILDREN'S BOOKS by PICTHALL & GUNZI LIMITED

*Edited by* Deborah Murrell
*Designed by* Dominic Zwemmer

*DTP Design* Yahya El-Droubie
*Design Assistance* Anthony Cutting
*Editorial Assistance* Jane Bawden

*Editorial Direction* Christiane Gunzi
*Art Direction* Chez Picthall

Reproduction by Colourscan, Singapore
Printed and bound in Italy by Graphicom

British Library Cataloguing in Publication data available

Library of Congress Cataloguing in Publication data available

ISBN 1-901881-10-5

Publisher's note:
This book uses American English spelling and punctuation.

# CONTENTS

## THE MIND

# THE BODY

# THE SPIRIT

# THE EARTH

# INTRODUCTION

IN MANY ways, the roots of this book go back a very long way. I remember as a child wondering why we were all here on Earth and if there was anything beyond it. I needed answers to my unending questions about us, the World, and the Universe. This thirst for knowledge has taken me on a fascinating journey in life to discover some of the mysteries of this amazing and extraordinary planet that we live on.

Some years ago, my husband and I decided to take a break from our television careers and go in search of a more meaningful life. Along with our two eldest children (the third one arrived at the end of that adventure!) we travelled the World for a year, living in eco-friendly and spiritual communities to see if we could find a better alternative to the stressful life that we had carved out for ourselves.

We didn't find any one answer, but instead we discovered a wealth of knowledge and experience that celebrated human potential and the Earth's natural resources in all sorts of new and exciting ways.

Back in Britain, we've been living in a spiritual community for over three years, but leading conventional lives in every other sense. It's been a wonderful adventure, with eye-opening results. Living a more holistic and more meaningful way of life has been both empowering and exciting.

Our three children, who are aged between 3 and 9 at the time of writing this book, have truly benefitted from increasing their knowledge about matters of the Mind, Body, Spirit, and Earth. It's added another dimension to their lives and has helped them to make more sense of the unexplained.

Here's a picture of a "dream diary." It appears in *Dreams and Visions*, which you can find on pages 16 and 17.

We've also found that more and more people from all walks of life are asking themselves those same questions that intrigued us – "Why?" "What if?" and "I wonder?" Realizing that spiritual values and powers are just as important as scientific and technological advances, people want to know more about the subjects that we have experienced and learned about.

So I wrote this book! In it, you'll find different theories about where we come from, where we go to after death, and lots about all the interesting bits in between!

This encyclopedia in no way tries to make any decisions for you. It's really a collection of thoughts, beliefs, and ideas about our World and the invisible worlds. This is a book of signposts, and it's totally up to you which road you choose to take. The most important thing of all is that you enjoy it!

JOANNA CROSSE

# ABOUT THIS BOOK

THESE TWO PAGES explain how this book works. As its name suggests, the encyclopedia is divided into four sections – the Mind, Body, Spirit, and Earth. One of the main topics from each of the four sections is shown below. To find out some more about a subject that interests you, look in the contents list at the front, or the index at the back.

## RUNNING HEADS
The running head is a way of finding the subject you want from within the four Parts. This one shows you that you're in the Mind Power section of Part One.

## THE MIND

THE MIND REPRESENTS our thoughts, intelligence, memory, and imagination, and it's also where we get our creativity and our ability to concentrate from. It's about our rational response to situations rather than our emotional response. In Part One we look at everything that's connected to the mind, and at the amazing abilities we all possess to do quite extraordinary things. For example, you can teach yourself to meditate, levitate, or bend spoons, just through the power of thought!

## INTRODUCTIONS
The introduction reveals the content of the page, discussing in general terms what you can learn from the subject. This one deals with Martial Arts, their origins, and their benefits.

## QUOTATIONS
The encyclopedia includes several quotations, which bring another dimension to the book. They are all chosen from well-respected sources and are directly related to the text.

## THE BODY

OUR BODY IS LIKE the engine of our being. It's also connected to what goes on in our minds, and people are beginning to see this more and more. Mental and physical health are essential in bringing harmony to the mind, body, and spirit. What we eat and how we live also has an enormous influence on our body. The many aspects of life, including birth, death, health, and healing are dealt with in Part Two.

## TRY IT YOURSELF BOXES
These boxed pieces of information encourage the reader to put his or her knowledge into practice, with step-by-step "try it yourself" instructions on a variety of different subjects.

# THE SPIRIT

JUST BECAUSE WE can't actually see our spirit or the energy field that exists in the Universe doesn't make it any less real. If it weren't for the spiritual part of ourselves, we might not be here at all! Spirit is about our connection with everything else – our ability to communicate with other worlds and our belief in a source, or God, of creation. In Part Three, we look at all things psychic, magical, and wonderful, and you'll have the chance to learn about reincarnation, mediums, miracles, magic, and oracles.

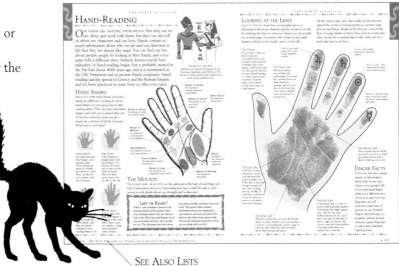

## SEE ALSO LISTS

Along the bottom of the page, you'll find a list of other topics in the book that relate to some of the information on the subject that you're reading about.

## PICTURE CAPTIONS

Captions accompanying the photographs and specially commissioned illustrations give the key facts and make learning simple and enjoyable.

# THE EARTH

IN PART FOUR, we take a look at the Earth we live on – not just the physical planet but our environment, our relationship with the animal, plant, and mineral kingdoms, and how our actions affect Mother Earth. The way that the planets and stars relate to the communities we live in is all part of our experience here on Earth. We take a look at how science and spirituality are moving closer together and find out how everything is connected to everything else! Subjects range from Feng Shui to Faith Systems.

## FACT BOXES

Fact boxes have a "Did you know?" flavor. They may inform the reader of something unusual or extraordinary to do with a subject that he or she takes for granted.

# GLOSSARY AND INDEX

AT THE BACK OF THE ENCYCLOPEDIA there is a detailed glossary of terms. This explains the meaning of all the unusual words and phrases that appear throughout the book. There is also a comprehensive index to make it easy to look up subjects that interest you, and a bibliography in case you'd like to find out more about a particular subject.

# THE MIND

# MEDITATION

ANYONE OF ANY AGE CAN MEDITATE, in any situation. It's a way of slowing down and getting in touch with that calm space inside. By using good breathing and concentration techniques, a few moments of silent meditation can help you relax both mentally and physically. It really does bring about a feeling of well-being, and helps us to get connected to the spiritual part of ourselves. Meditating also does us an enormous amount of good. There's evidence to show that people who meditate visit their doctor far less often than those who don't meditate.

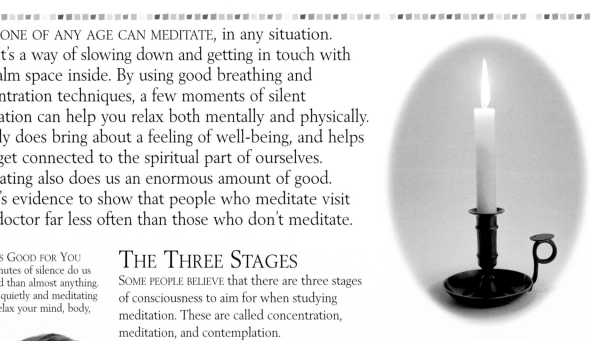

**SILENCE IS GOOD FOR YOU**
A few minutes of silence do us more good than almost anything. By sitting quietly and meditating you can relax your mind, body, and spirit.

**CONCENTRATION POWER**
A good way of meditating is to imagine an object, such as a candle flame or a flower. The idea is that you concentrate on this image and clear your mind of all other thoughts. As you do this, you begin to relax.

## THE THREE STAGES

SOME PEOPLE BELIEVE that there are three stages of consciousness to aim for when studying meditation. These are called concentration, meditation, and contemplation.

The first stage is to concentrate, or focus, on one thing, for example, a candle flame. When you concentrate for long enough, the second stage of meditation should happen naturally, and without any great effort.

During the second stage, you go beyond the chattering of your conscious mind, forgetting everyday chores and concerns. Thoughts drift slowly, and you begin to receive information from your subconscious mind.

The third stage is called contemplation, when not a single conscious thought crosses your mind. It may take years of practice, and people who reach this stage are said to be in touch with the pattern of the whole Universe.

This hand position is a visual sign representing the sound *"om."* Like the mantra itself, this sound helps concentration.

## BREATHE NATURALLY

BELIEVE IT OR NOT, many of us don't breathe correctly. We take shallow, quick breaths, as though we were nervous. Breathing more calmly can help us relax our mind and body and leave the worries of the day behind.

Buddhists believe that every breath we take should be a form of meditation. But they don't teach a way of breathing. Instead, they emphasize that you should breathe in the way that is natural to you. As you grow calmer during meditation, or sitting, your breathing will slow down and become deeper anyway.

Some people think that Zen Buddhism teaches breathing "from the abdomen." In fact, this way of breathing was used for a time in Japan when many monks had the lung disease tuberculosis. The disease made them cough during sitting, and breathing from the lower part of the lungs helped to stop their coughing.

**SHRI YANTRA MANDALA**
This Nepalese Shri Yantra mandala is about 300 years old. The four outer arms represent doors for the mind to enter or leave by during meditation. The triangles represent the male and female parts of the Universe, and they are surrounded by circles to unite them.

## MANDALAS

MANY PEOPLE, including Buddhists, use mandalas to help them meditate. Mandalas are symbols of the Universe. They're often in the shape of a circle or square and they contain complex and beautiful geometric patterns. Each part of the pattern has a special meaning, and is said to help the user to focus his or her mind on the Universe.

A mandala can be very useful as an object to concentrate on while you empty your mind of all other thoughts and begin to meditate.

## TRANSCENDENTAL MEDITATION

A FAMOUS HINDU teacher, or guru, called Maharishi Yogi developed a special way of meditating that allowed the mind to transcend, or go beyond, the physical limitations of the body. In this method, called transcendental meditation, people use a mantra to help them to become more aware.

## MANTRAS

A MANTRA IS A word or sound, usually one with a special meaning. In transcendental meditation you chant or repeat the mantra silently to yourself, concentrating on its meaning and your inner self at the same time.

One mantra that people often use in meditation is the phrase "I am." Another common mantra is the sound "om." It is a Sanskrit word made up of three letters – "a" is for waking consciousness, "u" is for dreaming consciousness, and "m" is for sleeping consciousness. This mantra is believed to wake up the three parts of our being and move us beyond the physical and onto the spiritual level.

## ZEN SITTING

ONE OF THE MAIN aims of Zen Buddhists is to live in the present, experiencing everything fully and seeing things as they are. A special form of meditation, called Zen Sitting, helps them do this. For a period of time they sit very still, in one of six positions. This allows the mind to be quiet. Zen masters sometimes call this "sitting like a mountain." While sitting, they become aware of all that surrounds them, the Earth, the sky – even the grass growing. After sitting still for long periods, the body needs to get moving again, so another technique is used, called Zen Walking. This is a slow, flowing motion that involves being aware of your contact with the Earth and all your movements. It also helps the blood circulate freely to all parts of the body.

> 66 *What does one think of while sitting?* a monk asked a Zen Master. *"One thinks of not-thinking,"* replied the Master. *"How does one think of not-thinking?"* asked the monk. *"Without thinking,"* said the Master. 99
> A ZEN BUDDHIST STORY

## YOGA

THIS FORM OF exercise uses many meditation techniques, so it is excellent for the mind and spirit, as well as the body. Some of the techniques you learn in yoga are posture, breathing control, and self-awareness. Using these techniques, yoga students hope to reach a state of super-consciousness.

Yoga not only relaxes your mind and body, but it also helps with balance, strength, suppleness, and coordination.

### IMAGINE A MANTRA

SIT QUIETLY AND comfortably and try to relax your mind. Think of a word or a sound that you particularly like, and repeat it over and over, either aloud or in your head. Try to concentrate on the word as you repeat it, and empty your mind of all other thoughts until you find yourself in a more relaxed and peaceful state. You can use this special word as your secret mantra whenever you meditate.

# SUPERSTITIONS

IF YOU'VE EVER OPENED an umbrella indoors, walked under a ladder, or gone out on Friday the 13th, superstitious people would say that you've tempted bad luck. They might even cross their fingers or knock on wood for good luck. Superstitions go back to ancient times, and they are a way of explaining the forces of Nature, or Fate. They're based on magic, religion, and folklore, and sometimes they actually work. If you believe something may happen, it's more likely that it will.

Superstitions can be powerful, because to a certain extent our lives are governed by our thoughts. Subconsciously, you can make your hopes or fears come true.

## LUCKY RITUALS

A LUCKY RITUAL IS doing something that you think will bring you luck. You might think that avoiding the cracks in the sidewalk will help you get a good grade, or score a goal. A well-known lucky ritual is knocking on wood, but it really doesn't matter what you do, because if you believe it'll help, it probably will.

## CHARM BRACELETS

THE CHARM BRACELET has been popular since the time of the Ancient Greeks. They wore gold and silver charms of all sorts hanging from chains around their wrists, just as we do today. The word "charm" comes from the Latin word *carmen*. This was a song or incantation that people chanted over an amulet or talisman to give it power and to make it "charmed." The charms on a charm bracelet are said to protect the wearer from harm, and bring them good fortune. Some people say that a charm that is given to you by someone else is luckier than one that you buy for yourself. Apparently the goodwill in the gift gives the charm extra power.

CHARM BRACELET
The charms on a bracelet are said to bring the wearer good luck and to keep bad luck away.

LUCKY NUMBERS
The most popular lucky number is seven, and the unluckiest is generally said to be 13.

ST. CHRISTOPHER
Patron saint of travelers, St. Christopher is said to have carried Christ across a river. A medallion or other jewelry with a picture of St. Christopher on it is supposed to keep you safe while traveling.

## AMULETS

FOR THOUSANDS OF YEARS, people in all parts of the World have worn charms called amulets to protect the wearer against evil spirits. These included garlic to protect against vampires, posies of flowers to protect against the Plague, and bells in a baby's crib to protect against evil spirits. The Ancient Egyptian sailors wore the symbol of a fish as an amulet, made from lapis lazuli or turquoise, to protect them against drowning. The image of an open hand was used as an ancient amulet against the Evil Eye. Amulets of all kinds are still used today.

ANKH
The ankh is said to represent the Key of Life and immortality. The Ancient Egyptians wore ankhs to give them a long life on Earth, and were even buried with them, ready for the afterlife. Since the 1960s the ankh has been a symbol of peace and truth.

KEY
These are a symbol of wisdom and maturity. In some countries, people are given a key when they reach 21. This represents the key to the door of the family home, and also to adulthood and responsibility.

 SEE ALSO: CRYSTALS PP.118-119, DEMONS AND DEVILS P.79, SIGNS AND SYMBOLS PP.138-139

# TALISMANS

WHEREAS AMULETS PROTECT YOU from bad luck, charms called talismans bring you good fortune. A rabbit's foot was said to bring good luck because of its contact with the Earth's energy. Sapphires and moonstones are believed to be powerful bringers of luck because of their ability to store and reflect light. The swastika, which means "good fortune" in Sanskrit, was a talisman in many Eastern cultures. It is now regarded as sinister since Nazi Germany adopted it as a symbol during World War II.

SCARAB
To the Egyptians, the scarab beetle is a powerful amulet. The bright blue color is often used in Eastern countries to put off evil, perhaps because the blue color is a reminder of the sky and, therefore, the gods.

BLACK CATS FOR LUCK
Many years ago at the Savoy Hotel in London, England, there were 13 guests at a dinner table. Some time later, the host was killed. This tragic news reached the Savoy and, ever since, if there is a party of 13, the waiters lay an extra place at table for Kasper, a black china cat.

## OMENS

THESE ARE EVENTS or sightings which are seen as predictions, either happy or otherwise. To many Native Americans, a black crow's feather is a symbol of death. In Christian countries, the shiny black plumage of the raven is a bad omen, as black is traditionally linked with Satan and sin. The number 13 is regarded as an unlucky omen, too. This is based on the fact that there were 13 people present at Jesus's Last Supper. In the story of *Jane Eyre*, by Charlotte Brontë, the old chestnut tree splits in a storm, and is an omen of the destiny of the two lovers. In different parts of the World, the same omen can have the opposite meaning. For example, in some countries a black cat crossing your path is a lucky omen and in others it's unlucky.

HORSESHOE
A horseshoe hung this way up is said to bring good luck. If it is hung upside down, it is said that all the luck will run out. Horseshoes are said to ward off the Evil Eye because they are made of iron, which is strong.

CROWS
The crow family has always been associated with omens and prophecy. Magpies in pairs are said to be symbols of joy, but if you see only one, it's a sign of sorrow. To the Norse people, the sight of a raven with its wings outstretched meant victory. It is said that if ravens desert their home, disaster will soon follow.

## EVIL EYE

THE POWER OF THE Evil Eye is one of the most widespread and ancient fears. It appears to be based on people's mistrust of those with an unusual appearance. In countries where most people were brown-eyed, blue-eyed people were seen as a threat. In countries where most people were blue-eyed, dark eyes were feared. Today many people in the Mediterranean and Middle East still wear charms in the form of eyes to protect themselves from the harm of the Evil Eye.

GARLIC
Like the cross, cloves of garlic are supposed to help ward off devils and vampires, perhaps because of their strong smell.

THE EYE OF HORUS
In Ancient Egypt the "Eye of Horus" was an amulet worn to outstare anyone who might have "the Evil Eye." Horus was the sky god. His left eye, or "wadjet" eye symbolized the power of light, and his right eye was his "solar" eye.

# DREAMS AND VISIONS

THERE ARE LOTS OF IDEAS ABOUT dreams and what they mean, but one worldwide belief is that we all dream when we're asleep, even if we don't remember it. Dreams have always been a source of fascination, and people once believed they were messages from the invisible world. In ancient times the interpretation of dreams was a great art, and we can see from the dreams and visions in the Bible that they were used to foretell the future. Today, some people believe that wherever we live we all share the same information, which we tune into when we're dreaming. This could explain why people dream about the same things the whole World over, from Africa to America.

## TYPES OF DREAMS

THERE ARE SO MANY sorts of dreams that people who study them divide them into groups. Here are some of the main types.

● CREATIVE DREAMS Many writers and artists are inspired by images that appear to them in dreams. Some of the best stories and paintings ever produced were created in this way.

● LUCID DREAMS This is when people are aware that they are dreaming and can actually control their dream – a bit like directing a film. It is an acquired skill, and some lucid dreamers claim that they meet up with each other in their dreams, then when they wake up they find they've dreamed about the same things.

● NIGHTMARES Dreaming about monsters can mean that there's something you're frightened of that needs to be confronted. A feeling that you can't move is often a sign that you feel stuck in a rut.

● PREDICTIVE DREAMS In these dreams the dreamers claim to be able to see into the future and predict certain events.

● RECURRING DREAMS If you have the same dream over and over again it usually means something's troubling you in your waking world, so try talking it through with someone to see if you can sort it out.

● SEXUAL DREAMS All of us can dream about sexuality and it's especially common during puberty. It is a perfectly natural thing to happen at this stage of our lives.

THE GOD OF DREAMS
In Greek mythology, the god Morpheus entered the mind by day or night to bring the precious gift of dreaming.

DREAMS MADE REAL
The famous psychologist Sigmund Freud believed that dreams reveal our most secret wishes. Whatever you think, it's fun figuring out what dreams might mean.

## KEEP A DREAM DIARY

WHY NOT MAKE A DREAM DIARY to see what your dreams might mean? As soon as you wake up write down or draw exactly what you remember from your dream. Then see if it fits in with any of the dream symbols described below. You can also try to dream your way through problems.

● BEFORE you go to sleep think about what it is that you want to resolve.

● IMAGINE how you could find the solution to the problem.

● IN THE morning write down or draw what you dreamed. You never know, great scientists, writers, artists, and politicians have found answers in their dreams.

# VISIONS

PEOPLE WHO HAVE VISIONS usually see a picture of something that will happen in the future. This may appear in a dream, or even when the person is awake. Many of those who have had visions believe they're messages from another world.

One of the best known visions in the Old Testament is Jacob's dream about angels on a stairway between Heaven and Earth. This vision convinced Jacob that he was in a holy land, which he named Beth-El. Mohammed was also given most of the words for the holy book, the Koran, in a vision.

In the nineteenth century a French girl called Bernadette Soubirous claimed to see the Virgin Mary in visions. In these, Mary told her about a healing spring near a town called Lourdes, in France. Each year millions of people from all over the World visit the spring, and many claim they have been cured of an illness or disease.

# DREAM SYMBOLS

THERE ARE MANY ways to understand dreams, so it's often best to follow your own feelings. Here's a guide to some of the common dream symbols.

● BIRTH can literally be a dream about a baby but it can also mean the start of something new in your life.

● BUILDINGS represent the self. If you dream about rooms and corridors you may be trying to understand yourself.

● CROSSROADS could mean there are many different paths to choose in life, and the markings on the signposts may help you to make a decision.

● DEATH is not always about the death of someone. It can mean the end of a phase of your life or the end of something that is no longer useful.

● FLYING is a classic symbol. It can come in the form of birds or airplanes, but the main theme is one of freedom.

● FOOD OR DRINK can pop up in a dream and, apart from meaning you're hungry or thirsty, it could mean that you need something extra in your life.

● GARDENS can represent how you're feeling, so if you dream about a garden try to remember how it looked, and whether it was full of flowers or not.

● MAPS can show us which way to go, and could be a sign of travel.

● MOUNTAINS can be symbols of what you want to do in life. They can also mean there are obstacles to overcome.

● NUMBERS are significant because each one has a different meaning.

● TREES are symbols of life, and they can also be about the family.

# IMAGINATION

THE PART OF OUR BRAIN that deals with our emotions and intuition also controls our imagination. This is the ability to create an image in our mind. We can call up any picture in the Universe, simply by imagining. It's rather like a mental paintbox that gives us total freedom to see what we want to see, and go where we want to go. Some people believe that the pictures their imagination creates are reality on another level, from another time and place. People see ships, castles, lakes, and other people, only to discover that they don't exist in what we call reality.

## USING YOUR IMAGINATION

OUR IMAGINATION IS a wonderful gift. It can give us a break from the stresses and strains of school work or chores at home! It's through our imagination that we can write wonderful words, draw amazing pictures, and tell tall tales. Some people discourage children from using their imagination, and this makes it harder for them to do so in later life. Luckily, we can train our imagination just by practicing. The more we use it, the easier it gets.

## DRAMA

WHEN YOU WATCH A play on television, where do you think the idea came from? Think of some of the great movies you've seen or the thrilling plots you've read in books. All of these began in someone's imagination.

## GO YOUR OWN WAY

WHAT YOU DO in your imagination can be just as much fun as what happens in reality. Your life can be as exciting and happy as you want, and you can choose the final outcome. Close your eyes and imagine you're at a crossroads. Go down each road in turn and see what happens! This mental exercise can teach you a lot about making choices in your life.

## MIND OVER MATTER

THE POWER OF THE mind is amazing. The statement "I am getting better and better every day" can be used in all sorts of situations. People who are sick but have a positive attitude are much more likely to recover than those who give up. For some people, positive thinking has literally been the difference between life and death.

## VISUALIZING

OUR IMAGINATION can really help us, if we learn how to use it properly. When people are sick, they are sometimes told to visualize an army attacking and defeating the diseased cells in their body. For many people, using their minds to create positive images like this works wonders.

 SEE ALSO: ANIMALS PP.114-115, DANCE PP.70-71, EMOTIONS PP.24-25, MIND POWER P.21, STORY-TELLING PP.40-41

# HYPNOSIS

THE WORD "HYPNOSIS" COMES from the name of Hypnos, the Greek god of sleep. Historians believe that the practice of hypnosis, or putting someone into a relaxed, trancelike state, was used long ago in Ancient Greek, Egyptian, and Indian civilizations.

Scientific studies have shown that at least one in five people can go into a deep, sleeplike state during hypnosis. These people will do almost anything they're told to do by the hypnotist. There are also those who can become very relaxed through hypnosis, or even go into some kind of a trance. Others simply don't respond to any suggestion!

## RELAXATION

THE FIRST THING the hypnotherapist does in a relaxation session is to make sure the patient is comfortable and feeling good about his or her surroundings. They then gradually talk the patient into a deeper state of consciousness, using visualization and suggestion. The patient doesn't lose sense of what's going on around him or her, but feels so relaxed that he or she doesn't notice it as much.

## ALTERED STATES

HAVE YOU EVER been at a sports match or other event, surrounded by clapping, chanting people, and felt light-headed? That's how it feels to reach an altered state. Groups of people can generate enormous power.

In some churches, people go into a group trance, and hand around dangerous snakes as a way of proving their faith. The trance, and the group, help to control their fear.

Many people believe that trancelike states can cure disease and sickness. People in African tribes use them to get in touch with their warrior spirits, or ancestors, and receive messages from the other world. Drumming can help an ill person go into trance and cast out their sickness. Shamans in South American tribes cure diseases while they are in an altered state, receiving information from the spirits.

## HYPNOTHERAPY

IN MODERN SOCIETY, MANY of us are highly stressed. This can lead to illness, but, for many people, learning to relax through hypnosis has solved the problem. In countries all over the World hypnotherapy is now an approved medical practice. People claim to have been cured of problems as varied as cancer, depression, phobia, and addiction after treatment using hypnotherapy. With the patient under hypnosis, a hypnotherapist can feed positive suggestions, such as giving up smoking, into the subconscious mind.

## WHO'S IN CONTROL?

MOST PEOPLE SAY that, even under hypnosis, people won't do anything they really don't want to do. However, some stage hypnotists persuade people to do things on stage that they would never normally do, such as eating raw onion. Many stage entertainers use special devices, such as a pendulum, or a ticking clock, to help their subjects to focus their minds.

## REGRESSION

MANY CULTURES AND FAITH systems believe that we have more than one life. This may be why we sometimes have fears or phobias we can't explain. For example, somebody who drowned in a former life might be afraid of water. Regression therapists use hypnosis to take their patients back to earlier in their life, or a former life, to trace the origins of a problem or anxiety. Once they know how and why the problem started, it's much easier to deal with.

SEE ALSO: DANCE PP. 70-71, EMOTIONS PP.24-25, MEDITATION PP.12-13

# EXTRASENSORY PERCEPTION

FOR A LONG TIME extrasensory perception, or "ESP," was used as a term for all sorts of psychic abilities through mind control. Nowadays, it means the ability to receive information through the mind without using any of our five physical senses of sight, smell, hearing, touch, and taste. People have talked about the subject of ESP for centuries, and many tests have been done to find out whether people can actually get information in this way.

A very simple example of ESP happens when you decide to call a friend and you dial the number only to find it's busy because they're trying to get hold of you!

## PRECOGNITION AND DÉJÀ VU

THE TERM "PRECOGNITION" is used when a person knows something before it happens. It's a psychic message, or "gut feeling," and it can relate to the person, someone close to them, or even the planet. Have you ever had a conversation, or been in a situation or a place that's felt strangely familiar? This is known as *déjà vu*, which is French for "seen before." Some people think that déjà vu is a memory from a past life.

## INTUITION

YOUR INTUITION IS your sixth sense, or the instinctive feeling that sometimes gives off mental alarm bells, and helps you to make decisions. If someone you're close to is in danger or sick, it's sometimes possible to sense things using your intuition. You might have a strong feeling that you need to contact that person for no obvious reason, or just decide to go around and see him or her without really knowing why.

There are times for all of us when we're in the company of someone whom we don't feel at all comfortable with. There might be no apparent explanation for this, but it could be your intuition warning you to keep away. It's a very useful tool in life, and it's well worth taking notice of.

## PSYCHOMETRY

THE ABILITY TO READ experiences, facts, feelings, and thoughts about someone from an object is known as psychometry. Thoughts are energy, so they have the power to make things happen. Our own energy can be stored in the objects around us – think of it as the object taking on some of our own vibrations. An old teddy bear, or a favorite piece of jewelry, for example, may have been with you through many different situations, both happy and sad. Some people believe that objects like these can actually record your experiences in life.

### FEEL THE FORCE

WHY NOT TRY PSYCHOMETRY for fun? You'll probably be surprised by the results! Hold an object, such as a piece of jewelry, that belongs to someone you're trying to get a "reading" from. Close your eyes, or simply concentrate on the object, and note any reactions you may feel. In order to receive the information you need to be relaxed, and open to any thoughts and feelings that you have when you're holding the object.

 SEE ALSO: LIFE FORCE AND ENERGY PP.90-91, PSYCHICS AND CLAIRVOYANTS PP.104-105, THE HUMAN BODY PP.50-51

# MIND POWER

THE HUMAN MIND CONTAINS our thoughts, memories, opinions, imagination, and ideas. We sometimes talk about our imagination "running away with us," to describe the feeling that we are not in command of our mind. But if we can learn to control our mind, rather than letting it control us, we can use its power to help us achieve all sorts of things. If your mind is saying you can't do something, it may be because other people have told you that in the past. If you change the message and tell yourself you can do it, more often than not you'll succeed.

**BENDING FORKS AND SPOONS**
People known as psychic metal benders demonstrate their power by bending spoons or forks in front of an audience. They seem to be able to do this with hardly any physical effort, although they often rub the metal gently with their fingers. People claim that focusing on the metal gradually makes it warmer, and soft enough to bend.

## LEVITATION

LEVITATORS CLAIM they are able to focus the mind and use its power to lift their body from the ground. The practice of levitation is often mentioned in Hindu writings, and it's a great achievement of mind over matter. There was a time when Roman Catholic monks and priests were famous for levitating, but it wasn't always when they wanted to! St. Joseph of Copertino, a Franciscan monk, was constantly levitating. Once, he took off in the middle of a church service and his sandals landed on the heads of the congregation!

**COMBINED POWER**
Some people claim they can levitate another person's body. The two people in the picture above appear to be combining their mind power to raise the girl's body off the ground.

## TELEPATHY

THE PRACTICE OF telepathy is being able to use the subconscious part of our mind to read someone's thoughts or to communicate to a person without even speaking.

All of us are capable of telepathy and you may well have done it without even trying – for example, if you've ever been in someone's company and found that both of you said the same thing at the same time. You can send pictures as well as words to another person's mind. You need to be able to clear your mind and focus on whatever you're trying to send. It helps if the other person's expecting a message from you, so that they can open their mind to your thoughts.

Scientists say that we only use a small part of our mind. This means either that a huge amount of it is not used, or that it's used for doing things that we can't yet understand.

## PSYCHOKINESIS

USING THE POWER of the human mind to move or change a physical object is known as psychokinesis. It includes the ability to bend spoons, stop or start watches, and move objects around, simply by using the power of the mind. Psychokinesis is a skill that gets better with practice. Some people think that when someone is using this skill, the magnetic field around him or her changes, and this is part of the energy that affects the objects he or she is focusing on.

One of the most well-known people to practice psychokinesis is Uri Geller, who is famous for stopping clocks and bending cutlery. He says the most important thing about psychokinesis is believing that you can do it. Children are great at doing this because they haven't become disbelievers like some adults!

### MIND MAIL

JUST FOR FUN, why don't you see if you can send a message or an image to someone? Make sure you're telling yourself you can do it and remember to visualize what you want to send in your mind before you attempt to mail it off!

The most important thing is to be absolutely clear about what you're trying to communicate. If you're not sure what you want to send, then obviously the picture or message that's received the other end is going to be fuzzy, a bit like a poor telephone line. Sometimes it helps to look at a picture of the image you are trying to send. It can also help to tell the person that you are trying to transmit something!

SEE ALSO: HYPNOSIS P.19, IMAGINATION P.18

# PERSONALITY

THE PART OF US that makes each of us individual and special is usually described as our personality. It's the way we think and behave. Although we're all different, there are some basic personality types, known as "enneagrams." These are part of an ancient system that emerged from the Middle East. We all have a certain set of personality traits that serve us during life, especially if we understand ourselves and make the best of our assets.

## KNOWING YOURSELF

IF YOU KNOW MORE about yourself, you can learn to accept who you are, including any negative traits. Learning to understand your own strengths and weaknesses helps you to understand other people too. If you're sensitive and can often feel other people's pain, you'll probably be appreciated for being kind and caring. However, you might need to learn how to separate your own feelings from those of other people.

The journey of discovering ourselves is a fascinating trip, and a lifetime's work. But the more we know ourselves, the easier life will be. Understanding who you are is a bit like being given a mental tool bag. If you know that certain things upset you then you can find the tools to deal with situations where you feel more vulnerable – or, even better, you may be able to avoid putting yourself in them in the first place!

## ECCENTRICS

AN ECCENTRIC personality is unusual, and may seem a bit odd. The word eccentric literally means "not centered." We might say that people are eccentric if, for example, they have a great deal of money but never spend it, or if they spend it on unusual objects that most of us would not want. Eccentric people are often very outgoing, and they can enjoy giving their opinion on almost anything and everything!

## SELF-CONFIDENCE

NEARLY EVERYONE WOULD like a bit more confidence, or faith in his or her personality. A lack of self-confidence can cause difficulty and confusion. Some people seem to be born confident and sociable, but for most of us these are personality skills that we build up as we get older. By coming to understand who we are, and by appreciating the way other people see us, we can begin to make sense of our lives, develop our strong points, and worry less about our weaknesses.

### THE NINE ENNEAGRAMS

HERE ARE THE BASIC characteristics of each enneagram. Of course each of us has more qualities than these. We may even start off with one character type and change or add others as we grow older. Which type, or types, are you?

● PERFECTIONISTS These are idealistic, hardworking types with strong principles.

● HELPERS These people are caring, kind, and sensitive.

● SUCCEEDERS These are happy-go-lucky, energetic, and ambitious people.

● ROMANTICS These people are loving, perceptive, and sensitive.

● OBSERVERS These types are inquisitive, and enquiring factfinders.

● ADVENTURERS These types have lots of energy and enthusiasm.

● QUESTIONERS These people are loyal, trusty, and responsible.

● ASSERTERS These are confident, direct, and independent people.

● PEACEMAKERS These people are talkative, perceptive, and harmonious.

# INTELLIGENCE

WE ARE ALL INTELLIGENT in different ways. You don't have to be a genius to be inventive, creative, or practical. Men and women have different sized brains, but that doesn't affect how bright we all are. The development of artificial intelligence means that computers can now do tasks that, in the past, only a person with strong academic skills could do. If this development continues, people with strong emotional or social intelligence may become more valuable in society, because these kinds of intelligence cannot be programmed into a computer easily.

## COMMON SENSE

DO YOU KNOW PEOPLE who are incredibly brainy, yet couldn't boil an egg for themselves? Or maybe someone who seems very sensitive and tuned into other people's feelings but isn't so successful in the classroom? Reliable, dependable, practical types – people with common sense – are vital in our World. We wouldn't have achieved what we have if people didn't have different types of intelligence.

## ACADEMIC INTELLIGENCE

WE ARE ALL GOOD at different things in life, and academic subjects are no exception. Most people have favorite subjects, such as languages or sciences, and they are best at these. Some people are good at a wide variety of subjects, whereas others seem to have difficulty with anything academic. Both groups of people need equal amounts of support in their different ways, so that every individual can develop his or her abilities as fully as possible.

STEPHEN HAWKING
Famous for his work on how the Universe began and the different kinds of matter contained within it, Professor Stephen Hawking is one of the World's most brilliant scientists. He is also a fine example of victory over severe physical disability, and an example of how modern technology serves us all by enabling him to communicate his immense knowledge to the rest of us through his computer.

## EMOTIONAL INTELLIGENCE

BEING IN TOUCH WITH your feelings, knowing what they are and how to deal with them, shows emotional intelligence. Anger, for example, can be a useful feeling if we know how to express it and use it correctly. But if it's out of control it can be very destructive. It's important for all of us to learn how to listen to our emotional self, get the message, and express ourselves appropriately. Emotions are there to help you and they're never wrong. Being aware of your own feelings and those of others is a gift in itself.

## SOCIAL INTELLIGENCE

IT'S IMPORTANT TO DEVELOP our social intelligence because it helps us to mix, make friends, and work with other people. Sometimes the brightest of people lack social skills, and the way they behave means that they can't get along easily in a group. We develop our social intelligence through mixing with other people. Other people's reactions tell us whether we have done or said something funny, interesting, upsetting, or ridiculous. We use and build on this information to improve our social skills throughout our lives.

SEE ALSO: EMOTIONS PP.24-25, THE HUMAN BODY PP.50-51

# EMOTIONS

■■▪▪●▪■□■▪▪■■▪▪●▪■□■▪■▪▪■●▪■□▪■▪▪■●▪■□▪■▪▪■●▪■   ▪▪■■▪▪

SOMETIMES OUR EMOTIONS seem to spring up from nowhere. We can be bursting with happiness, filled with fear, or boiling with anger. Emotions are triggers, or launch pads for action. They are automatic responses to situations, and cause biological reactions in our body, such as moving away from a dangerous situation.

Our feelings have a powerful effect on the body, and that's why there's such emphasis today on being in touch with our emotions and expressing them openly. Laughter can solve many problems, and even helps cure illness. Smiling makes the brain release chemicals that make you feel happy.

POSITIVE ANGER
Anger isn't always negative.
A mother's anger often stems from love. It's possible to convert anger into energy and determination to achieve great things.

## EXPRESSING EMOTION

THERE'S EMOTION IN just about everything we do, including listening to music, watching a movie, celebrating, or grieving over the loss of a loved one. However, for many years, some cultures have encouraged us to hide our emotions, and this has caused all sorts of problems.

We can usually see how people are feeling from their facial expression, hand gestures, or behavior. Watching a sad movie makes most of us cry, but some people hold back their tears, because they don't want others to see them. People who don't express their emotions can build up tension and anxiety, and can become sick.

Recently, it's become much more acceptable to show our emotions, even from an early age, and nowadays children and young people are more open about their feelings than they were a hundred years ago. These days, it's popular to go to a therapist, and learn how to express yourself.

However, it isn't always appropriate to express your innermost feelings, and doing so may even hurt someone else. We all need to learn when it's O.K. to be expressive, and when it might be better to keep quiet. Our emotions are a way of measuring up a situation, and we can learn to use them, together with our rational mind, to everyone's advantage.

# TYPES OF EMOTION

● FEAR This is a feeling of distress which can be caused by a sense of danger or pain. It can give us the sensation of our blood running cold. The brain's emotional centers go on full alert and we're ready for action!

● ANGER If we're angry, our heart rate goes up and our blood starts rushing, so we have loads of energy. Anger can be an opportunity to release negative feelings but only if we use it positively.

● HAPPINESS This is a feeling of joy and lightness. Happiness wipes out any negative emotions that might be lurking around us, and it can help us to feel more energetic. It can also give us enthusiasm, and a sense of determination to achieve.

● SADNESS We probably wouldn't be able to appreciate happiness if we didn't ever feel sad. Sadness lowers our energy levels and can make our lives feel dull and gray instead of bright or colorful. But it is necessary to be sad sometimes, such as when we are grieving over a loss of some kind.

● HATE Some people say that there's a thin dividing line between love and hate, and that if you feel strongly enough to hate someone, it's not far off from loving them. Hate is a passionate response that can come from a resentment toward someone or something.

● COMPASSION To care for others is to be compassionate. It's not to be confused with pity, which is feeling sorry for someone but being helpless to do anything. Compassion can help us to help others.

# FEARS AND PHOBIAS

WE ALL KNOW WHAT it's like to feel anxious. Phobias are an extreme form of anxiety. People have phobias about all sorts of things, from deep water to great heights! Phobics tend to avoid situations they fear, but this is a sure way to keep the phobia going. One fear can also lead to another. Some aquaphobics don't like flying because planes usually have to go over water!

Some people think that phobias come from past lives. Someone who drowned in a previous life might fear water in this life. This might explain an otherwise illogical phobia.

# LOVE

THERE ARE many different types of love. Some people say that love in a spiritual sense is the basis of all creation. Without love we would be nothing.

The range of love, like all feelings, is incredibly wide. Worldly love can include feelings of tenderness for someone else. Parental love is said to be unconditional, which means that mom and dad love their children no matter how they behave or what they do. We can fall desperately in love with someone, and we can care for and sympathize with many people. We can love animals, and sometimes even objects, such as a cuddly toy! It's important in life that we also learn to love ourselves, despite our faults. In a physical sense, love has the opposite effect on our body from that of fear and anger. It can give us a real sense of warmth, calm, and well-being.

## FACE YOUR FEARS

PHOBIA IS A RECOGNIZED condition and there's a wide range of help available, including hypnotherapy. The best way to treat a phobia that won't go away is to face the problem and understand where it's coming from. Most phobics are aware of what makes them afraid, and they might even know why.

They can help themselves by confronting their fear, especially with the support of friends and family. Some people, for example, are phobic about snakes because they think they're cold and slimy to touch. In fact, snakes are dry and warm. With the help of friends, you can overcome your fear just by touching a snake once!

# ADDICTIONS AND OBSESSIONS

THERE ARE MANY KINDS of addiction, and as many substances to become addicted to. An addiction is a habit that is very difficult to give up. An idea or thought that is continually in someone's mind is called an obsession. We can obsess about ourselves, our houses, another person or persons – almost anything, in fact. Addicts and obsessors often lack something in their lives. However, it is possible to get all the answers and contentment we need, just by taking time to go inside ourselves.

**NO FUN AT ALL**
Drugs and alcohol might seem like fun things to try but they are potentially dangerous and damaging, and can ruin a person's life.

## ADDICTIVE PERSONALITIES

PEOPLE WITH ADDICTIVE personalities can get hooked on almost anything, from glue to exercise. They may be more susceptible to habit forming, whether it's watching TV, smoking, or working late. Addiction can be a wrong road we've taken on our spiritual journey, with whatever it is we're addicted to acting as a replacement for something we really need, such as stability, friendship, or other support. The answer often lies in developing our inner strength and self-esteem, loving ourselves, and accepting ourselves for who we are.

**SMOKE HARMS**
Smoking harms the heart, blood vessels, and lungs, and affects all the tissues in the body.

**PASSIVE SMOKING**
People who are around smokers, and breathe in their smoke, are also harmed by it.

## DRUGS

A DRUG IS ANY CHEMICAL substance that affects the organs of the body. Drugs include medicines prescribed to treat diseases, and remedies to cure minor ailments. Many foods and drinks, such as coffee, tea, cola, and chocolate, contain small amounts of drugs. Certain drugs can alter our mood and give us temporary relief from unwanted feelings. Unfortunately, some people take mood-altering drugs for pleasure rather than as a medication. These substances have been glamorized to appear exciting, but they are not. They can change your behavior drastically, so that you are no longer being true to yourself. Drugs can also lead to chronic dependency, personality change, and criminal behavior. People who take drugs for fun may find themselves addicted, in jail, or going through terrible withdrawal symptoms in an attempt to kick the habit. A much better answer is to look at whatever is making you unhappy or dissatisfied and to try to do something to change it.

## TOBACCO

THE TOBACCO THAT'S USED in cigarettes, cigars, and chewing tobacco has strongly addictive properties. It contains nicotine, which is a harmful drug. Some youngsters take up smoking because they believe it looks good and makes them seem grown-up. The truth, as any adult smoker (who's probably been trying to give up for years) will tell you, is that it's an expensive habit that makes your clothes, hair, and breath smell and, more importantly, can lead to heart disease and chronic respiratory problems.

# ALCOHOL

ALTHOUGH ALCOHOL IS legal in many countries, it is also a drug. For an adult, drinking socially can be a pleasure. Drinking too much turns the pleasure into a problem. Often people become dependent on drink because they don't have much self-confidence, and find that a drink can help them feel better. But that feel-good factor doesn't always last and as time goes on they need to drink more to achieve the same effect. As with any drug, it's a vicious circle. In the end it's down to us to learn to feel O.K. about who we are and what we're doing with our lives.

ALCOHOL
Many people enjoy a glass of wine or beer occasionally but more than a couple of drinks in a day can be harmful.

# OBSESSIVE BEHAVIOR

LIKE ADDICTION, OBSESSIVE behavior is a dependency, and it often takes a habitual form. Repeatedly dusting shelves or tidying up might reveal an obsession with cleanliness – or it could be a need to keep busy. Obsessive behavior usually fills a gap in someone's life. The solution is to find out where that gap is, and to develop a more appropriate way of filling it, such as finding a new interest in life.

CONSTANT CLEANING
Cleanliness is a common obsession. It may begin with someone being very house-proud, or wary of catching a disease, but it can develop into an obsession. People who continuously clean their houses, or repeatedly wash their hands, and feel ill at ease when they are not doing so, may well be obsessive.

# DRINK OR DRUG?

COFFEE, TEA, COLA, and cocoa contain a drug called caffeine. This boosts physical energy, gives you a mental lift, and is one of the most popular drugs in the World. In fact, coffee first came to Europe from Arabia as a medicine, rather than a drink. However, more than a few cups a day can literally make you shake or find it difficult to sleep, and can even cause heart disease.

CHOCOLATE
The cocoa in chocolate causes the release of chemicals in your brain, called endorphins, which make you feel good. Unfortunately, the effect doesn't last long.

COFFEE
One or two cups of coffee in the morning can improve your brain power for up to six hours – more may make you feel very ill!

TABLETS AND PILLS
Some tablets or pills that are prescribed by doctors can be addictive, such as certain anti-depressants.

# EATING DISORDERS

WE NEED FOOD TO LIVE, and mealtimes can be special times with our family and friends. Sadly, for some people eating is not an enjoyable, sociable event, but the opposite. Eating disorders such as anorexia, bulimia, and compulsive eating seem to be increasingly common. It's easy to blame newspapers, magazines, and television for their images of slim, beautiful, happy people, and say we feel obliged to try to be like them. But eating disorders are really about our feelings. If you find yourself using food or anything else as a prop, just ask yourself, "What am I trying to run away from? What am I afraid of?" If you think it through you'll get some of the answers you need so that you can begin dealing with the problem.

## TRY SOMETHING ELSE

PREVENTION REALLY IS better than cure. It's usually very easy to start a habit but it's never as easy to give it up.

If you think you have a dependency or an addiction, or you know someone else who does, you may be able to do something about it. Recognizing that you have an addiction to something means that you're more than halfway to dealing with it. These days there is plenty of help available through counseling and various organizations, so it should be possible to get the care and support that you need.

Talking to family or your friends about addiction can often be far more help than you would ever imagine. The first step you can take is just to try talking to someone else about it.

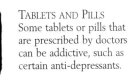

# EDUCATION

WHAT WE LEARN AT SCHOOL is only a small part of our education. Everything in the World has some kind of lesson we can learn. Going for a walk can teach us about Nature. With other people we learn how to make friends, share things, and support each other, how to express ourselves, and how to care for others.

We learn best when we are enjoying our learning. For example, to win a swimming race you need to put in hours of practice. If you didn't enjoy the practicing, you wouldn't be successful at the sport.

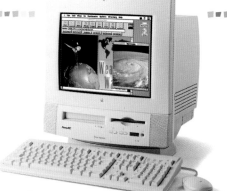

GLOBAL LEARNING
Today, the computer is one of our most useful teaching aids. With the introduction of the World Wide Web, people in many parts of the globe can now be linked by computer. This enables us to learn new skills, share information, make friends, and swap ideas on masses of different subjects.

## LIVING AND LEARNING

SOME PEOPLE BELIEVE that life in itself is an education. Earth is sometimes described as being like a school. That's probably why we have to go through so many varied experiences, including all of life's ups and downs. If things were good all the time we wouldn't learn to appreciate them. Equally, if we only had bad times we wouldn't be able to experience joy and happiness. Life is full of opposites. In a way, opposing situations bring about a sense of balance. The many and varied experiences that are put in front of us give us endless opportunities for educating ourselves.

When we are infants and children our parents look after us. They guide us through childhood and adolescence as we learn about our World. As we mature, our relationship with our parents changes constantly, and we may end up looking after them. This is a learning opportunity for all concerned.

LIFE'S LESSONS
Education is not just about going to school. It's about becoming aware of our surroundings, and learning about all the other life forms that share the planet with us.

# WHY SCHOOL?

AT ONE TIME, AND in some countries still, people thought it was pointless to send children to school if the only way for them to earn their living was by learning a trade, for example, becoming a blacksmith. It was better to become an apprentice, and learn and work at the same time. Today, a general education is seen as a good thing for everyone. For example, by being able to read, a farmer can learn about modern developments, and may be able to improve his working methods. We can still learn after leaving school by becoming an apprentice, but many schools include crafts and practical skills, such as woodwork, in their normal curriculum. Schools also teach more formal subjects, such as math. Exams are less important to people than they once were.

FINDING OUT IS FUN
The easiest way of learning about something new is when you're enjoying yourself and having fun.

# LEARNING THROUGH PLAY

THE KINDERGARTENS of Germany were set up by Friedrich Froebel in the 1830s because he believed children learned through play. He invented lots of toys specially for schools, and the pupils were encouraged to care for animals and plants, and to sing and play games! This proved to be such a popular form of teaching, for the teachers as well as the children, that there are now kindergartens all over the World.

# ALTERNATIVE EDUCATION

HOW WOULD YOU LIKE to go to a school where you did what you liked, when you liked? These days there are many such "free" schools.

A.S. Neill believed there was no such thing as a bad child, only an unhappy one. He said that if children were encouraged rather than punished, they would flourish, and he was proved right. Today, allowing a child to direct his or her own education is encouraged by many teachers and parents.

In America, John Dewey disliked late 19th century schools, where the children sat still, listened to their teachers speak, and learned facts by heart. In his schools, children learned by doing experiments and making things. American schools today owe a lot to people like Dewey.

Some teaching methods take into account the whole mind, body, and spirit aspect of education. Two of the most famous ones are the Steiner and Montessori schools.

# MONTESSORI

MARIA MONTESSORI believed that children should learn through their own initiative. She introduced a method of teaching where children decide what they want to do in the classroom. The teacher acts as a support and guide to the children but lets them get on and try things and retry things so that they build up levels of inner confidence and feelings of self-esteem, or feeling good about oneself.

# STEINER

RUDOLF STEINER wanted to encourage the development of a person's spiritual side through science, philosophy, arts, and religion. Steiner believed that people developed most in the first seven years of life, and that during that time the emphasis should be on play, color, and Nature rather than on training the mind.

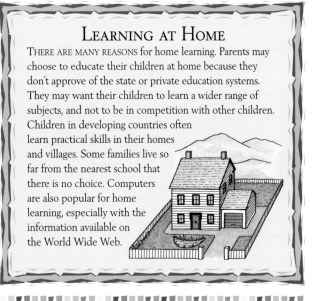

## LEARNING AT HOME

THERE ARE MANY REASONS for home learning. Parents may choose to educate their children at home because they don't approve of the state or private education systems. They may want their children to learn a wider range of subjects, and not to be in competition with other children. Children in developing countries often learn practical skills in their homes and villages. Some families live so far from the nearest school that there is no choice. Computers are also popular for home learning, especially with the information available on the World Wide Web.

# PHILOSOPHY

THE WORD PHILOSOPHY means "love of wisdom." To find wisdom you need to ask questions, and the most famous philosophers, from Socrates to Sartre, have asked very simple questions, such as "Why are we here?" "Where do we come from?" "What happens to us when we die?"

Our early ancestors had to struggle just to survive. They didn't have time to wonder if they really existed! In today's World, most of us don't have to protect ourselves from dangerous wild animals or worry about where the next meal's coming from. So we have the luxury of time and space to start asking questions about life. That's why philosophy is seen to be a mark of a civilized society.

> " *If a man will begin with certainties, he shall end in doubts; but if he will be content to begin with doubts, he shall end in certainties.* "
> FRANCIS BACON

## ASKING QUESTIONS

WE ARE ALL BORN philosophers. You only have to listen to a small child to hear the question "Why?" over and over again. Grown-ups will often start by answering the questions with the word "because," but as they run out of answers the conversation often ends with the simple statement "Just because!" Somewhere along the way most of us grow up to accept the answer "Just because!" and we stop being philosophers.

If you enjoy asking questions, don't be put off by the fact that you don't always get the answers you want. Keep asking and you may end up a philosopher.

## PHILOSOPHERS

- PYTHAGORAS Pythagoras was one of the first Greek philosophers. He believed that there was a harmony in the Universe and that everything related to numbers.
- CONFUCIUS The philosopher Confucius believed that knowledge was found in people, not in something mystical. He was in favor of education and an orderly society.
- ARISTOTLE Aristotle believed that we should strive for the good in life, and happiness for all people, but he realized that different things made different people happy.

- SOCRATES Socrates thought that all truth is within our souls. He strongly encouraged his pupils to think for themselves.
- PLATO Plato believed that evil was really lack of knowledge, and that finding out how to live a good life was like solving a math problem.
- SHANKARA The Indian thinker Shankara thought that Brahma, the self, was the only reality. Everything else was due to a lack of knowledge.
- LAO-TZU The Chinese philosopher Lao-tzu felt that we should follow the Tao, or way of life, and live in harmony with the Universe.

- FREUD The Austrian physician Freud believed that we are all driven by unconscious needs and desires, which our conscious mind can't always control.
- JUNG The Swiss psychiatrist Jung invented the idea of a "collective unconscious." This suggests that the same ideas and mythical events are found in the unconscious minds of everyone in the Universe.
- SARTRE The French philosopher Sartre believed that existence is the only important thing, there is no higher meaning, and we are each responsible for our own life.

# CONSCIOUSNESS

BEING CONSCIOUS IS being awake, or having an awareness about ourselves and the World. Awareness of others and their feelings develops into our conscience, a set of mental rules that controls the way we deal with people.

The unconscious mind is hidden from us, but it can give our conscious mind information and experiences. If you go into an altered state of awareness you can discover all sorts of things about yourself that you didn't know.

Somewhere between the conscious and the unconscious mind is the subconscious. This contains information that we are only aware of in the form of instinctive reactions, or habits. The subconscious affects our everyday life and it can control our actions without our conscious knowledge.

> " Whoever saves
> one life saves
> the World entire. "
> TALMUD

## SELF-AWARENESS

FOR THE FIRST FEW WEEKS of our lives, we have no self-awareness at all. We can't tell where our body ends, and the rest of the World begins. Gradually we develop a sense that we are separate. Physical characteristics help us to see ourselves as individuals and recognize others. We may share some of our opinions, beliefs, and dreams with others, but each of us is different, and special.

Throughout life, every thought, sight, sound, and smell we experience helps to make up our awareness. As we grow older and learn new things, most of us change our beliefs and attitudes to the people and things around us. This is our self-awareness developing.

## RAISING AWARENESS

HAVE YOU EVER felt really angry, upset, even outraged, by something you've heard on the radio or seen on the television? It's your social consciousness that makes you angry. Environmental campaigners raise people's awareness of issues that concern our planet and the lives of future generations. Campaigners have much more power in a group than they would by themselves. It's by raising awareness of important issues that civilization moves on. Who knows what the future holds? Maybe the next campaign could be one for equal rights and votes for children!

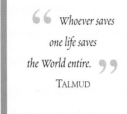

PEOPLE POWER
Peaceful marches can be a positive way for people to get together and show how they feel about issues that affect us all. This kind of "people power" makes us all more aware of what's going on in the World.

### PSI TIME

ONE WAY OF "switching off" from the hustle and bustle of our everyday life is to go into an altered state of consciousness, called "Psi Time." In psi time we are more able to receive help from the Universe. You can try the following exercise any time.

Make sure you're sitting comfortably, shut your eyes, and relax. Then imagine yourself turning a switch off, or imagine a blank screen. You may find images appearing on that imaginary screen, or it may stay blank. After a while you should find yourself moving into "the gap," which is supposed to be the area between Heaven and Earth. You'll feel your mind clearing and your anxieties slipping away as you begin to see things as they really are.

SEE ALSO: DREAMS AND VISIONS PP.16-17, ENVIRONMENT PP.110-111

# ASTROLOGY

THE STUDY OF THE Sun, Moon, and planets and their influence on us here on Earth is called astrology. You've probably read your horoscope in a newspaper or magazine. For lots of people it's good fun to look up their "forecast" for the day and see what's mapped out for them. The word astrology comes from the Greek words *astron*, meaning "star," and *logos*, which means "knowing." Astronomy, the scientific study of the stars, and astrology were closely linked for a long time, but in the 17th century, new scientific evidence split the two.

## MAPPING THE HEAVENS

SINCE ANCIENT TIMES, PEOPLE have tried to understand the patterns and movements of stars, planets, and moons. They help us to measure time and predict the seasons. Unusual events, like comets and meteors, are useful as reminders of a particular year, and are often seen as omens, or signs for the future. In most countries of the World, the stars and planets are named after the gods and goddesses of the people – probably because of their place in the sky, or Heaven. The planet Neptune, for example, is named after the Ancient Roman god of the sea. Venus is named after the goddess of love.

## WHAT ASTROLOGERS DO

AN ASTROLOGER WORKS OUT your chart or horoscope by using your date, time, and place of birth. This shows the position of the Sun, Moon, and planets at the exact time of your arrival on planet Earth!

The wheel of the zodiac acts as a kind of clock. Depending on where and when you were born, the planets will have a particular effect on your personality and your life. It's as though you chose a window through which to come into the World. In astrology, everyone has a unique chart, because the Sun, Moon, and planets will never be in the same spot for anyone else.

### CAPRICORN THE GOAT,
*EARTH SIGN*
*(December 22-January 20)*
Like the goat, those born under the sign of Capricorn will climb mountains to achieve their ambitions. Capricorns can be serious, responsible types. This sign is linked to the skeleton of the body, and these types like to have structure in their lives. Capricorns can sometimes be shy and reserved.

### AQUARIUS
THE WATER CARRIER, *AIR SIGN*
*(January 21-February 18)*
Aquarians are independent souls and communicators with a strong need for equality. They're humanitarians who care about the World as well as themselves. Aquarians are connected to the blood so they like to move new ideas!

### PISCES THE FISHES, *WATER SIGN*
*(February 19-March 20)*
Pisceans are usually very sensitive and can be dreamy. As a result, they can find it hard to face reality, and can be weak-willed and easily led. Pisceans are caring types who often love music and art. They rule the feet!

### ARIES THE RAM, *FIRE SIGN*
*(March 21-April 20)*
If you were born under Aries you're friendly and probably have an adventurous spirit, full of energy. You can be brave, and come up with lots of ideas. Aries is linked to the head so you may be quite headstrong.

### TAURUS THE BULL, *EARTH SIGN*
*(April 21-May 21)*
Taureans are usually practical, down-to-earth types who love Nature. They're loving and strong and, like the bull, can be stubborn! Taureans make good singers because this sign is linked to the throat.

### GEMINI THE TWINS,
*AIR SIGN*
*(May 22-June 21)*
Geminians, like their sign, often seem to have two personalities, but they can see both sides of an argument! They're great communicators and are adaptable and lively. Gemini rules the lungs, hands, arms, and shoulders, which means they can be good with their hands but are restless.

# THE ZODIAC

HAVE YOU EVER NOTICED when you look up into the sky at night that the stars appear to form shapes and patterns? These patterns are known as constellations. The constellations relate to the twelve signs of the Zodiac. The word Zodiac is Greek for "circle of life." Each constellation has a name that describes its shape in the sky, and human beings are said to take on the characteristics of the "Sun sign" that they were born under.

## SAGITTARIUS THE ARCHER,
*FIRE SIGN*
*(November 23-December 21)*
Sagittarians love to find out about things and always rise well to a challenge. They are optimistic types, have a good sense of humor, and are great thinkers. People born under this sign can get restless so travel is often high on their agenda. Sagittarius is linked to the thighs.

## SCORPIO THE SCORPION, *WATER SIGN*
*(October 24-November 22)*
As a water sign, Scorpios can have very strong, but hidden feelings.

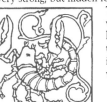

They are often powerful people who are fascinated by the mysteries of life. Scorpios can be jealous types but this often encourages them to do well in their own life. This sign is linked with the sexual organs.

## LIBRA THE SCALES, *AIR SIGN*
*(September 23-October 23)*
Fairness is a typical characteristic of this sign. Librans need beauty, balance, and harmony, although they can be indecisive. Romance and relationships are very important and a Libran would much rather make peace than war! The physical area is the kidneys.

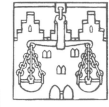

## VIRGO THE MAIDEN, *EARTH SIGN*
*(August 24-September 22)*
Practical, tidy, and efficient sums up Virgoans. They are perfectionists, so they can sometimes be critical of others. They can make fine artists, teachers, or writers. Virgoans are usually keen on keeping fit. This sign is linked to the intestines.

## LEO THE LION, *FIRE SIGN*
*(July 23-August 23)*
Leos are proud and strong and they often have great leadership qualities. They can also be bossy! Leo is linked with the heart which means anyone born under this sign is usually warm and big-hearted!

## CANCER THE CRAB,
*WATER SIGN*
*(June 22-July 22)*
Our feelings are often linked with water, and Cancerians can be emotional types who hide away like the crab when their feelings are hurt. Cancerians are kind, sensitive people but they can be moody. This sign's linked to the womb, which can mean that Cancerians like caring for others, and make very good parents.

# SUN AND MOON SIGNS

THE BIRTH CHART is divided into 12 "Houses," or sections which describe different aspects of our everyday lives. Our Sun sign is the House in which the Sun could be seen at the time of our birth. It is the guiding force in our lives, and has an exciting, strong, masculine energy. Each Sun sign, which is the main part of an astrology reading, represents a part of the body and certain characteristics.

The Moon, which moves around the Earth and through the Zodiac, is about the emotional side of our being. Our Moon sign has a feminine energy which shows us about our habits, our childhood, and our inner feelings.

Other planets that influence an astrology reading are Mars, Jupiter, Saturn, Uranus, Neptune, and Pluto.

## TWO FAMOUS SUN SIGNS
THE MAHATMA GANDHI, the political reformer, was born October 2, 1869. Like many Librans, Gandhi hated injustice and was sociable and sensitive to others. Diana, the late Princess of Wales, was born July 1, 1961. In many ways, she was a typical Cancerian. Home-loving, strongly maternal, and idealistic, she was known to be a person who loved unreservedly.

# CHINESE HOROSCOPES

ORIENTAL ASTROLOGY IS EVEN older than Western astrology, and has been in use for thousands of years. Apart from sharing the word "astrology," the two systems are quite different. For a start, they use different calendar systems. The signs of the Zodiac used in Western countries are arranged in a 12-month cycle, whereas the cycle of the East uses a 12-year cycle, with each sign named after an animal. In fact, if you take into consideration the animal of each year, and the five elements that also influence it, the full Chinese cycle takes 60 years to complete!

## HOW IT WORKS

THE CHINESE DAY IS divided into 12 equal hours, each of which lasts for two Western hours. The animal linked to the hour of your birth tells you about your outer self, or the personality you show to others.

The animal of the year in which you were born, together with the element and the Yin or Yang forces, tells you about your inner self, or your true personality. To get a full reading, you must take into account both the year and the hour of your birth.

## WHAT ANIMAL ARE YOU?

THE ANIMAL OF THE HOUR of your birth describes your outer self. The hour of birth has been important in astrological readings for thousands of years, but the hours were only recently given the names of animals. Look at the list below to work out which animal you are. The hours shown are standard time, so if you were born in summer, or daylight-saving time, you need to work out the standard hour of your birth first.

23:00-00:59 Rat
01:00-02:59 Ox
03:00-04:59 Tiger
05:00-06:59 Rabbit
07:00-08:59 Dragon
09:00-10:59 Snake
11:00-12:59 Horse
13:00-14:59 Sheep
15:00-16:59 Monkey
17:00-18:59 Rooster
19:00-20:59 Dog
21:00-22:59 Pig

## OX
If you're an Ox then you're reliable and strong. Oxen enjoy working hard but can be determined and stubborn. They enjoy home life and make good and loyal friends.

## TIGER
Tigers are courageous, passionate, and freedom-loving. They'll stick by their decisions and their friends. Tigers enjoy a challenge, but they can sometimes overdo things!

Yang years are described as positive and active. They are linked with daytime, fire, and the Sun. The even years, such as 1998, are Yang years.

## RABBIT
Rabbits are tidy, sociable, tactful, emotional, and sensitive. They avoid argument and can be hurt by criticism. Rabbits have a sense of fun and enjoy fashion, the arts, and beautiful things.

## DRAGON
Dragons can be fiery creatures. They enjoy attention and adventure, and are confident and enthusiastic. Dragons are easily stressed, but they're optimistic, and prone to taking risks.

THE YEAR 2000
The Western millennium, the year 2000, will be a Metal Dragon year, influenced by the positive qualities of the Yang. Dragon years are generally dramatic in character, and often contain great projects and extraordinary events. There may be important worldwide developments. The Dragon brings good fortune, so a Dragon year is a good time to start a new project or business.

## RAT
Rats are bright and sociable, and see both sides of an argument. If you're a Rat, you're probably brave, resourceful, and a natural leader. Rats are also charming, good with money, and enjoy travel and home life too.

## SNAKE
Snakes enjoy a party, but also need their own space. They are calm, intuitive people, interested in the mysteries of the Universe. A Snake loves luxury and finds it easy to relax.

 SEE ALSO: ASTROLOGY PP.32-33, LIFE FORCE AND ENERGY PP.90-91, THE ELEMENTS P.123, MILLENNIUM P. 143

# THE INNER YOU

THE ANIMAL FOR EACH year influences worldwide events and the inner personalities of those born during that year. Each year is associated with an element as well. For example, there are five kinds of rabbits – Metal, Water, Wood, Fire, and Earth rabbits.

The qualities of the elements are:
Metal – strength
Water – sensitivity and persuasion
Wood – imagination and creativity
Fire – passion and energy
Earth – practical skills and stability.
Use the table below to work out the animal and the element for the year of your birth.

## PIG

Pigs, or Boars, are great fun and utterly dependable. They would rather give than receive. Peace, harmony, holidays, and food are their favorite things. The Pig usually has plenty of friends and very few foes.

## DOG

Dogs are loyal and helpful, but they can worry and hang on to resentments. Dogs are honest, cheery types who rate friends more than money or status.

## ROOSTER

Roosters enjoy dressing up for parties. They're outspoken, but dependable, and make good and honest partners – it's said that a Rooster's heart is made of gold.

Yin years are described as negative and passive. They are linked with night, water, and the Moon. The odd years, such as 1999, are Yin years.

## MONKEY

Monkeys are quick thinking, clever, and chatty. They also have lots of interests, and are curious and good fun to be around. Monkeys often have jobs in the world of finance.

## SHEEP

Sheep, sometimes called Goats, love art, music, nature, and their home. They are charming, shy, and sympathetic, caring deeply about others, but can also be rather manipulative.

### NAMING THE YEARS

According to legend, just before the Buddha left this World, he invited the animals to celebrate with him. Only 12 of them arrived. The Ox was leading the way, but the Rat ran ahead and arrived first. The Buddha decided to reward the twelve animals by naming a year after each of them, in the order of their arrival. Each cycle of twelve years begins with the Rat, and ends with the Pig.

## HORSE

Honest, lively, and popular, the Horse is ruled by its heart. It tends to be physically strong and optimistic. Horses love freedom, travel, and change, and can be impulsive, but trustworthy.

| Year | Dates from and to | Animal | Element | Aspect |
|---|---|---|---|---|
| 1936 | January 24, 1936 - February 10, 1937 | Rat | Fire | + Yang |
| 1937 | February 11, 1937 - January 30, 1938 | Ox | Fire | - Yin |
| 1938 | January 31, 1938 - February 18, 1939 | Tiger | Earth | + Yang |
| 1939 | February 19, 1939 - February 7, 1940 | Rabbit | Earth | - Yin |
| 1940 | February 8, 1940 - January 26, 1941 | Dragon | Metal | + Yang |
| 1941 | January 27, 1941 - February 14, 1942 | Snake | Metal | - Yin |
| 1942 | February 15, 1942 - February 4, 1943 | Horse | Water | + Yang |
| 1943 | February 5, 1943 - January 24, 1944 | Sheep | Water | - Yin |
| 1944 | January 25, 1944 - February 12, 1945 | Monkey | Wood | + Yang |
| 1945 | February 13, 1945 - February 1, 1946 | Rooster | Wood | - Yin |
| 1946 | February 2, 1946 - January 21, 1947 | Dog | Fire | + Yang |
| 1947 | January 22, 1947 - February 9, 1948 | Pig | Fire | - Yin |
| 1948 | February 10, 1948 - January 28, 1949 | Rat | Earth | + Yang |
| 1949 | January 29, 1949 - February 16, 1950 | Ox | Earth | - Yin |
| 1950 | February 17, 1950 - February 5, 1951 | Tiger | Metal | + Yang |
| 1951 | February 6, 1951 - January 26, 1952 | Rabbit | Metal | - Yin |
| 1952 | January 27, 1952 - February 13, 1953 | Dragon | Water | + Yang |
| 1953 | February 14, 1953 - February 2, 1954 | Snake | Water | - Yin |
| 1954 | February 3, 1954 - January 23, 1955 | Horse | Wood | + Yang |
| 1955 | January 24, 1955 - February 11, 1956 | Sheep | Wood | - Yin |
| 1956 | February 12, 1956 - January 30, 1957 | Monkey | Fire | + Yang |
| 1957 | January 31, 1957 - February 17, 1958 | Rooster | Fire | - Yin |
| 1958 | February 18, 1958 - February 7, 1959 | Dog | Earth | + Yang |
| 1959 | February 8, 1959 - January 27, 1960 | Pig | Earth | - Yin |
| 1960 | January 28, 1960 - February 14, 1961 | Rat | Metal | + Yang |
| 1961 | February 15, 1961 - February 4, 1962 | Ox | Metal | - Yin |
| 1962 | February 5, 1962 - January 24, 1963 | Tiger | Water | + Yang |
| 1963 | January 25, 1963 - February 12, 1964 | Rabbit | Water | - Yin |
| 1964 | February 13, 1964 - February 1, 1965 | Dragon | Wood | + Yang |
| 1965 | February 2, 1965 - January 20, 1966 | Snake | Wood | - Yin |
| 1966 | January 21, 1966 - February 8, 1967 | Horse | Fire | + Yang |
| 1967 | February 9, 1967 - January 29, 1968 | Sheep | Fire | - Yin |
| 1968 | January 30, 1968 - February 16, 1969 | Monkey | Earth | + Yang |
| 1969 | February 17, 1969 - February 5, 1970 | Rooster | Earth | - Yin |
| 1970 | February 6, 1970 - January 26, 1971 | Dog | Metal | + Yang |
| 1971 | January 27, 1971 - January 15, 1972 | Pig | Metal | - Yin |
| 1972 | January 16, 1972 - February 2, 1973 | Rat | Water | + Yang |
| 1973 | February 3, 1973 - January 22, 1974 | Ox | Water | - Yin |
| 1974 | January 23, 1974 - February 10, 1975 | Tiger | Wood | + Yang |
| 1975 | February 11, 1975 - January 30, 1976 | Rabbit | Wood | - Yin |
| 1976 | January 31, 1976 - February 17, 1977 | Dragon | Fire | + Yang |
| 1977 | February 18, 1977 - February 6, 1978 | Snake | Fire | - Yin |
| 1978 | February 7, 1978 - January 27, 1979 | Horse | Earth | + Yang |
| 1979 | January 28, 1979 - February 15, 1980 | Sheep | Earth | - Yin |
| 1980 | February 16, 1980 - February 4, 1981 | Monkey | Metal | + Yang |
| 1981 | February 5, 1981 - January 24, 1982 | Rooster | Metal | - Yin |
| 1982 | January 25, 1982 - February 12, 1983 | Dog | Water | + Yang |
| 1983 | February 13, 1983 - February 1, 1984 | Pig | Water | - Yin |
| 1984 | February 2, 1984 - February 19, 1985 | Rat | Wood | + Yang |
| 1985 | February 20, 1985 - February 8, 1986 | Ox | Wood | - Yin |
| 1986 | February 9, 1986 - January 28, 1987 | Tiger | Fire | + Yang |
| 1987 | January 29, 1987 - February 16, 1988 | Rabbit | Fire | - Yin |
| 1988 | February 17, 1988 - February 5, 1989 | Dragon | Earth | + Yang |
| 1989 | February 6, 1989 - January 26, 1990 | Snake | Earth | - Yin |
| 1990 | January 27, 1990 - February 14, 1991 | Horse | Metal | + Yang |
| 1991 | February 15, 1991 - February 3, 1992 | Sheep | Metal | - Yin |
| 1992 | February 4, 1992 - January 22, 1993 | Monkey | Water | + Yang |
| 1993 | January 23, 1993 - February 9, 1994 | Rooster | Water | - Yin |
| 1994 | February 10, 1994 - January 30, 1995 | Dog | Wood | + Yang |
| 1995 | January 31, 1995 - February 18, 1996 | Pig | Wood | - Yin |
| 1996 | February, 19, 1996 - February 7, 1997 | Rat | Fire | + Yang |
| 1997 | February 8, 1997 - January 27, 1998 | Ox | Fire | - Yin |
| 1998 | January 28, 1998 - February 15, 1999 | Tiger | Earth | + Yang |
| 1999 | February 16, 1999 - February 4, 2000 | Rabbit | Earth | - Yin |
| 2000 | February 5, 2000 - January 23, 2001 | Dragon | Metal | + Yang |
| 2001 | January 24, 2001 - February 11, 2002 | Snake | Metal | - Yin |
| 2002 | February 12, 2002 - January 31, 2003 | Horse | Water | + Yang |
| 2003 | February 1, 2003 - January 21, 2004 | Sheep | Water | - Yin |
| 2004 | January 22, 2004 - February 8, 2005 | Monkey | Wood | + Yang |
| 2005 | February 9, 2005 - January 28, 2006 | Rooster | Wood | - Yin |
| 2006 | January 29, 2006 - February 17, 2007 | Dog | Fire | + Yang |
| 2007 | February 18, 2007 - February 6, 2008 | Pig | Fire | - Yin |

# CALENDARS

PEOPLE HAVE BEEN FINDING ways to measure time since the beginning of history. Knowing what time or season we are in gives us a way of controlling our lives, telling us when to do certain tasks, and when to celebrate events. The years, months, and days that make up a calendar can be based on almost anything, as long as it happens on a regular basis. Many peoples measured the year by the appearance of a star in a particular place in the sky, or how long it takes the Earth to orbit the Sun.

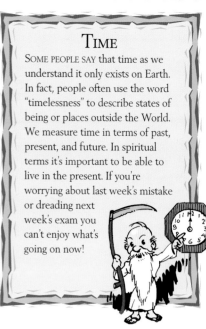

### TIME
SOME PEOPLE SAY that time as we understand it only exists on Earth. In fact, people often use the word "timelessness" to describe states of being or places outside the World. We measure time in terms of past, present, and future. In spiritual terms it's important to be able to live in the present. If you're worrying about last week's mistake or dreading next week's exam you can't enjoy what's going on now!

## GREGORIAN CALENDARS

THE ORIGINAL Roman Calendar was based on the lunar or Moon cycle, but Emperor Julius Caesar introduced the Julian calendar, which measured time by the Earth's journey around the Sun. Later on, a team set up by Pope Gregory XIII made the system more accurate, and it became known as the Gregorian calendar, which is still used in most of the Western world today.

The most recent calendar system is the Baha'i calendar. Baha'i people want everyone to adopt it to show that we're all linked. The 19 months in a Baha'i calendar represent divine qualities such as Beauty, Light, Power, and Knowledge. The seven days are Glory, Beauty, Perfection, Grace, Justice, Majesty, and Independence.

## TYPES OF CALENDAR

● ASTROLOGICAL  The astrological calendar is based on the movements of the planets. It's said that the position of the planets at the time of our birth influences our whole life.
● CHINESE  People in China use the modern Gregorian calendar for their business lives, but the traditional lunar calendar for celebrations. Each year is represented by one of 12 animals.
● BUDDHIST  Early Buddhists adopted the Hindu calendar and, as Buddhism spread, each group adapted it to their own needs. Many calendars measure time from the death of Buddha.
● HINDU  The traditional Hindu year is split into four months. Modern Hindu calendars use the same months as the astrological calendar, with Sanskrit names.
● MUSLIM  People of the Islamic faith use a lunar calendar. The ninth month is very important to Muslims because a month-long fast, called Ramadan, starts with the full moon.
● JEWISH  The Jewish calendar has 12 months, with a 13th month put in seven times during a 19 year cycle. The most important day of the week is the Sabbath, Saturday.

## EARLY CALENDARS

IN THE EARLY YEARS of human society, people needed to know what season was coming next, and how soon. This told them what the weather would be like, and whether or not to plant crops. A wise person, perhaps a priest, might check the position of the stars to find out what part of the year it was. Later, people wanted to know the dates of important religious festivals, such as the birth or death of a leader. The wise people learned to be more accurate, and some began to record what they knew in the first written calendars.

### SOLSTICES AND EQUINOXES
The January solstice is the longest night in the northern hemisphere and the longest day in the southern hemisphere. The July solstice is the longest day in the north and the longest night in the south. The March and September equinoxes are when day and night are equal in length. In many cultures, solstices and equinoxes provided the dates of important religious ceremonies.

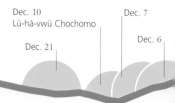

Dec. 10
Lü-há-vwü Chochomo

Dec. 7

Dec. 21

Dec. 6

 SEE ALSO: FAITH SYSTEMS PP.130-133, PLANETS AND STARS P.122

# CENTRAL AMERICA

THE MAYAN AND AZTEC cultures in Central America worked from two calendars, based on the movements of the planets, and a sacred almanac. The Mayan Haab, or 365 days consisted of 18 months, each of which had 20 days. This left five unlucky days, which the Mayas called *uayeb* and the Aztecs *nemontemi*, or "days left over and profitless." The religious calendar had only 260 days, so although the two calendars meshed together to form a very accurate dating system, they began on the same day only once every 52 years. Not surprisingly, when this happened there was a very important feast!

Highly decorated calendars like this one were used to calculate the years, months, and days in Central America.

This calendar would have been carved from stone.

# DAYS

ACROSS THE WORLD, early peoples decided that a day included a period of light, and a period of darkness. When it began and ended was more difficult. Ancient Babylonian, Egyptian, Chinese, and Hindu people began and ended their day at sunrise. Ancient Hebrews measured from sunrise to sunrise, and the Romans from midnight.

# MONTHS

THE ROMANS began all their months at a fixed time, and they soon didn't match up to the Moon's phases. Every two-and-a-half to three years, the Roman, and therefore our Gregorian calendar, has two full moons in one calendar month. The second is called a Blue Moon, a term also used for other rare events.

# LEAP YEARS

THE MAYANS REALIZED THAT the solar year was slightly longer than 365 days, and they developed a very accurate way of compensating for it, by adding an extra day into certain years. This system of leap years was developed over 1000 years earlier than the equivalent European system.

# UNWRITTEN CALENDARS

CULTURES WITHOUT A WRITTEN language found other ways to record time. North American tribes counted the days by making notches on sticks, and some counted and named the moons. For example, "Wild Goose Moon" was the time when wild geese were seen in the sky. The Sioux tribe, who remembered their years by the winters, named 1834 the "Winter of Meteor Shower." For tribes who lived in the same place all year, such as the Hopi and Zuñi, the horizon provided a perfect way of measuring time. The Zuñi Sun-priest watched for the Sun's position at dawn, and compared the shadow of their sacred mountain with a man-made column, so that he knew when the people should begin preparing the fields. A Hopi Sun-priest watched at sunset, tracking the Sun against a set of positions on the horizon. He knew that the winter solstice would happen around eleven days after the Sun set in the position of Lü-há-vwü Chochomo.

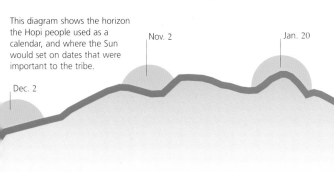

This diagram shows the horizon the Hopi people used as a calendar, and where the Sun would set on dates that were important to the tribe.

Nov. 2

Jan. 20

Dec. 2

Jan. 25

Sun sets over Cuñopove Feb. 17

# ART AND MUSIC

WHEN WE MAKE A work of art, we use our skills and creative imagination to express something that we feel. We can be inspired by an emotion, or a beautiful landscape. Have you ever seen a picture or heard a piece of music that's brought tears to your eyes? That's the power of transcendence, where we are affected so deeply by something that we feel as though we are taken outside of ourselves. The arts have a kind of power that can really change our lives. Recently people have begun to use this power to fantastic effect in various forms of healing and therapy.

## THE MAGIC OF MUSIC

LISTENING TO MUSIC can really change your mood! Sometimes, if you're feeling low, it's tempting to play slow, sad music, but this will probably make you feel worse! An uplifting tune or a cheerful song can instantly improve your energy levels and your emotional well-being.

## BEING CREATIVE

ART, IN ANY FORM, is a way of expressing yourself from the depths of your being. Early people used the walls of their caves for some amazing creative visualization! They drew pictures of what they wanted to happen, such as the capture of some animal in a hunt. They hoped that the drawings could help bring about what they wanted to happen in real life.

Throughout the history of art, people have drawn what they'd like to be true, as well as what was true, or real. It's fine to draw an idealized view of the World, or to copy things that you see in real life.

You can also work the other way around, and paint or draw exactly what you feel, then try to work out what the images mean. Sometimes you may find that they work as symbols, which can help you to understand feelings that you might not otherwise recognize.

ROCK PICTURES
These ancient stone carvings in Namibia were created thousands of years ago.

### AN INNER SELF-PORTRAIT

GET SOME PAPER AND colored pens or crayons together, then sit in a comfortable position, close your eyes, breathe deeply, and relax. After a while, an image may come to you. Focus on it, and when you're ready, open your eyes and try to draw what's in your head. Use the colors that feel right, rather than the colors that look right on the paper.

The colors and the strokes you use to draw the object, for example, hard, solid strokes, or light, feathery ones, may show you lots of different things about yourself. It's all open to interpretation. You could try the exercise with a friend, then interpret each other's pictures afterward.

## HEALING ARTS

YOU MAY FIND DRAWING, painting, or playing an instrument "therapeutic," or healing. Across the World, people are using art in therapy to help those with physical, mental, or emotional problems. They're having very good results, too. There are many different types of therapy, including some that use imagery to express emotions that people find difficult to talk about. Other types of therapy use music as a way of learning to communicate more freely and work with a group of people.

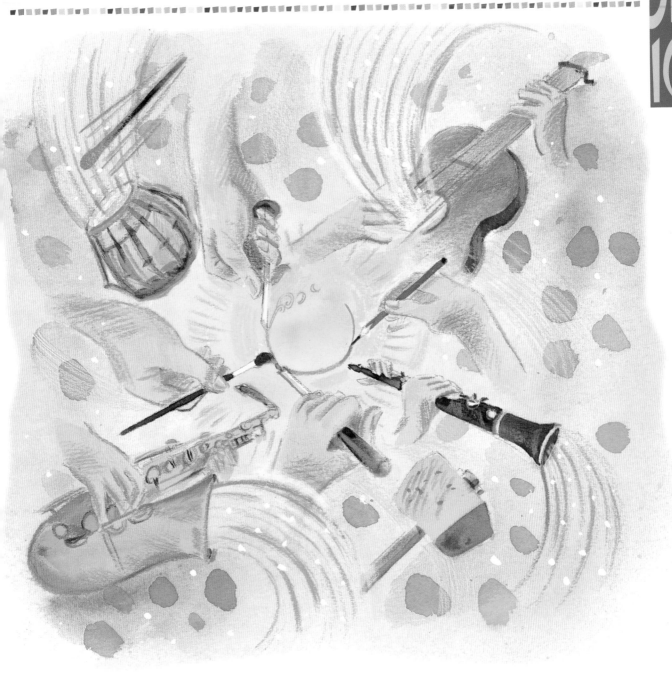

# EXPRESS YOURSELF

THERE ARE TIMES WHEN all of us feel like taking our temper out on a set of drums and, in fact, it would almost certainly help us to feel better. Unfortunately, it's not always possible to express yourself quite so loudly, especially with other people around, but all forms of art and craft can help you to release tension and let out your inner feelings. Singing, playing an instrument, painting, or making something allows us to express how we feel, without having to use words.

Of course, these are just some of the many different ways we can express ourselves. Creativity of all kinds allows us to let go of some of our anger or fear, and make space for happier, more positive emotions. In fact, learning a new artistic skill can act like a safety valve to avoid stress in the first place, and practicing it keeps our stress levels low. If we constantly release our emotions by being creative, we're less likely to become upset by life, and we're better able to deal with a crisis when it happens.

# NEW AGE MUSIC

COMBINING THE musical styles of different cultures and playing them on electronic instruments, such as a synthesizer, produces a kind of music known as "New Age." The rhythm is usually quite slow, so that it has a relaxing effect on the person listening to it. Some musicians also add natural sounds, such as whalesong, birdsong, waves, or gentle rain, to help produce a feeling of calm and relaxation. New Age music is often played in healing centers to help relax the patients.

# STORY-TELLING

ONE OF THE MOST ancient arts in human history is that of telling stories. Before people had a written language, they shared information by speaking to each other. Stories passed on the history of the tribe or race, and taught people about their ancestors and their beliefs. There are still peoples whose history is recorded like this, in the mind, rather than in writing. A story-teller needs a good memory, and skill with language and expression.

## STORY-TELLERS

EVERYONE ENJOYS listening to a good story, and throughout human history, story-tellers have been highly valued, respected members of society. Even today in most parts of the World, a person who can tell a good story is greatly appreciated. In the past, a story-teller would have to memorize all the history and myths of his or her culture, then pass them on to the next generation.

## BARDS

CELTIC POETS who told legends in verse about their tribes, were known as "bards." The Celts, who lived in Europe from about 750 B.C. to A.D. 100, didn't have a written language but they had an alphabet called the Ogham. They may have used this for passing on messages. The spoken language of the Celts was very sophisticated and their story-tellers, or bards, were highly regarded. They had to study for many years before they were allowed to perform, and they had to learn the whole history of the tribes they belonged to.

STORIES AROUND THE FIRE
In many parts of the globe, people still gather around the fire to listen to stories or hear the news. Story-tellers are still important members of society, especially in remote places, where people have no books or newspapers. A story-teller has to have a good imagination and an excellent memory.

## FOLK TALES

FOLK TALES ARE often passed down through many generations of family and friends, and can be hundreds of years old. They're often about people and their homes, and animals, or they may be about the local neighborhood. Folk tales are just as interesting as fairy tales, but they're different because they don't contain the powerful psychological meaning that fairy tales do. *The Story of the Little Red Hen* is a well-known animal folk tale.

### THE STORY OF THE LITTLE RED HEN

ONE DAY THE LITTLE RED HEN found some corn. She was excited, and said to her friends, a dog, a cat, and a rat, "we can plant these ears of corn, and when it grows, we'll make flour and bake a cake." "I'm too tired," said the dog. "I can't get my paws dirty," said the cat. "I'm far too busy," said the rat. So the little red hen planted the corn by herself. When the corn grew, she asked her friends to help cut it to make it into flour. They made the same excuses as before. So the little red hen did it by herself. When the flour was ready, she asked her friends to help carry it, but they made excuses. So the hen brought the heavy bag of flour home all by herself, and baked a cake. When the dog, cat, and rat walked by, they smelled the cake baking, and went into the kitchen. They looked at the cake and said, "Oh, what a delicious cake you've made. We can all sit down and enjoy it." The hen said to the dog, "You're too tired to eat it." To the cat, she said, "This cake isn't good enough for you," and to the rat, "I'm sure you're too busy." Then she sat down and ate the cake all by herself.

 SEE ALSO: DEMONS AND DEVILS P.79, EDUCATION PP.28-29, MAGIC PP.86-87

# FAIRIES AND ELVES

PEOPLE WHO'VE SEEN FAIRIES say they're like tiny people, with delicate, colored wings. There are many stories of fairies dancing around together in rings. Fairies are linked with one of the four elements – fire, earth, air, or water, and they work closely with Nature. They have magical powers, which they use to help the plant, animal, and human kingdoms. However, there are some mischievous fairies, who use their power to play naughty tricks on others! Elves are also spirits of Nature, but are said to be larger than fairies. "Light" elves are kind, happy creatures, who live in the air. They are famous for helping Santa with the presents at Christmas. "Dark" elves are rather gloomy and unpleasant, and are said to live underground.

**PICTURE A FAIRY**
Most of us imagine fairies to look a bit like this one, with a flowing gown, dainty wings, and a magic wand. This fairy is from a painting by John Atkinson Grimshaw called *Spirit of the Night*.

# FAIRY TALES

SOME PEOPLE BELIEVE that fairy tales, such as *Cinderella* or *Little Red Riding Hood* are only useful for sending children to sleep. Recently, however, people have become more aware that these stories contain basic truths about how humans think and behave. Changing the stories can actually be damaging. For example, at a school in Chicago, U.S.A., traditional fairy tales were rewritten and told without some of the elements, such as the violent scenes in which heroes and heroines fought with the monsters. The children who had been told only the new versions had much more difficulty accepting the way that other people behaved in everyday life.

**JACK AND THE BEANSTALK**
THE STORY OF Jack and the Beanstalk is one of the best-known fairy tales. The tale describes how, as a boy grows up to be a man, he must eventually leave his mother's protection and go out into the big, wide World. This can often appear to be a frightening thing to do, like facing the giant, which is what Jack has to do in the story. But if the boy is prepared to use his cunning and his common sense, then he can overcome even the most frightening problem. In this fairy tale, each time Jack has the courage to climb up the beanstalk to the giant's house, he is rewarded with gold, a golden goose, or a harp. Finally Jack masters his fear and lives happily ever after.

# AESOP'S FABLES

DO YOU KNOW THE story of *The Tortoise and the Hare* or *The Dog in the Manger*? These wonderful stories were written down long ago by the famous Ancient Greek, Aesop. They are usually grouped under the title of *Aesop's Fables*, although Aesop probably didn't make them all up himself, but perhaps collected at least a few from other people!

Fables are different from folk tales and fairy stories because they are stories with a moral. The idea is that they teach the reader what sort of behavior is good, and what sort of behavior is bad, from the point of view of living with other people in a civilized society.

**THE TORTOISE AND THE HARE**
ONE OF AESOP'S FABLES IS ABOUT A HARE who teased a tortoise for being slow. The tortoise surprised the hare by challenging him to a race. The hare accepted, and boasted that he would win easily. Soon the hare was so far ahead of the tortoise that he decided to stop for a nap, and fell asleep. The tortoise plodded on, slowly but surely, and overtook the hare. Just as he was getting to the finish line, the hare woke up, and ran as fast as he could, but he was too late. The slow, steady tortoise had won the race.

# MYTHS AND LEGENDS

PEOPLE HAVE ALWAYS TRIED to understand the World and how it works. Myths and legends often explain events, like a great storm or battle. Some cultures tell their myths and legends through dance, without using words. Generally, myths are stories about gods, goddesses, and other superhuman beings, and legends deal with people who perform heroic feats. Myths and legends pass on beliefs from one generation to another, and help people to understand their roots.

## DREAMTIME MYTHS

ONLY 40 YEARS ago there were Aboriginal peoples living in Australia whose lifestyle had been the same for 20,000 years. Their myths are very important because they can show us what people thought about the World all those years ago.

Aboriginal myths are about what people call the Dreamtime, which exists on two levels, the past and present, the visible and invisible. The people believe that each part of their land was created through a sacred song. Each tribe member has a sacred part of land to visit and care for and to sing its song to. Like other ancient peoples, Aborigines are very close to the Earth and see animals as their relations.

## THE GIFT OF SONG

ONE DREAMTIME MYTH TELLS HOW the Creator gave gifts to the animals. He gave the gift of song to the frog, who became full of himself and forgot to thank the Creator. The frog told the other animals his song would charm the Moon from the sky, so they gathered to watch. The Creator learned what the frog was doing, and took away the gift. When the frog tried to sing, a harsh croak came out. He was so ashamed he dived into the pond and hid in the mud. The song was in the form of a piece of string, which the Creator picked up. Then He noticed the lyrebird, who hadn't been given a gift. The Creator snapped off a piece of string and threw it to the bird. To this day the lyrebird sings more sweetly than any other creature.

 SEE ALSO: GODS AND GODDESSES PP.44-45, STORY-TELLING PP.40-41

# MYTHICAL BEASTS

LEGENDS ARE FULL OF TALES of mythical beasts, often fantastic to look at and with special talents, such as strength, intelligence, or courage. Some of them are on the side of goodness, and help rescue people in danger, or give good advice. Others are on the side of evil, and may keep people imprisoned, or play tricks on them. Legendary creatures are sometimes said to represent the different qualities in humans, showing both their good and bad sides.

## ANCIENT GREECE

THE ANCIENT GREEK gods often joined in the lives of men and women, but the myth of Icarus and Daedalus shows that any mortal who tried to be like the gods would be punished.

Daedalus, a great inventor, had a quarrel with King Minos, ruler of the island of Crete. He and his son Icarus were locked up, but Daedalus made wings out of feathers and wax, and he and Icarus flew off the island.

Icarus swooped around like a bird, saying he was as powerful as a god now that he could fly. Daedalus warned him not to fly too close to the Sun, in case the wax melted.

Some versions of the myth say Icarus ignored his father's advice and flew too near the sun. Others say that Apollo, the Sun god, was so angry when he heard Icarus boasting that he used all his heat to melt the wings. Either way, Icarus fell to his death.

### THE MINOTAUR

Before his imprisonment, Daedalus designed the Cretan labyrinth, or maze, which Minos used to imprison the minotaur, a mythical beast with the head of a bull and the body of a man. Each year, seven boys and seven girls were sacrificed to the minotaur.

### THE UNICORN

Unicorns appear in many legends, often preventing evil, or helping people in danger. The unicorn's white or silver coat symbolizes purity. In one legend, the unicorn and the lion are constantly arguing, and a chase begins. One of the unicorn's magical powers is that it never becomes tired, and the lion becomes more and more frustrated. Then the unicorn's horn gets caught in the branches of a tree, and the chase is over.

## ARTHURIAN LEGEND

THE LEGENDS OF King Arthur and the Knights of the Round Table were probably invented by the Celts, who lived in Britain and North Western Europe from around 750 B.C. These stories are about the adventures of an English king and his knights, or soldiers, who travelled around the countryside doing good deeds, protecting people from harm, and rescuing innocent prisoners.

King Arthur gave his knights the task of finding and protecting the Holy Grail, a sacred cup or bowl.

The Celts believed that warriors who had died in battle were given the gift of immortality by plunging into a big pot of water called the Cauldron of Life, which rejuvenated anyone who dived in. This could have been the original Holy Grail of the stories.

After the arrival of Christianity, however, the story was changed to fit in with the new religion, and the Grail was said to have been the cup from which Jesus drank at the Last Supper.

## NATIVE AMERICAN LEGENDS

THERE WERE HUNDREDS OF different tribes all over North America before the Europeans arrived there. Very few had any form of written word so, as the tribes were scattered or destroyed, their stories were lost. Around the beginning of the 20th century, some people realized what was happening and began to record the myths and legends of the first peoples of America. This wasn't easy because the stories were believed to have magical properties and people were afraid to repeat them to others outside the tribe. People wrote down a few stories, but the lost ones are thought to be so powerful that some tribes believe they're alive and sleeping under the ground. It's said that only the most skillful story-tellers can persuade them to come out of their hiding holes and visit humans, and they do this with music and chanting.

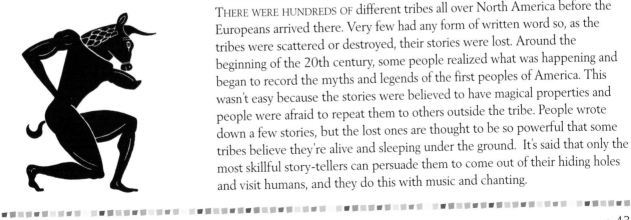

# ...ND GODDESSES

...S OF ancient times were gods ... Early civilizations didn't ...ut many. Our ancestors had to ...xplaining the workings of their ...things they wanted to explain were the seasons and the weather. They believed these were the work of individual gods. Such beliefs were handed on from generation to generation through myths. The more they were repeated, the stronger the belief in the gods became.

**ZEUS**
The Greek king of gods, Zeus was god of the skies. He was wise and compassionate, and only answerable to Destiny. His Roman counterpart is Jupiter.

**ARTEMIS**
The Greek goddess of hunting, woodlands, and of moonlight, Artemis was a lover of mountains, valleys, and music.

## GREEK AND ROMAN GODS

THE PANTHEON, or family, of Greek gods began with Gaia, the Earth goddess, who gave birth to the sky, the mountains, and the sea. With Uranus, the god of Heaven, she bore other gigantic children, called the Titans. Uranus hated his children, and imprisoned them in the body of Earth. With Gaia's help they defeated Uranus and put Kronos on the throne. Kronos was later defeated by his son, Zeus, who went with his supporters to live on Mount Olympus.

The Roman gods were similar to the Greek ones, and may have simply been renamed when the Romans overthrew the Greeks.

**QUETZALCOATL**
The plumed serpent god of the Aztecs, Quetzalcoatl was given a human face by his brother, which made him feel ashamed. The coyote, Xolotl, made him a coat of Quetzal bird feathers and a mask, to help disguise his face and make him look more like a serpent.

**NEPTUNE**
The Roman god of the sea, Neptune also ruled lakes and rivers, causing them to dry out. His rage took the form of great tempests. His Greek counterpart is Poseidon.

## CELTIC GODS

CELTIC PEOPLE BELIEVED that ordinary people lived in one of three worlds. Above, in the Upper World, lived the gods, and below, in the Underworld, lived the fairy forces. Many stories about Celtic gods involve men and gods slipping back and forward between the different worlds. Legend mixes tales of kings and queens with those of mythical gods, and so the distinction has become blurred. Nobody's quite sure what the facts are and what the fiction is! Perhaps this is why there were later beliefs that the Celtic kings had been handpicked by the gods!

## AZTEC GODS

QUETZALCOATL WAS THE AZTEC serpent god, in charge of the city of the gods. He was so humble that he swept the paths for the rain gods to make sure that they would bring rain. His father was the Lord of the Dead, who lived in the Underworld. Quetzalcoatl went to visit him to bring back precious bones, with which he made the people on Earth. Quetzalcoatl's brother was Tezcatlipoca, god of warriors, and of the night sky, and he was constantly playing cruel tricks on his kind brother. His name means "smoking mirror". Stories say he could read the thoughts of others.

 SEE ALSO: CREATION PP.120-121, HEAVEN AND HELL P.78

**THOR**
When the thunder rolled, the Vikings believed it was Thor, the sky god, sounding his hammer as a warning to the giants of Jotunheim. The hammer he threw always came back to his hand.

**RA**
The Egyptian Sun god, Ra, or Re, was thought to fight every night with the serpent of chaos, called Apep. He must have won every night, since the Sun rose every morning!

**ISIS**
The twin sister of Osiris, Isis was also his wife, and the greatest of the four goddesses of the dead. She could turn herself into a sparrowhawk.

**OSIRIS**
The great good king of Egypt, Osiris went to rule the land of the dead, where he judged souls. He was married to Isis.

**FREYA**
The Norse goddess of love, fertility, and magic, Freya was the beautiful sister of Frey. She could turn herself into a falcon, and travelled in a carriage drawn by two cats.

## SUN GODS

ALMOST EVERY culture has myths telling of a Sun god. A god was the only way to explain the huge ball of fire giving out light and heat. Sun gods often have other jobs, too. Apollo, the Greek god of the Sun, was also in charge of healing, poetry, music, and light, and his temple at Delphi was famous for its oracles.

## EARTH GODDESSES

EARTH GODS ARE usually goddesses, who give birth to the Earth and protect everything on it. Gaia is the Greek Earth Mother. Russian peoples still say prayers to the Earth, calling her Mati-Syra-Zemlya, which means "Moist Mother Earth." They ask her to control the elements, so that they can grow crops successfully.

## THE UNDERWORLD

IN GREEK MYTHOLOGY, souls had to pass through gates guarded by Cerberus, a three-headed dog on their way to the Underworld. Once through, they had to pay a ferryman to carry them across the Styx River. Ancient Greeks were often buried with coins for this payment. On the other side of the river, a group of people would judge whether they had been good enough in their life to go to a place called the Elysian Fields. If not, they would be sent to Tartarus, the world of the damned.

## NORSE GODS

THE NORSE GOD who created Heaven and Earth was Odin, the All-father. He was the most powerful god, and represented wisdom and battle. When the warm air from the south met the cold air from the north, the ice melted and created a giant called Ymir. Thor, the sky god, was the son of Odin. Frigg was goddess of childbirth and wife of Odin. Some of the days of our week are named after Norse gods – Tuesday, after Tyr, Wednesday, after Woden, or Odin, Thursday, after Thor, and Friday, after Frigg.

## EGYPTIAN GODS

RA, OR RE, WAS THE GOD whom the Egyptians believed created the Universe. In art he is usually shown as a scarab beetle. When Ra spat he produced Shu, the god of air, and Tefnut, the goddess of moisture. Together they produced other gods and goddesses. Osiris, god of the Underworld and spirit of creation was married to Isis, the most important Egyptian goddess. They had a son, the sky god Horus, usually shown with a falcon's head and the Sun and Moon for eyes. Another son, Anubis, had a jackal's head, and was responsible for taking souls to be judged.

# THE BODY

# BIRTH

**A FLYING START**
Some folk tales say that new mothers found their babies under a gooseberry bush, or that they were brought by a stork.

BIRTH IS A MIRACULOUS, creative process. From a tiny speck of an embryo, after nine months growing in our mother's womb, out we go into the big, wide World. We've only quite recently found out how babies are formed. Before that, people used symbols and myths to explain how they arrived on Earth. Birth is a word that's used in many different ways, but its original meaning was the birth of a human being on this planet. It's the beginning of a new physical existence.

## THE BREATH OF LIFE

AS SOON AS WE enter the World we take our first breath. In some cultures, breath is seen as a symbol of the cosmic, creative forces in life. Taoists believe that there are nine different streams of breath, which together create the space for everything that exists.

The Bible teaches that God woke Adam, the first man, with his breath, and that's how human life began!

Breath is believed to be the spirit of life, connecting us to all of creation. Has anyone ever said to you if you've been upset, "take a deep breath?" If you breathe in a shallow way, it will add to your anxiety. If you take deep breaths it helps you to feel more centered, relaxed, and at ease with whatever's going on around you. Next time you feel upset or scared, try breathing properly and you'll discover it works wonders!

### THE FIRST LESSON

BABIES IN THE WOMB BREATHE the liquid that surrounds them, using special gills, rather like a fish's gills. When they are born, they quickly have to learn how to breathe air. You might have heard of doctors or nurses slapping a baby just after it's born. They sometimes have to do this to clear the baby's lungs of liquid, so that it can begin to breathe in the way it will breathe for the rest of its life on Earth – by taking in air.

## BEING BORN

IF WE COULD REMEMBER OUR BIRTH, we probably wouldn't want to. Imagine being safe and warm in your mother's body for months, then suddenly having to get used to lights, noises, people touching you, and a whole load of other new sensations. It must be a great shock! Soon after birth, we have to learn how to communicate, and not long after that we take our first steps.

# BIRTH RITUALS

PEOPLE HAVE ALWAYS celebrated the arrival of a baby with rituals and ceremonies. In many ways, this is to initiate, or introduce the baby into its family and their way of life. The family's belief system dictates the ceremony they will go through.

In some faith systems, the rituals begin as soon as the baby arrives in the World. For example, the minute a new baby arrives in a Muslim family, the father whispers to it "I witness there is no God but Allah, and Mohammed is the Prophet of God." A newborn Hindu baby has a prayer whispered into its ear.

However different each culture's rituals may be, they all have one thing in common, and that's a sense of joy, happiness, and thanksgiving.

Buddhist parents say their child isn't a Buddhist until it's old enough to know what the word means. The children in a Buddhist family will learn about their faith in the coming years, as they learn about everything else. They will only become truly Buddhist when they understand the rules, and agree with the beliefs held by other Buddhists. Other religions, including Judaism and Christianity, also believe it's important for children to choose their faith for themselves, so they have rituals when the child is older, as well as when it's born.

## CLEANSING RITUAL
This newborn's father and grandmother are holding the baby over the smoke of a wood fire to cleanse it. Smoke is used in birthing rituals in Ghana, Africa and in other countries because it is believed to cleanse and purify.

# BONDING

CAN YOU IMAGINE what life would be like if you didn't love anyone or have a special relationship with your friends or family? We all need someone to love. These days there's a lot of emphasis on parents "bonding" with their baby as soon as it arrives in the World. It's important for the baby to have a cuddle immediately after the shock of being born. How we're loved right from the start can have a big influence on the rest of our lives.

Even as adults, we all need comforting from time to time. If babies don't learn that comfort is available, they may not be able to ask later in life when they need love and support.

## THE PHOENIX
The Ancient Greeks and Egyptians believed that this legendary Arabian bird set fire to itself in a nest of cassia twigs and frankincense when it was old. Every 500 years it rose again from the ashes. For this reason, the phoenix became a symbol of rebirth and reincarnation.

# REBIRTHING

THE REASON WE CAN'T recall our own birth is that the memory's tucked away in our unconscious. We can't remember the event at all unless we find a way of getting in touch with our unconscious mind.

Rebirthing is a way of doing just that. Most of us have no present memory of being a tiny baby but all the information is stored away, a bit like information on a computer disk, so it's possible to access it.

Many people believe that illnesses or problems have their roots in prenatal experiences, in other words before we were born, or while we were in the process of being born. Others believe that they may have begun in a past life, but are affecting the present life.

You may have a fear of dogs, but you don't know why. You might discover through the process of rebirthing that your mother was badly bitten by a dog while she was pregnant with you, and her fear and pain were transmitted to you in the womb. Of course, you have no conscious awareness of that. However, understanding or even reliving the birth process can help us to release pain and emotions that are no longer useful to us.

# THE HUMAN BODY

WHILE WE LIVE ON EARTH, the human body is the house for our spirit. The only major generality you can make about bodies is that they can be roughly divided into the category of male and female. Even though we may share some similar physical characteristics, the make-up of each human body and face is different. So the good news is that you're unique!

The human body is sometimes said to be the most amazing machine in the World – it moves, thinks, communicates, and even takes care of unconscious but vital things, such as breathing. But the body is not a machine. Computers can't match the incredibly complex workings of the human brain, and it's unlikely that they'll ever be able to do so.

## THE PHYSICAL BODY

YOUR BODY IS AN amazing thing. Your skeleton acts like a frame to support and protect all the softer organs. Muscles allow you to move, and give you strength and flexibility. Your heart pumps blood containing oxygen from your lungs to every bit of you. Your skin not only allows you to feel things, such as heat and pain, but keeps out water and helps ensure you don't get too hot or cold. Even your hair can help keep in the heat on cold days.

Gymnasts and dancers must have a combination of strength, flexibility, balance, and elegance to perform well. Achieving this can take years of practice.

## PHYSICAL ABILITIES

WE ALL HAVE DIFFERENT physical abilities, just as we all have different talents and mental skills. If someone is physically different, it's hard for him or her to come to grips with and can be difficult for family and friends to know how to deal with it. Being differently abled makes us stand out from the crowd. Some people say that our physical body in this life can be affected by a past life. Others say that all our attributes, mental and physical, are given to us to help us learn whatever we need to learn for our spiritual well-being.

## SPATIAL AWARENESS

YOUR SPATIAL intelligence controls how you coordinate your body in the physical World. Spatial awareness is the way we relate to our environment. It includes the way we touch, feel, sense, and generally experience everything that's around us. Do you have a natural sense of balance which makes you feel confident about trying new things? Tightrope walkers can do what they do because they have a highly developed sense of balance, which they've spent years improving, and they're confident. If you're centered in space, as a tightrope walker must be, then you can move anywhere with ease.

## THE BUSY BRAIN

ALL OUR THOUGHTS, IDEAS, and memories are stored in our brain. It's the body's nerve center, and controls all our physical movements, such as heartbeat, breathing, and digestion, as well as our senses. The brain has two sides. Each looks after one side of the body. The right side is used for thinking intuitively and creating visual images, and looks after the left side of the body. That's why very creative people, such as artists and musicians, are often left-handed. The left side is the part of the brain that you use to communicate through speech. It's also the one that helps you to learn practical skills, such as tying a shoelace or working out a math equation. The left side of your brain rules your logical processes and looks after the right side of your body. Scientists and other people who are good at thinking logically are usually right-handed.

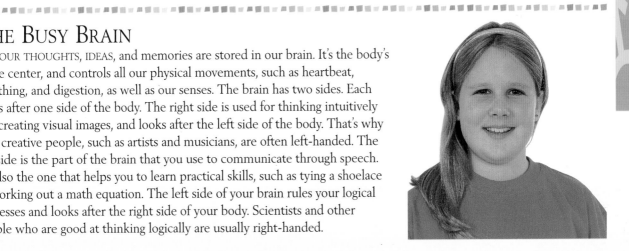

## THE GENES

YOU MAY physically resemble either your mother, your father, or both. This is because you've inherited some genes from them. Genes are found in the cells of the body in a structure known as DNA. Half of your genes come from your father, and half from your mother. Genes carry the instructions that tell your body how you're going to grow and what you'll look like. We all have a unique set of genes, except for identical twins, who have exactly the same genes.

## THE SENSES

MOST OF US ARE aware of our physical sense organs, our eyes, ears, nose, mouth, and skin. Did you know that we can also receive and send information through hidden senses? These are said to be in the energy wheels of the body known as chakras. In this busy, noisy world of ours it's become increasingly difficult for us to use our inner senses, but they're invaluable tools. If you get confused by the messages your mind's giving you, go with your instinct.

## FACIAL EXPRESSIONS

YOU CAN SEE ALMOST immediately what kind of mood somebody's in by studying the expression on his or her face. When we look in the mirror we see the reverse of what everybody else sees. Perhaps that's why it's difficult to see ourselves as others do, because we're usually more critical of our appearance than others are. We can learn about ourselves, though, as well as learning about other people, by watching their faces react to what we're saying or doing.

## BODY LANGUAGE

LANGUAGE IS A WAY of communicating with other people. People of different cultures use different sounds, or language, to speak to their family and friends. But we don't need words to have a language. Our body can speak volumes – so much, in fact, that people with limited hearing have invented a whole sign language of their own. If you feel defensive or you're trying to hide your feelings, you might cross your arms or fold them over your solar plexus, the emotional response area just above your navel. If you're feeling sad or down, then that's just how your body will look. During those wonderful, victorious times in life, when you've won a race or passed an exam, your elation will be there for all to see!

## THE BODY'S CYCLES

MANY PEOPLE BELIEVE THAT our well-being is at the mercy of our biorhythms, the cycles of our body. There's said to be a physical cycle of 23 days, which looks after our energy, immunity, strength, and confidence. The 28-day emotional cycle rules our emotions, moods, and creative phases. The 33-day intellectual cycle affects learning, reasoning, memory, and decision making. It's possible to work out your biorhythmic cycles and use them to help plan your life.

# CHAKRAS AND MERIDIANS

THE BODY IS AN IMPORTANT form of physical energy, but we also have invisible energy fields around us which are just as important! You can tell how someone is by looking at their aura, a colored energy field which some people can see surrounding the body. Chinese people believe that the energy of the Universe, or Ch'i, flows through our bodies, carried by a network of channels known as meridians. There are also invisible energy centers, called chakras, along the spine. By looking at the body's energetic system, we can detect illness before it becomes physical.

## ENERGY BOOST

IF YOU FEEL off color, your chakras may need balancing. To do this, some people place a crystal on each chakra. You can use colored pieces of paper just as well. Cut out pieces of paper that match the color of the chakras. Once you've got them together, lie on the floor and, looking at the diagram, place the paper on the relevant chakra. Leave them for a while and each color will start to transmit its particular frequency or vibration through your body. Take your time in getting up and once you're on your feet again you should be feeling much better!

## THE SEVEN CHAKRAS

THE WORD "CHAKRA" IS the ancient Sanskrit word for wheel. Indian Yogis were the first to write about the seven chakras in the human body. They're believed to be powerful centers, which bring in the Universal life energy and send it flowing through our systems. You can't see the seven colored spinning disks of light with your normal vision, but it's possible to see them in your mind's eye.

**CROWN CHAKRA**
The Crown chakra is the highest spiritual center of the body and it's a violet color. It's a place of wisdom and a "spiritual doorway."

**THIRD EYE CHAKRA**
The Third Eye chakra is in the middle of our forehead and is a deep blue or indigo color. This is the spot where we can use our intuition and psychic abilities to see things in the invisible world.

**HEART CHAKRA**
The Heart chakra is green and is our place of connection with the spirit. It's a healing center and one from which we can feel unconditional love, sympathy, and care for ourselves and others.

**THROAT CHAKRA**
The Throat chakra is blue and the first of the three spiritual centers of the body. In other words it has no relation to our Earthly, or physical, existence but looks after our spiritual connection with the Universe. It's the chakra of creativity, communication, and the search for truth.

**SACRAL CHAKRA**
The Sacral chakra, colored orange, is just below the navel, and it's the seat of our intuition. It's also the chakra which helps us to put our imagination to good use.

**SOLAR PLEXUS CHAKRA**
The Solar Plexus chakra, just above the navel, is yellow. This is the main chakra that the Universal energy flows through and it's related to our feelings, happiness, and health. If you've ever felt as though someone has punched you in the stomach when they've said something hurtful or told you some bad news, that's because you've received that message in a very powerful energy center.

**ROOT CHAKRA**
The Root chakra, which is colored red, is at the base of the spine. It gets its name because it keeps us rooted to the Earth. It deals with our survival issues, such as how we're going to eat, and who's going to love us and look after us.

# THE BODY'S MERIDIANS

THE MERIDIANS ARE LIKE a map that covers the whole body. There are 12 main meridian channels, with acupuncture points along them. They connect the Ch'i, or life force, with the blood flow round the body. The Chinese believe that there are 59 meridians, although Indian healers say there are hundreds!

The twelve main channels are in pairs that match the six Yin organs and the six Yang organs of the body.

The meridians send energy to the whole of the physical body. The body is connected to our mind, emotions, and spirit, and we can become ill through events or emotions. Those who work with the meridian system can find and treat any blockages that appear in the flow of energy before they result in illness. They work with the channel that relates to the particular Yin or Yang organ that needs healing.

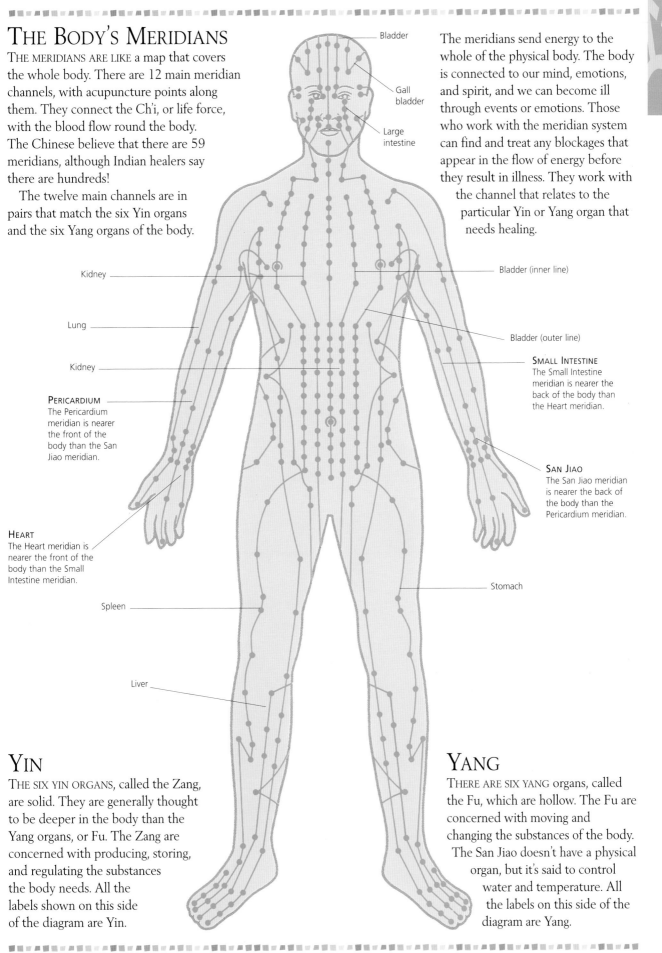

Bladder

Gall bladder

Large intestine

Kidney

Lung

Kidney

**PERICARDIUM**
The Pericardium meridian is nearer the front of the body than the San Jiao meridian.

**HEART**
The Heart meridian is nearer the front of the body than the Small Intestine meridian.

Spleen

Liver

Bladder (inner line)

Bladder (outer line)

**SMALL INTESTINE**
The Small Intestine meridian is nearer the back of the body than the Heart meridian.

**SAN JIAO**
The San Jiao meridian is nearer the back of the body than the Pericardium meridian.

Stomach

# YIN

THE SIX YIN ORGANS, called the Zang, are solid. They are generally thought to be deeper in the body than the Yang organs, or Fu. The Zang are concerned with producing, storing, and regulating the substances the body needs. All the labels shown on this side of the diagram are Yin.

# YANG

THERE ARE SIX YANG organs, called the Fu, which are hollow. The Fu are concerned with moving and changing the substances of the body. The San Jiao doesn't have a physical organ, but it's said to control water and temperature. All the labels on this side of the diagram are Yang.

# COLOR AND LIGHT

CAN YOU IMAGINE HOW drab the World would be without color? It would be dark, too, because colors only exist as part of light. Colors appear in Nature, in homes and schools, and they're important in our lives.

Have you ever wondered why you choose to wear green clothes one day, and blue another? Energy frequencies give colors individual qualities. We make choices depending on the way that we feel at the time.

Some people believe that colors can be heard. High musical notes are light and bright, and lower notes are darker. Each day of the week has a color, as does every number and every letter.

DRESS FOR JOY
The saffron, or bright orange color of these Buddhist monks' robes is said by color therapists to have a gentle, feminine energy. It can help to lift depression and bring about happiness and joy.

## COLORS IN NATURE

SOME OF THE COLORS of Nature can be so beautiful that they are almost hypnotic, for example, a dramatic sunset, or moonlight shining on a deep blue sea. The bright colors of a field or garden full of flowers and insects can be amazing.

Throughout history, people have used the natural colors of the Earth, called pigments, to decorate their homes and heal their bodies. Native Americans still work closely with the Earth's colors in their clothing and crafts, and they even paint their bodies with the red and brown ochers of the land.

All around the World, colors are used in celebrations and ceremonies. There's no doubt about it, life is a rich tapestry full of color!

## SACRED COLORS

COLORS HAVE STRONG associations for many religions and philosophies around the World. They can mean different things to different people.

● BLACK can be a color of mourning or darkness for Indians or Christians, whereas the Ancient Egyptians connected black with transformation, resurrection, and rebirth.
● RED is the luckiest color for the Chinese, but Celtic people believed it symbolized doom and gloom.
● ORANGE represents happiness and love for the people of Japan and China.
● YELLOW is important to Buddhists and to Christians.
● GREEN is considered to be a very sacred color for Islamic people.
● BLUE seems to be popular with religions all over the World and sky blue is sometimes known as the Great Mother. The Romans believed blue was linked to Venus, the goddess of beauty. Purple and Violet are used in many religious ceremonies and rituals.
● GOLD usually represents the Sun, light, and truth in many cultures.
● SILVER is linked with the Moon and the deeper side of life.
● WHITE is the color from which all others are born. It's seen as a color of illumination and is used in ceremonies of birth, marriage, and death.

# COLOR ENERGIES

THERE ARE THREE "primary" colors – red, blue, and yellow. The others are made by mixing these three. Each color has both negative and positive qualities. Some are shown here.

- RED gives strength and energy.
- GREEN is for balance, and also for imbalance, such as selfishness.
- ORANGE is for independence and happiness.
- YELLOW is for mental activity.
- TURQUOISE is for calmness and purity.
- BLUE is for peace and sleep.
- VIOLET is for mysticism and hope.
- MAGENTA helps us to let go and move with the flow of life.
- WHITE is for purity and truth.

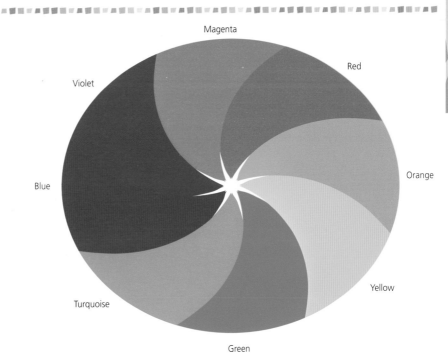

# RAINBOWS

RAINBOWS ARE SO magnificent that we've adopted them as a symbol of luck, fortune, and happiness. They're caused by drops of water falling through the air in sunlight. They usually happen at the end of a shower, and you can often see the same effect in the spray of waterfalls.

When a ray of light travels through a raindrop, it's split into the colors of the rainbow – red, orange, yellow, green, blue, indigo, and violet.

White light consists of all the colors of the spectrum. Each color has a different frequency, or wavelength. Spiritually, the different frequencies of the colors are said to give them their different characteristics.

# COLOR HEALING

OVER THE CENTURIES people have used color and light to help them recover from illness. These days colors are used a great deal in healing. Many people believe that color therapy has helped cure a lot of conditions, from learning difficulties to cancer. Colors affect us in invisible, but dramatic ways. You need a balance of colors that vibrate at different frequencies to make you feel healthy in body, mind, and spirit. Color therapists help us find any areas that are out of balance. Then they decide on a particular color, or group of colors, to work with to help us restore our mental, physical, and spiritual color balance.

## COMPLEMENTARY COLORS

EVERY COLOUR HAS AN OPPOSITE and complementary color. For example, orange and blue, and green and magenta, are complementary colors. You can see this for yourself by doing the following simple experiment. Cut out a circle, or any other shape, of colored paper. Make sure it measures about six inches across. Place the colored paper on top of a white piece of paper. Now stare at it for 15-20 seconds, then quickly take away the colored paper. Look at the blank white paper and after a while you should see a shape. It will be the same shape as the paper that you removed, but it will be its opposite, complementary color. Often the color is very bright and glowing, almost like a light.

# SADS

SEASONALLY AFFECTED Disorder Syndrome, or SADS, is caused by a lack of natural light. Some people seem to need sunlight in their lives more than others. When the days are short, and nights are long, these people can suffer from depression and lack of energy and motivation. It may well be a symptom caused by our unnatural modern lives. More research needs to be done on which part of light it is that people need, but artificial light that contains all colors of the spectrum seems to help them.

# LIFE

WHAT IS LIFE? It's a word that we use for plants and creatures that feed, grow, and reproduce to survive on Earth. There are four kingdoms of life on Earth, plant, animal, mineral, and human. It is said that all forms of life have a soul, which is midway between the physical and the spiritual. In life the soul is housed in a physical body for a given amount of time in order for it to be on Earth. There's a multitude of possible experiences on Earth, but in Universal terms there's really only one aim. That's to learn valuable lessons that will enable us to grow and expand in our consciousness, or awareness.

## BEING ALIVE

WHEN THE LIFE FORCE or energy of the Universe is pumping through your veins, you know you're alive! Of course, we sometimes feel more or less alive, depending on how we spend our time, what we put into our bodies in terms of fuel, and how we look after our mind, body, and spirit. Some people talk about vitality, which is how vital, or strong, our energy field is. The way we live depends enormously on the frequency level at which our bodies function. Many other factors, such as age, circumstances, and environment, also play a big part in being alive.

## EVOLVING

THE THEORY OF EVOLUTION, which the naturalist Charles Darwin developed, describes how humans "evolved" from apelike creatures. All living creatures come in different shapes, sizes, and colors. This is called individuality. A particular shape, or color, might give one individual a better chance of surviving to adulthood and having young. These young have a good chance of inheriting the shape or color that helped their parents to survive. Over many generations, animals can change quite a lot in their appearance, mainly because of this process, which is known as "natural selection."

In this family of Emperor penguins, both parents play an equal part in bringing up their young.

**AMMONITES**
These are fossilized ammonites, sea creatures that lived on Earth millions of years ago. Their nearest living relative is the nautilus.

# LIFE CYCLES

IN A COSMIC SENSE, life may be eternal, and for each of us, the journey may be far longer than the time that we spend on Earth. It's not just a question of eating, drinking, sleeping, and enjoying ourselves, although those things do take up a lot of our time. There is a cycle that exists to help us learn about ourselves and others, including how to face problems, cope with loss, overcome fears, and achieve in different areas of our life. Our parents start off by looking after us, then by the time they're old we're taking care of them. That's the cycle of life. In it are lessons for us to learn how to receive, how to care and give, and how to be tolerant and loving. Of course, some of us don't make all the stages of life, and there may be a divine reason for some people living much longer than others.

## SYNCHRONICITY

HOW MANY TIMES IN your life have you come across coincidences? How about that time you bumped into somebody that you hadn't seen for ages and had just been thinking about? Or, on a bigger scale, when things happen in your life that seem to be connected but which you've simply put down to coincidence? Another term for coincidence is "synchronicity." Carl Jung used this term to describe two seemingly separate incidents that turn out to be related. We discover throughout life that we have all sorts of connections to other people and things that previously seemed unrelated.

## ADOLESCENCE

RESPONSIBILITY INCREASES as we grow into puberty and the teenage years, when we become less dependent on our parents and guardians and start making choices and decisions about our future. For many people, adolescence can be a difficult time.

## ADULTHOOD

IN ADULTHOOD WE BECOME independent and have to try to support ourselves in this World without relying too much on anybody else. If we become parents, or guardians, the cycle of caring and looking after others begins.

## THE MIDDLE YEARS

THE FOURTH STAGE of our lives is when any children we have had are grown up, and some of us are in the position of enjoying our freedom again, although in an older and wiser way!

## CHILDHOOD

AS INFANTS, OR babies, we are totally dependent on other people to care for us. As we grow into childhood, we take the first steps of responsibility by learning how to feed, talk, and do things for ourselves. This is when we learn how to make friends and get on with other people.

## OLDER AGE

AS WE GROW older, we may slow down and become less strong physically, but we have a wealth of experience to draw on. Sometimes grandchildren arrive to give us a new lease on life.

# DEATH

THE WORD "DEATH" often causes negative feelings. It's the end of life as we know it. However, in spiritual terms, death is simply moving from one dimension, in this case Earth, to another. Death comes to us all in the end, and it shouldn't frighten us. The trouble is, we don't know how it feels, and we are often scared of the unknown. Of course, we won't know until we experience it, but it might even be quite pleasant!

## BELIEFS ABOUT DYING

NEARLY ALL FAITH systems believe that when someone dies the soul goes to another place. Hindus, Sikhs, and Buddhists believe that we have more than one life and that the soul comes back in many physical forms on Earth before staying in the spiritual realms. Christians, Jews, and Muslims believe we can only have one life on Earth. Taoists say that a dead person's soul crosses a bridge to the next life. Jewish people believe that a human soul goes to the world to come. Sikhs believe that to die is to be one step nearer to God and that the soul will come back again in another life.

## WHAT HAPPENS WHEN WE DIE?

THERE ARE MANY COMFORTING stories about how, when we die, we are met by loving souls who have died before us. They could be from your family, such as your grandparents, or other people you knew well on Earth and loved very much. It's said we also have our spirit guides or guardian angels with us after death. Some people believe that we experience something close to dying every night when we go to sleep. It's said that while we sleep, our soul temporarily leaves the physical body to travel in the astral body, just as it does after death.

## GRIEF AND GRIEVING

IN SOME CULTURES IT can be difficult for people to show their grief and upset over someone's death. For a long time in many places, death was a subject that people didn't talk about. These days, we're usually encouraged to grieve openly – to show our feelings and let them out as a way of healing our hurt over someone's death. It's said that there are three main stages of grieving – disbelief, anger, and acceptance. Bottling up your feelings can make you ill. It's as though all the sadness and anger you're keeping in contaminates your body. Some people say it's important to grieve properly, or the soul you cry for is trapped between Earth and the invisible realm. A soul can't move on until it's freed by those who loved it on Earth. One expression says "Loving someone is letting them go." You can show your love for someone who dies by expressing your feelings and letting his or her spirit go.

THE LADY OF SHALOTT
In the legends of King Arthur, Elaine, the Lady of Shalott, died of love for Sir Lancelot. Her body was sent up the Thames River to King Arthur's Court, carrying with it a letter telling him what had happened.

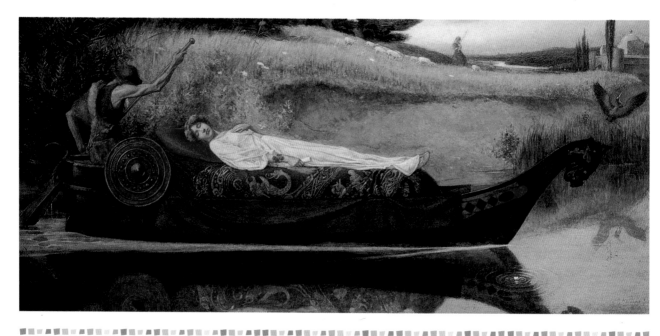

**DAY OF THE DEAD**
The Mexican Day of the Dead is a festival, when people light candles and make offerings to welcome souls back to Earth. This shop is selling edible sugar skulls and other objects that are used in the celebrations.

# DEATH RITUALS

ALL CULTURES HAVE THEIR own special ways of saying farewell to a loved one. As well as the funeral, there are many rituals that people observe, depending on their faith. These rituals help give people a structure to work with, which helps them to grieve properly. Many cultures, for example, wear clothes of a particular color to the funeral, and for some time after that, while they are "in mourning."

● ORTHODOX JEWS won't go to any kind of entertainment for a month after someone they were close to has died. Jewish people say a prayer for the dead person every day for at least a year after his or her death.

● VIKINGS used to put gold and other precious metals into the graves of the dead so that they could pay for the journey to Heaven.

● JAPANESE PEOPLE have special funerary bowls which contain food. These are placed with the dead to make sure they have spiritual nourishment for the next part of their journey.

● BUDDHISTS often use special urns for the ashes of the dead as a symbol of good luck.

● TAOIST mourners sometimes completely cover themselves from head to toe as a mark of respect for the dead.

● CHINESE PEOPLE burn colored paper on their funeral pyres. This is meant to bring good luck to the soul as it journeys in the after life.

● ANCIENT EGYPTIANS had a special god for the dead, Anubis, who was said to take the dead to be judged, and to guard the tombs. Egyptian bodies were mummified, or preserved, to last into the next life.

# FUNERALS

A FUNERAL IS A CEREMONY in which we say goodbye to a loved one who has died. Funerals vary depending on the culture we have been brought up in, or the faith system we believe in. The dead person's body is often buried in the ground, in a grave marked with a stone or other object. This gives friends and relatives a place to visit to remember the person's life, and feel that he or she is still with them in spirit. Many people prefer the idea of being cremated, and have their ashes stored for their friends and relatives to visit. Some people choose a different type of ceremony, such as burial at sea. Most funerals have special rituals to represent the cycles of life, and symbols to help the family and friends accept what has happened. The ceremony is usually seen as a celebration of the person's life, and a chance for those left behind to grieve openly.

## NEAR DEATH EXPERIENCES

IN TECHNICAL TERMS, A NEAR DEATH experience, or NDE, means that you've died, returned to life, and can remember the life force leaving your physical body and the reason for returning to the planet.

Accounts of NDEs are incredibly similar. Many of them happen on the operating table. A person who dies usually sees the events of their life flashing by as if on film, and then a tunnel of bright light. A lot of people say they sense a wonderful feeling of light and love. Sometimes they're met at the end of the tunnel by friends and relatives who've already died. When they realize that there are still things they need to do in this lifetime, they decide to return to their bodies.

People who've had an NDE say it reassures them that death is an enjoyable experience, but also makes them more keen to live their lives to the full and to achieve something while they are on Earth.

# REINCARNATION

T HE WORD INCARNATION COMES from the Latin *in carne* which literally means "in the flesh," or "having a physical body." Reincarnation means to be born more than once into Earthly existence.

There are various theories about what happens when we die. Many people believe that we come back in different bodies so that we can have lots of experiences and learn new things. Eventually, there comes a point when, in spiritual terms, we don't need to come back to Earth again and we can move forward to the next stage of our personal journey.

### DIFFERENT PEOPLE
In one life you might be a crusader in the Middle Ages, and in another a 20th century engineer. You'll have learned at least something valuable from all your lives.

SEE ALSO: BIRTH PP.48-49, DEATH PP.58-59, EMOTIONS PP.24-25, SOULS AND SPIRITS P.76

# BEING REBORN

SOME PEOPLE SAY IT makes sense that we should be reborn several times, to experience famine and riches, fatherhood and motherhood, community and loneliness. In our many visits to Earth, we might have lived in different parts of the World and in more than one period in history. We might experience living in various cultures, be born under a new astrological sign, be rich in one lifetime but poor in another. We could meet all sorts of different people, and adopt different attitudes to those we have in this life. A variety of existences would give us a much fuller experience of what life has to offer.

## SOUL GROUPS
Some people believe that each of us incarnates, or begins a life on Earth, with a particular soul group, which means that we are quite likely to meet the same people in more than one life, although probably in a different kind of relationship.

# KARMA

MANY PEOPLE, PARTICULARLY in the Eastern countries of the World, believe in reincarnation and multiple lives. Those who do often also believe in the idea of karma, which is that all actions have a consequence of some kind, and not necessarily in the same life. If you do something that doesn't seem to have any consequences in one life, you'll probably find that they happen in the next. For example, if you were cruel to someone, you might find that in a later life you are treated cruelly by someone else. On the other hand, if you're generous and kind to others, including animals, you won't always be thanked, but you'll be building up good karma for the next life, so you'll benefit eventually. It's not always as obvious as that, of course, but we all have lessons to learn, and for people who believe in karma, there is simply not enough time in one life to learn them all.

## FLY AWAY
If you're frightened of spiders, it might be because in one of your past lives, you were a fly!

## PAST LIVES

HAVE YOU EVER VISITED somewhere new but felt as if you'd been there before? Have you met someone for the first time but sensed a strong bond and familiarity? People say they feel drawn to certain periods in history, or are fascinated by a particular subject, yet don't quite know why.

These could all be instances of past lives you've had, which have left a ghost of a memory in your awareness that's reawakened when you visit that place or meet that person. We may even have phobias about certain things because of an event that happened in a past life.

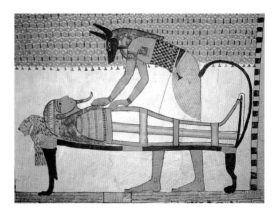

## ANOTHER LIFE
This painting is from a tomb in Luxor, Egypt. It shows Anubis, the jackal-headed god of the dead, preparing a body for judgment. The Ancient Egyptians believed that their bodies would live again in another world, and preserved them carefully after death for the next life. They preserved the bodies of cats in the same way.

# HEALTH AND FITNESS

IF WE ARE TO MAKE the most of our life, we need to keep ourselves healthy and fit in all senses of the word. There are five types of fitness, and they are physical, mental, emotional, social, and medical fitness. Each of the five types needs looking after in a different way, but they are all of equal importance for a balanced, happy life. The best way to stay healthy and happy is to develop good habits, such as eating a balanced diet, taking regular exercise, and managing stress. There are times in all our lives when we need to be able to draw on our reserves, and general fitness means that energy is there when we need it.

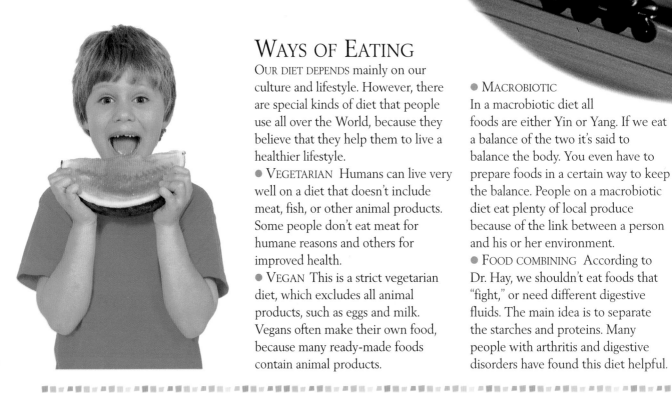

## A HEALTHY BODY

PEOPLE WITH healthy bodies can do all the things they need to do in their everyday lives and still have a little energy, extra strength, and motivation left. If you exercise regularly, eat and drink healthily, and have regular check-ups by the doctor and dentist, you should find you feel good most of the time, and become ill less often. Your body, just like a machine, will work better if it is looked after properly. People who've looked after their bodies throughout their young life usually find that they have fewer problems in older age, too. They may even look young for longer!

## WAYS OF EATING

OUR DIET DEPENDS mainly on our culture and lifestyle. However, there are special kinds of diet that people use all over the World, because they believe that they help them to live a healthier lifestyle.

● VEGETARIAN Humans can live very well on a diet that doesn't include meat, fish, or other animal products. Some people don't eat meat for humane reasons and others for improved health.

● VEGAN This is a strict vegetarian diet, which excludes all animal products, such as eggs and milk. Vegans often make their own food, because many ready-made foods contain animal products.

● MACROBIOTIC
In a macrobiotic diet all foods are either Yin or Yang. If we eat a balance of the two it's said to balance the body. You even have to prepare foods in a certain way to keep the balance. People on a macrobiotic diet eat plenty of local produce because of the link between a person and his or her environment.

● FOOD COMBINING According to Dr. Hay, we shouldn't eat foods that "fight," or need different digestive fluids. The main idea is to separate the starches and proteins. Many people with arthritis and digestive disorders have found this diet helpful.

Sports and Fitness
Learning a new sport, such as rollerblading, not only keeps your body moving, but it can keep your mind alert as well.

# PHYSICAL EXERCISE

EVERYONE SHOULD take some form of exercise every day, even if it's only a walk in the park or a quick swim. Doctors also recommend that people take half an hour of moderate exercise three times a week. Lots of people play sport at school, but stop as soon as they leave. Many of these people quickly gain fat, and their energy levels get lower and lower. This can be a vicious circle, because the more unfit you are, the less you feel like doing anything about it. A gentle swim or dance class can be as much fun as it is good for you, and can become a very good habit!

# BODY BUILDING

YOU MAY HAVE SEEN PEOPLE flexing their muscles in competitions on television, or at the local gym. Building muscle is good for improving posture, or the way we stand, and strength. It also improves the body's metabolism, the system for producing energy from food. However, if muscles get too big, they can get in the way of ordinary movement. People who overdo their weight training can lose flexibility. If you want to be good at a wide range of activities, you need a mixture of strength, flexibility, stamina, balance, and coordination.

# MENTAL HEALTH

IT'S OFTEN SAID THAT a healthy body leads to a healthy mind, and it's true that exercise can help beat stress and help you think clearly. However, we need to take special care of our mental health, too. There are many professionals who specialize in mental problems, but as with physical health, prevention is better than cure. We can learn to avoid situations that cause us stress and pain, and we can learn to deal with difficult situations that we can't avoid.

# NUTRITION

THE HUMAN BODY HAS a digestive system that can adapt to all sorts of different foods, and teeth that can crunch, grind, and chew most things into tiny pieces. This means that we can choose what we eat, and most of us have a great range of foods available to us. Unfortunately, many of us choose processed foods for convenience. These often have added fat, sugar, and salt, but few vitamins, minerals, and other nutrients. Although they take time to prepare, fresh, natural foods such as beans, grains, vegetables, and fruit are far more valuable, and easier to digest.

## SLIMMING

YOU CAN MEASURE the energy in food in calories or joules. Many people try to slim by limiting the amount of energy they eat each day. However, it's much better to increase the amount of exercise you do, and make your diet healthier, rather than simply lower in calories. For example, eat less fat and refined sugars and starches, such as white bread, and eat more raw fruits, vegetables, and unrefined starches, such as wholemeal bread. Begin exercising by taking a brisk walk, or going for a swim more often.

# HEALING

I N THE PAST, MOST people used to let their doctors decide how they should be healed. Today, we have more choice, and our attitudes have changed. Many people now decide for themselves what kind of healing they prefer, and which health practitioner they need to help them. Our attitude toward ourself, our illness, and the treatment we choose plays a large part in how we mend. Incredibly, for some people, the power of positive thinking can mean the difference between life and death.

It's important to choose the way of healing that feels right for us. For some people this might be a visit to the doctor, for others it could mean a trip to the homeopath or chiropractor, or even a combination of several kinds of medicine.

**HEALING SNAKES**
In ancient times, people believed that snakes knew the secret of eternal life. Even today, snakes coiled around a staff are a symbol of the medical profession.

## CONVENTIONAL MEDICINE

IT'S AMAZING TO THINK that only three centuries ago most people thought they were lucky if they lived into their thirties. Today, our expected lifespan is more than double that. This is mainly because we have discovered new ways to prevent, treat, and cure many kinds of illness.

In ancient times, illness was seen as a curse from the gods, and many people believed that only magicians and priests had the power to heal them. However, Hippocrates, who is thought to be the founder of modern medicine, believed that Nature was at the root of illness. His belief started the search for causes and cures of disease. This formed the idea of conventional medicine, which is still going on today.

**MEDICINES**
Conventional medicines come in many different forms, including syrups, tablets, powders, capsules, and pills.

**TRICOSANTHUS FRUIT**
These are used in Chinese herbal medicine for coughs, especially chesty coughs.

**LILYTURF**
This herb is used mostly for sore throats, and for clearing the skin by cleansing the body of toxins, or poisons.

**WOLFBERRY FRUIT**
This fruit is used for people who have problems in their eyes or their kidneys.

**MILLETTIA STEM**
This is used for improving blood circulation. Millettia is equally effective for both men and women.

**CHINESE ANGELICA**
This is good for treating poor blood circulation, especially in women.

## HOLISTIC MEDICINE

AS THE NAME SUGGESTS, holistic medicine is about treating the whole person. Many alternative practitioners believe that we need to take care of ourselves on all levels.

Conventional medical practitioners usually treat specific illnesses. But holistic practitioners believe that the mind, body, and spirit are related, and must all be treated. Often they don't believe in immunization because they think that chemical medicines hold the illness inside the body instead of allowing it to be released in a more natural way.

## HERBALISM

HERBS HAVE BEEN USED in healing for as long as people have existed. Many cultures believe that disease is caused by an imbalance of the emotional, mental, and physical bodies. Herbs can help to correct these imbalances.

Herbal practitioners believe the whole of a plant is useful in the healing process. They often make up mixtures, called infusions, by boiling the herbs with water. Remedies may also come in the form of compresses or poultices for wounds, and herbal tinctures, which are concentrated solutions of herbs.

 SEE ALSO: CRYSTALS PP.118-119, HEALTH AND FITNESS PP.62-63, MAGIC PP.86-87, NATURE PP.108-109

# HOMEOPATHY

IN THE 18TH CENTURY, a German doctor called Samuel Hahnemann founded the practice of homeopathy. The term is from the Greek word *homios*, which means "like" and *pathos*, which means "suffering." This is exactly what the treatment's about – treating like with like. For example, bee stings are treated with a very diluted solution of *Apis*, which is made from bee stings! The theory is that by adding a little more of the cause of the problem, the body is able to build up an immunity against the cause of the illness, infection, or other problem.

In the last 20 or 30 years, homeopathy has become more and more popular as a form of medicine in all parts of the World. It's useful for both short- and long-term illnesses, and for accidents and injuries, such as burns and bruises. Homeopathy is safe, and can be used on children, old people, and even animals. You can treat minor problems, such as coughs and colds, at home, using remedies that are available from pharmacies or health stores.

**SILICEA**
Most rocks consist mainly of *Silicea*, also known as silica. In humans, it helps keep our teeth, hair, and nails strong. *Silicea* can be used for many different problems, including colds, skin and bone complaints, tiredness, stress, and problems with the nervous system.

**BEES**
Whole bees are used to produce *Apis*, which is mainly used as a remedy for insect stings. Their honey, beeswax, royal jelly, which is food for young queen bees, and propolis, a sticky fluid used in the hive, are also used in various remedies, including fever and dry skin.

**CALENDULA**
The *Calendula* is also known as pot marigold. It's a popular garden plant, and is usually made into creams and lotions. These are used as an antiseptic and to reduce swelling, in problems as simple as dry skin, and as serious as skin cancer. A tincture can be used on cuts.

# FLOWER REMEDIES

ABORIGINAL PEOPLES in Australia and Native Americans have worked with flowers for many centuries, but one of the best known flower-remedy users is an Englishman called Dr. Edward Bach. Bach recovered from a hemorrhage after being told he had only three months to live. Bach believed that positive thinking had helped him to recover, and he began to work with homeopathy and other natural therapies. He made up essences from flowers that he believed would cure the negative emotions causing illness. By the time he died Bach had created 38 flower remedies, which covered every negative emotional state that he could think of. Today, Bach flower remedies are used all over the World.

# ALEXANDER TECHNIQUE

THIS IS A VERY popular therapy created by a man called Matthias Alexander. He was an actor who suffered from a hoarse voice. When he tried to find out what was causing it he realized it was because he wasn't holding his body properly. His techniques help to balance the head, neck, and spine. Correcting our posture and breathing like this can greatly improve our general health and well-being.

# CRYSTAL HEALING

GEMSTONES AND CRYSTALS are said to contain properties that can help us in our daily lives. They come in different shapes, sizes, and colors and each is said to have a special gift to help heal the Earth and those who live here. Some people use crystals to heal the human body. They can be held, worn as jewelry, or simply placed on the areas that need healing.

# FELDENKRAIS

THIS PARTICULAR type of therapy is very popular with people who have spinal problems, and people suffering from stroke or arthritis. It teaches you to become more aware of your body by using movement, both as part of a group and as an individual. Many sports people, such as athletes, and dancers use Feldenkrais because it helps them to strengthen their backs and improve their postures. This, in turn, helps them to give better performances.

## HEALING CAN HARM

SOME TYPES OF HEALING use parts of animals as medicines. This is why some animals have become so rare. Traditional Chinese medicine is partly to blame for the illegal killing of tigers that are hunted for their bones. They are now endangered. Many new medicines and types of surgery are tested on animals, and can cause them a great deal of pain, even death. Replacement heart valves, for example, may come from a pig, although artificial valves are also available. If you are concerned about the animal kingdom, find out if all the medicines, soaps, and shampoos that you use are "animal-friendly."

# HYDROTHERAPY

HAVE YOU EVER FOUND that going for a swim in the local pool makes you feel better? Being in water can be very healing. It's the ultimate in natural therapy. People drink natural spring water and also take treatments in it. In Roman times, special spas were set up throughout Europe, and they're still popular today.

Whether you go for saunas (hot steam), or use Turkish baths or sea water baths, or have water sprayed in jets onto your body, hydrotherapy is great for improving the body's circulation and relaxing the nervous system.

# IRIDOLOGY

THE NAME IRIDOLOGY means "the study of the iris," which is exactly what this holistic treatment is about. Those who practice iridology believe that they can work out a person's health by looking at their eyes. Every organ and gland of the body is shown on the iris as either streaks, dots, spots, or flecks.

Iridologists can detect allergies, and can tell you how to change your diet and lifestyle in order to get better. As with other holistic therapies, an iridologist can tell you what's out of balance, but it's up to you to correct it yourself by changing your lifestyle.

CHOLESTEROL
A blurred outline on the iris can mean that the level of cholesterol in your blood is a little too high.

THE BRAIN
This area of the iris can show up problems in the brain.

METABOLISM
Dark areas can mean poor metabolism, which is the body's energy production system. They may also reveal toxins in the body.

THE LOWER BODY
These three dark areas suggest that there may be toxins in the area of the lower body.

# KINESIOLOGY

SOMEONE WHO practices kinesiology can find out about your energy levels by checking how your muscles respond to pressure. A kinesiologist might ask you to hold out your arm, and push down on it to see if the muscles are strong enough to resist. Once he or she has found the weakness and decided on the problem, they can help by using massage on the body's acupuncture and reflex points. This clears the blocked energy, and allows the body to heal itself. Sometimes the healer will also suggest you avoid eating certain foods that may cause muscle weakness. Kinesiology is popular in dental practices in the U.S.A., and with sports people all over the World.

# NATUROPATHY

THE FOUR IDEAS that form the basis of naturopathy are clean air, clean water, healthy food, and lots of exercise. If you visit a naturopathic healer, you'll find that rather than giving you a prescription for treatment, he or she will probably recommend a change, or changes in your lifestyle. This might mean avoiding some foods, and eating others that you don't normally eat. You'll certainly be encouraged to eat fresh, healthy foods, and to take more exercise. This should help give the body enough strength, vitamins, and minerals to heal itself of any problems. There's not much you can do about the air where you live, except to help stop pollution. If the drinking water in your house isn't great you could choose bottled water. If you follow the four principles of naturopathy throughout your life, you should find that you have fewer illnesses and injuries in the future, too.

# MAGNETIC HEALING

ACCORDING TO SOME PEOPLE, the Earth's magnetic field has a strong effect on the human body. Some people believe that for everyone there is an ideal direction to sleep in, depending on the effect of the magnetic field on their body. The theory that magnets placed on the body can heal someone's illness was popular in the 18th and 19th centuries, and is still practiced today.

## ACUPUNCTURE

THE CHINESE TREATMENT METHOD of acupuncture is more than 5000 years old. It works with the meridian system, which is a network of channels in the body that Ch'i, or life force, flows through. Acupuncture aims to cure any imbalance in someone's body, which affects their overall health, so it can be used to treat anything from depression to addiction. It involves putting small needles into certain points in the body to stimulate the Ch'i and restore balance and harmony.

## BIOENERGETICS

THERE IS A WAY OF releasing feelings and blocked energy through body movements, called bioenergetics, which has been developed by various people since the early 20th century. The theory is that unreleased anger and other emotions can cause physical pain. Massage, breathing, and exercise can all be used to help a patient release the emotion, and stop the pain.

## AYURVEDIC HEALING

THE WORD "AYURVEDA" MEANS science of life, and it's an ancient Indian form of healing. It's based on the belief that humans are simply a microcosm of the macrocosm. In other words we are part of the whole of the Universe and the four elements of air, fire, earth, and water. Ayurvedic healers believe the elements are directly linked to the body's five main senses – hearing, sight, touch, smell, and taste. They believe that heat and energy, known as *Pitta*, is linked with the Sun and looks after our digestion. *Kapha* is the water and tides, which are linked with the Moon and look after our body's metabolism, while the wind, known as *Vata*, looks after our nervous system and body movements. Diet, fasting, and purification, combined with meditation and yoga, are some of the Ayurveda healing methods. Long-term changes in lifestyle should help prevent future illnesses as well as curing existing ones.

## COUNSELING

IT'S IMPORTANT TO BE able to share our feelings and thoughts. Sometimes people go through a difficult experience, such as the death of someone close to them, and they need to talk to someone who'll listen to them with their full attention. Being listened to properly is a gift which many of us never truly receive, and it's not always someone's fault. People close to us may not be able to listen when we need them to, and sometimes we have things we need to talk about that we don't want to discuss with anyone close to us. These are situations where a professional counselor can be really useful. There are many different types of counseling, but they're all based on the idea of being heard. A counseling room is a safe space where you can explore your feelings without being judged or criticized. You can get to learn a lot about yourself in a counseling session, and leave it feeling much lighter and happier. As the saying goes, a problem shared is a problem halved.

## AROMATHERAPY

THE USE OF ESSENTIAL oils from plants, usually in combination with massage, is called aromatherapy. Lots of people go to aromatherapists because it's an enjoyable experience and can leave them feeling glowing with health. Aromatherapy is particularly good for stress-related illnesses. You can even enjoy a kind of aromatherapy treatment in your own bathroom, by buying some special oils and adding them to your bath. It's best to check with an expert which oils and how much to use. Essential oils that are often used are lavender, which calms you, eucalyptus, an antiseptic which is great for coughs and colds, orange, which lifts the spirits, and rosemary and basil, used to treat headaches.

USING AN OIL BURNER
Oil burners like this one have a candle that gently warms the oil and sends the scent into the air. First, you fill the bowl with water, then add just a couple of drops of your favorite essential oil. In this way, the smell is released slowly into the room.

# MASSAGE

BACK IN THE TIME of Hippocrates, the Greeks used massage for relaxation. The rhythmic stroking, pounding, and kneading movements of a masseur or masseuse can release stress and bring a sense of ease and well-being.

Massage can help people with back pain, sports injuries, headaches, and even insomnia (difficulty in sleeping). Over the centuries, people have developed different kinds of massage, such as aromatherapy, many of which are popular all over the World.

# CHIROPRACTIC

PROBLEMS IN THE BONES and joints can affect the nerves and muscles. This can lead to symptoms, including pain, appearing in other parts of the body. Chiropractors manipulate, or move, the joints to restore proper alignment, and free any tension caused by misalignment. Much of the work is centered on the spine. This is because the spinal cord is linked, either directly or indirectly, to everything in the human body. Chiropractors manipulate the spine exactly where the problem is, to correct it.

# REIKI

THIS IS A JAPANESE FORM of spiritual healing. Reiki therapists place their hands in certain positions on the body. They use sacred symbols, and believe that they act as a channel for the Universal energy to come through in order to help the patient heal. Reiki is becoming popular as an alternative treatment.

# SHIATSU

THE JAPANESE ART OF SHIATSU massage works with the same pressure points on the body that are used for acupuncture. The idea is to improve blood flow and release muscle tension, and to get the energy flowing smoothly throughout the body.

# ACUPRESSURE

THIS TREATMENT IS SIMILAR to acupuncture in that it comes from the Chinese way of working the body's Ch'i, or energy, and the meridian system. Instead of putting fine needles into the body, acupressure therapists press on the pressure point with their thumbs.

The body's meridians

# OSTEOPATHY

OSTEOPATHS, LIKE chiropractors, ask their patients lots of questions, and look at the way they hold their body. They can treat back pains, joint pains, headaches, and digestive problems. Osteopathy can even help someone get their body back into alignment after childbirth. Unlike chiropractors, osteopaths may manipulate areas of the body where pain is not found, in order to treat areas where it is. For example, an osteopath may manipulate the legs to treat a problem in the shoulder area. Osteopaths often use massage as part of the treatment, and you may find that a course of treatment over several weeks or months is needed to correct some problems, especially those that are caused by bad posture.

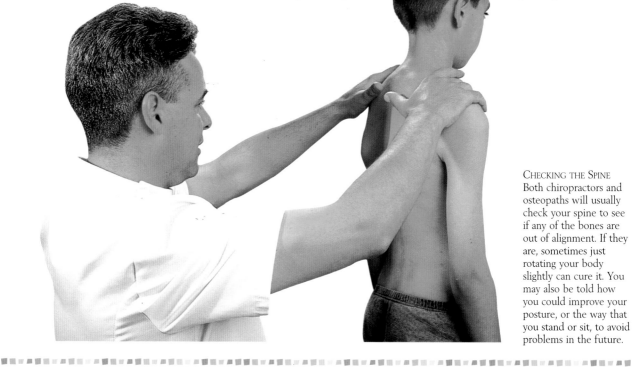

CHECKING THE SPINE
Both chiropractors and osteopaths will usually check your spine to see if any of the bones are out of alignment. If they are, sometimes just rotating your body slightly can cure it. You may also be told how you could improve your posture, or the way that you stand or sit, to avoid problems in the future.

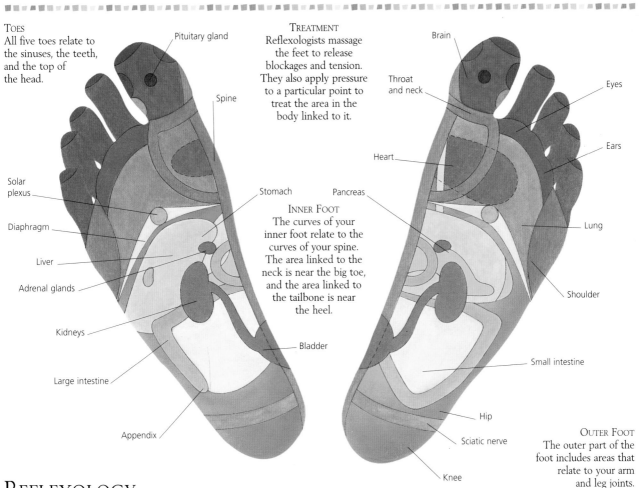

**TOES**
All five toes relate to the sinuses, the teeth, and the top of the head.

Pituitary gland

Spine

**TREATMENT**
Reflexologists massage the feet to release blockages and tension. They also apply pressure to a particular point to treat the area in the body linked to it.

Brain

Throat and neck

Eyes

Ears

Heart

Solar plexus

Stomach

Pancreas

**INNER FOOT**
The curves of your inner foot relate to the curves of your spine. The area linked to the neck is near the big toe, and the area linked to the tailbone is near the heel.

Diaphragm

Liver

Lung

Adrenal glands

Kidneys

Shoulder

Bladder

Large intestine

Small intestine

Appendix

Hip

OUTER FOOT
The outer part of the foot includes areas that relate to your arm and leg joints.

Sciatic nerve

Knee

# REFLEXOLOGY

THIS TYPE OF HEALING probably goes back to Egyptian times, and is also used by the native peoples of North and South America. Some people say that because we walk on our feet, they connect us to the Earth and therefore to the energies of the Universe. However, your feet do a lot more than carry you around. They can tell a reflexologist all there is to know about what's going on in your body. Every area on each of the feet represents a human organ, a gland, or other part of the body.

Reflexology is a holistic therapy. It's based on the idea that most modern illness and disease is caused by our thoughts and lifestyles. Given the chance, the body will heal itself. However, if the channels that the body uses become blocked, the healing can't happen. Reflexologists work with the foot's reflex points, releasing any blockages they can feel in the feet and toes. At the same time, blood circulation improves, toxins, or poisons are removed, and stress is released. The results can be incredible!

# PSYCHIC HEALING

PEOPLE WHO'VE been treated by a psychic healer often say that they can feel the energy flowing into their body. The healer puts their hands on or near a person's body and releases their pain. Apparently they do this by channeling, or using Universal energy. Some psychic healers claim to be able to heal people hundreds of miles away. They do this by sending their positive energy to the ill person through thought instead of actually touching them.

# THERAPEUTIC TOUCH

RECENTLY, A NON-RELIGIOUS version of "the laying on of hands" has become popular. This is known as therapeutic touch. It involves one person, called the sender, placing their hands on, or near, the affected part of the other person, or receiver. The sender sends relaxed, healing forces to the receiver through their hands. This can result in the patient becoming much more relaxed, with a quieter tone of voice, and slower, more relaxed breathing.

## HELPING HANDS
YOU CAN TRY therapeutic touch for yourself with a friend. Whoever is "receiving" should sit or lie down in a comfortable position. The "sender" places their hands on or near the part of the receiver that needs healing, and sends healing thoughts through their hands. After a while you should feel the energy flowing between the two of you.

# DANCE

HAVE YOU EVER FELT so happy or excited that you wanted to dance? Dance can be a form of art, and of magic. It's a way of moving that's often associated with joy, celebration, and happiness. In fact, you can dance to express any emotion you feel, on your own or in a group, in public or in private. Dancing is about moving energy. Whichever way you choose to move your body, it's a wonderful exercise. Next time you find yourself feeling a bit down or sluggish, put on your music and move that body. It works wonders!

## FOLK DANCES

MANY COUNTRIES AND cultures have special folk dances, with set steps that you can learn. They may be danced at certain times of the year, to celebrate a religious event, or at ceremonies such as weddings. Often the people dancing wear a particular costume, which adds to the way the dance looks. They may also carry objects, such as sticks or cloths, and dance around swords or other symbolic objects placed on the ground. Some dances have hardly changed for hundreds of years.

## EARLY FORMS OF DANCE

DANCING HAS ALWAYS BEEN a part of human life. Early dancing may have been similar to the dances that many animals do in courtship, or to protect their territory. People danced in lines, circles, pairs, and alone, and represented animals, historical events, and religious rituals. They danced to encourage rain to make the crops grow.

Even the changing phases of the Moon and the movement of the Sun inspired dances. Today, dancing is very often done at a social occasion, and knowing the steps to particular dances can help to make people feel that they have something in common with others. In a way, by dancing, we link ourselves spiritually to the Earth and everything on it, and to the Universe as a whole.

PERUVIAN COLORS
People often wear colorful costumes, like these from Peru, for traditional folk dances.

 SEE ALSO: CELEBRATIONS PP.140-142, EMOTIONS PP.24-25, FAITH SYSTEMS PP.130-133, HEALTH AND FITNESS P.62-63

# WHIRLING DERVISHES

MANY DANCES HAVE A DEEP spiritual meaning. Cultures across the World use dance as a way of tuning into their God. One Islamic group, called the Sufis, dance as "whirling dervishes," which they say makes them feel connected with God. By spinning on the spot for up to half-an-hour, they can lose their sense of themselves and gain a kind of spiritual ecstasy. Other groups around the World have similar dances, and they are thought to represent the circling of the stars.

# DANCING FOR JOY

AT THE ROOT OF all dances are the emotions. We can dance when we're happy, and we can dance when we're sad. We usually find we want to dance most when we are very happy. It's a way of celebrating an event or just a great feeling, and that's why people dance at parties, festivals, and other celebrations. But if we can do it when we feel sad, moving energy through the body is a way of releasing and clearing out old, unwanted feelings. It's a bit like dusting out the basement of a house. To begin with, it's hard work, but when you start to see the results and feel better you'll probably get more energetic as well as happier. You can start off dancing to express your sadness and end up dancing for joy!

# DANCE THERAPY

USING DANCE TO DISCOVER more about our inner selves is becoming increasingly popular. It's a way of expressing our imagination and using our creative skills. We can use dance to mime or to act out something in a game. Dance is a great way of communicating, so it's useful in therapy for people who find it difficult to express themselves in words. There are some beautiful dances, called Universal Peace Dances, which are choreographed, or designed, to bring inner harmony and peace. People sometimes sing words to these as well, but the graceful movements of the dance help give the individual or group a sense of well-being and happiness. It's a bit like a moving meditation!

# SOCIAL DANCES

FOR HUNDREDS, probably thousands, of years, people have danced together in pairs and groups. It's one way of meeting people and making new friends. Many people even meet their partner at a dance. Lots of couples continue dancing together throughout their lives. Like any way of communicating, social dancing can help keep people in a relationship happy and contented.

**IN A SPIN**
It's possible to change your state of awareness by dancing. Whirling dervishes do this regularly, to feel nearer to God in mind and spirit.

# DANCING FIT

TODAY, MANY PEOPLE dance to get fit as well as to have fun. Lots of fitness classes include dance moves, because it's a very good way of improving stamina. Some types of dancing, such as ballet and jazz, also help improve people's flexibility, or suppleness.

## DANCING'S EASY

EVERYBODY HAS EMOTIONS, such as anger, fear, love, joy, or happiness. Anyone can dance to express their emotions, so why not try it? Styles of dancing move in and out of fashion, but there's a multitude to choose from, including the graceful and elegant movements of ballet and the foot-stomping style of rock 'n' roll. Latin American, square dancing, jazz, break dancing, Spanish flamenco, waltzing, and traditional folk dances are other styles that many people enjoy. If you want to learn a particular form of dance, the best way is to try out a few classes in your area, and see which of the styles you like best.

# MARTIAL ARTS

IF YOU WANT TO develop your physical fitness and, at the same time, help bring harmony to your mind, body, and spirit, you might think about taking up one of the many different kinds of martial art. Most of these methods of combat were developed in China, Japan, and other parts of Asia. The techniques can be used in fighting or self-defense, and as competitive sports. They may also be practiced as a way of improving physical fitness. As well as physical moves, each martial art teaches you a kind of inner strength, involving concentration, control, and self-awareness.

> 66 *I hope martial artists are more interested in the root of martial arts and not the different decorative branches, flowers, or leaves... when you understand the root, you understand all its blossoming.* 99
>
> BRUCE LEE

IT'S ALL IN THE MIND
Every martial art requires self-discipline, concentration, and a calm, focused mind. Skilled martial artists never allow themselves to be distracted, and are always aware of their breathing and position.

In Karate, it's traditional to wear a white Karate-gi. The belt, or *obi*, is wound round the waist twice with a knot at the front.

The position of the feet is very important in martial arts, and a wide stance creates a stable base.

## THE EARLY FORMS

ALTHOUGH NOBODY REALLY knows when the martial arts were first practiced, most people agree that the styles we know today are based on the non-aggressive beliefs of the Buddhist faith.

In the sixth century, an Indian monk named Bodhidharma visited the Shaolin Temple in China, where he preached the teachings of Zen Buddhism. The Shaolin monks travelled widely, and they were often attacked on the way to their destination. Bodhidharma taught them eighteen exercises for self-defense. These exercises are now known as "Shaolin eighteen monk boxing" and they form the basis of all the Western martial art techniques.

The first part of this Tai Chi movement is a position called "Ward off."

The second step is called "Grasp bird's tail."

## SELF-DEFENSE

LOTS OF PEOPLE PRACTICE a martial art as a method of self-defense. In fact, many self-defense courses use elements of different martial arts as a part of their teaching. Everyone, both young and old, can benefit from learning some kind of self-defense, even though they may never need to use it. Improved balance and poise, and being ready to deal with an attacker, can give you great confidence in all sorts of other everyday situations.

 SEE ALSO: FAITH SYSTEMS PP.130-133, HEALTH AND FITNESS PP.62-63, MEDITATION PP.12-13

# BRUCE LEE

DURING THE Communist Revolution in China, soldiers attacked the temples and the monks fled. Many Kung Fu masters fled too. Some of them settled in Hong Kong and set up martial art schools. One of these masters, called Yip Man, taught the famous Bruce Lee a form of Kung Fu known as the art of Wing Chun.

Bruce Lee combined different martial art styles into a form of his own called Jeet Kune Do, which means "Way of the intercepting fist." Apparently, he would tell his students "I am no style, but all styles."

By the age of six, Bruce Lee was playing lead parts in films. He appeared in many martial art movies,

and unfortunately he died at the height of his fame, aged 32, just before his martial art film *Game of Death* was released.

The Kung Fu craze of the 1970s, led by Bruce Lee, made Hong Kong the action-movie capital of the World. Today, Hong Kong has the fastest-growing of all film industries.

# TYPES OF MARTIAL ARTS

● AIKIDO One of the gentlest of all the Japanese martial arts, Aikido uses flowing, circular movements that have great power over an attacker. The word Aikido means "Way of harmony."
● JUJITSU This is the traditional Japanese martial art of unarmed self-defense, once used by Samurai warriors. Jujitsu developed into what we know today as Judo.

● JUDO This method of self-defense was started in Japan in the late 1800s, and it has been an Olympic sport since the 1960s. The main idea is to turn your attacker's force to your advantage.
● KARATE The many forms of Karate all use the force of blows, rather than throws. The target areas are the opponent's face and head, stomach, chest, and back.

ANIMAL MOVES
With names like "Monkey Grabbing the Peach" and "Nine Dragons at Sea" it doesn't take much to work out that many martial art moves are based on the movements of animals. The boxing style called Bak Hok Pai is based on the flapping movements of a crane's wings.

● KENDO This traditional Japanese martial art involves fencing with bamboo staves, and sometimes with real swords. The fast footwork and jumps make it exciting to watch.
● KICK BOXING A Kick-boxing competition takes place in a boxing ring. This is an energetic sport, good for improving fitness.
● KUNG FU Like Karate, Kung Fu is a kind of Chinese boxing, and it's one of the most popular martial arts. The handsprings, leaps and falls, turns and dodges, make it great fun to watch as well as practice. Kung Fu is Chinese for "Well done."
● TAE-KWON-DO Full of flying kicks and punches, this Korean style of martial art is one of the more aggressive of the martial arts.

This Tai Chi position is known as "Snake creeps down."

The final step of this exercise is called "Press."

# TAI CHI

THIS GENTLE KIND of martial art has been around for more than 2000 years, but Tai Chi reached its present form in the 1700s. It's based on balancing the opposing energies of Yin and Yang. The idea is that you develop balance and flexibility while bringing the mind, body, and spirit into greater harmony. All the movements of Tai Chi are done slowly, and you usually learn one at a time. Eventually, these flowing movements become automatic.

## DO THE DUCK WALK

MANY TAI CHI MOVEMENTS are simple to try, and "The Duck Walk" is one of them.
● FIRST, bend your knees, and sit on your haunches with your hands resting on your thighs.
● POINT your toes outward at about 45.°
● NOW shift your weight to the left and take a step forward with your right leg.
● PLANT the heel first, then roll onto the ball of the foot.
● REPEAT the step with your left leg. Try to keep your back straight and your head up, and look ahead to help you maintain your balance.

# THE SPIRIT

# SOULS AND SPIRITS

I'T'S EASY TO GET souls and spirits confused, although they do mean different things. Both are a part of every individual, but they also link us with the non-physical world, or astral levels. Spirit is the energy of all the Universe. You could think of it as the spark of life. The soul is our intelligence and brings us that spiritual energy. When you feel you know something "deep down," it's probably your soul speaking.

**SCROLL IN THE SKY**
Some people imagine the akashic records as an enormous scroll in the sky, with notes about everyone who has ever lived.

## SPIRITUAL ENERGY

EVERY SINGLE ATOM in the cosmos is made up of energy, including our spirits. The energy is not good or bad, but neutral. Humans, and other animals, have an individual essence that is made out of this spirit. It helps form our character. We often refer to someone as "spirited," meaning that he or she has a strong energy for life. We have temporary highs and lows in our energy levels, which we call being low-spirited or high-spirited, and these can be linked to energy levels around us. On a cloudy, dull day, when the whole World seems to be moving slowly, we can feel sluggish and uninspired. But when we're with energetic, lively people, or when the Sun begins to shine, our tiredness disappears and we feel spiritually uplifted.

## SPIRIT GUIDES

AS WELL AS having Guardian Angels, it's said that we all have one or more spirit guides to help us. These are people or animals who once lived on Earth. Spirit guides never interfere in our lives because it's important for us all to have free will. But it's said that they're waiting to help us in any way they can. You just have to remember to ask!

## THE HIGHER SELF

SOME PEOPLE CALL the soul "the higher self." Many people believe that everything that lives has a soul, which creates the pattern for our lives. The soul affects, and is affected by, our feelings and our relationships with other people. The soul remembers every life we've had, and every lesson that we've learned, so we can develop different abilities in each lifetime.

## AKASHIC RECORDS

THE AKASHIC RECORDS ARE like a library of books in the Universe. Each soul has its own personal account of lessons past, present, and future. It's a record of all the thoughts and feelings each one of us has on Earth. What we think of as rights or wrongs, or successes and failures, are probably not listed as such, because the important thing in terms of our spiritual development is learning from our experiences.

## TRANSCENDENCE

THE SOUL CAN help us overcome obstacles in our lives. By connecting with the God within us, we move into a higher state of awareness and can deal better with problems. Transcendence happens when we pass through one stage in our development and go onto the next.

# AFTER LIFE

FOR MOST OF US, the idea that death is the end of everything is pretty bleak, but we don't know what really happens when we die. People who've come close to death and survived talk about seeing a bright light, feeling a great love, and being met by friends and family who've already died. Some cultures believe that we come to Earth many times, and some that there is another kind of life awaiting us after this one.

## ASTRAL PLANE

SOME PEOPLE SAY THAT very close to Earth there's a level called the astral plane, which is where we go to after we die. It's quite similar to Earth, although it isn't a physical place. Clairvoyants say it looks a lot like the World we know, but the people are neither male nor female. There's a great feeling of love, and also a feeling of timelessness. In the astral plane there's no night or day, but a sort of glowing twilight.

## ASTRAL BODY

MANY PEOPLE BELIEVE that when we die we leave our physical body and any pain and suffering behind. However, it's said that we have other bodies, called the astral, etheric, and spiritual, and these move into the astral plane after death. They are also said to do this temporarily while we're asleep, so dying may be as pleasant as going to sleep.

## THE SILVER CORD

SOME PEOPLE CLAIM TO have seen themselves lying asleep in bed. When we're sleeping, it's said that our astral body moves away from our physical body into the astral plane. It's linked to the physical body by magnetic energy, known as a silver cord. Have you ever woken up suddenly and felt strange and disorientated? This is said to happen when your various bodies have returned to the physical plane too quickly, and are temporarily out of line. It doesn't do any harm, but it can feel quite odd for a while.

## ASTRAL FLYING

IT'S SAID THAT PEOPLE can project themselves into the astral plane, and have experiences there while their physical bodies are asleep. This is called astral flying. Some people, especially children, seem to be able to do it without even trying. If you can fly astrally you can do things that wouldn't be possible in your physical body, such as walking through walls. You can travel anywhere simply by using your will. Just imagine yourself somewhere as you go to sleep and maybe you could be there in the astral plane!

Many adults become closed to experiences like this because they don't like to talk about things outside the earthly plane. Children sometimes lose the ability to fly astrally when an adult doesn't believe them. That's why it's important for everyone to have confidence in his or her own experiences.

SEE ALSO: DEATH PP.58-59, HEAVEN AND HELL P.78, PSYCHICS AND CLAIRVOYANTS PP.104-105

# HEAVEN AND HELL

THE IMAGES OF HEAVEN AND HELL that we see in story books can differ depending on who they were written by and where the images came from. Lots of people think that they are real places, and many cultures share the idea of a dreadful underworld Hell and a beautiful Heaven in the skies. Other people say they are really states of mind. Sometimes we feel good about being kind to people when we could have turned our backs on them. At other times we are troubled by something we've done that was dishonest or unkind. In situations like these we can feel that we know what Heaven or Hell is like!

## HEAVEN

YOUR IMAGE OF Heaven is probably like that of the people around you. It represents the best possible place you could go to when you die. You might see Heaven as a place full of fun and laughter, or peace and quiet. Native American peoples dream of a "happy hunting ground" in the sky, where the brave and the true will be rewarded. Christians often imagine a golden place, full of shining angels and light.

PARADISE
We often think of Paradise as a kind of Heaven on Earth. We may see it as a place of natural beauty, with none of the difficulties of life. In the Bible, the first people, Adam and Eve, were said to have lived in Paradise until they disobeyed God. As punishment, they were thrown out to live in the World.

## HELL

NOBODY REALLY KNOWS WHETHER Hell exists, or what it might be like, so people use their imagination to describe it in the best way they can. Hell could be almost anything, from flaming pits to icy, barren wasteland. Images like these are very effective at frightening people into following the rules of their faith. For some people Heaven and Hell are only temporary resting places anyway. Hindus and Buddhists, for example, say that we only pass through such places on our way to the next life.

 SEE ALSO: AFTER LIFE P.77, ANGELS PP.80-81, FAITH SYSTEMS PP.130-133

# DEMONS AND DEVILS

MANY OF US are frightened by the idea of demons and devils, but they only become terrifying if we let them! Some people say that devils and demons are the things inside us that we don't want to see. When we bring them out into the open they seem to be a lot less powerful. Sometimes if we face our fears and weaknesses we find ourselves in a place of courage, achievement, and personal power. The antidote to fear is faith. It doesn't really matter what you have faith in. It could be anything that makes you feel better and safer inside, and strong enough to overcome your own personal demons.

## TYPES OF DEVILS

MOST DEVILS ARE said to take on physically horrible forms, some with the heads of animals or monsters. Stories about demons and devils differ according to belief and faith systems. Some say there is a demonic pecking order, similar to the angel hierarchy. Satan is in the lowest pits of Hell, and the less evil devils are in the upper levels, which are not quite so far away from Heaven. People, and Earth, are said to be half-way between the angels and the devils.

**THE PRINCE OF DARKNESS**
One of Satan's many names is "Prince of Darkness," because Hell is pictured as a dark underworld, lit only by the fires made by the devils to punish people sent there.

## LUCIFER

ONCE, THE CLOSEST Archangel to God was Lucifer, whose name means "Giver of Light." Legends about him vary, but one story says that when God created Adam, the first man, he asked the archangels to bow before him. Lucifer refused, so God cast him out of Heaven. Lucifer became angry, and was foolish enough to challenge God's rule. For his bad deeds, Archangel Michael threw Lucifer into the abyss, or Hell, and he became known as Satan, the Prince of Evil, or Beelzebub, among many other names.

Satan is also said to have taken the form of the snake in the Garden of Eden, who tempted Eve to bite the apple of knowledge. In that form he represents the temptation to do something wrong that all of us face from time to time!

**ANGRY ASMODEUS**
Asmodeus, the demon of anger, has clawed feet and more than one head! Demons are often red, which may be a symbol of Hellfire.

## FALLEN ANGELS

IT'S SAID THAT WHEN Lucifer was cast out of Heaven he took with him a third of the other angels, who joined him in Hell. The fallen angels became the demons, or devils, who are said to tempt humans into doing wrong, and to lure them away from hopes of eternal life. They are also said to punish people for their sins.

## LILITH

IN JEWISH LEGEND, when Adam realized that the other animals had mates, he became jealous, and so God made him a wife, called Lilith. Instead of making her out of dust, like Adam, God used dirt and soil. The pair weren't compatible, so God made Eve to replace her, and Lilith became one of the wives of Satan.

# ANGELS

CLOSE YOUR EYES AND imagine an angel. What do you see? Is it a sparkling being with wings, a serene look on its face and a halo above its head? We almost always see angels like that. Some say the light represents the Universal source, or God, and the wings represent freedom and power, since angels have the ability to soar and fly. Angels have been all around us since the beginning of time, and there are many stories from around the World that describe them in very similar ways.

## ARCHANGELS

ONE OF THE ARCHANGELS' duties is to carry messages from God to humans, so they are the best known angels. Archangels, as well as Principalities and Angels, work closely with the material World. You may have heard of Michael, who protects us, Raphael, who helps to heal us, and Gabriel, who brings messages from God.

Michael, the highest of the Archangels, is said to have beaten Lucifer, or Satan, in the Heavenly battle. This myth is often retold as *St. George and the Dragon.*

Gabriel is the angel who appeared to Mary and told her that she would give birth to the Son of God.

Raphael is often seen with a snake, which is a symbol of healing. He guards the Tree of Life in Eden and watches over humans on Earth.

## GUARDIAN ANGELS

IT'S SAID WE EACH have a Guardian Angel, who looks after us from birth. The angel gives us support from the invisible realm, throughout our childhood and development into adults, and for the rest of our lives. If we have a problem, or we want to find a way to help someone out, we can ask our Guardian Angel for help. They've been with us since the first moment, so they know us as well as our family, if not better, and they can give us the best possible advice. We can also ask for help from other angels if we think we need it.

### GABRIEL'S SIGNATURE
Some people think that this is the Archangel Gabriel's signature. Magicians sometimes use angel signatures to symbolize days of the week. Gabriel's signature represents Monday.

## ANGEL SPEECH

ACCORDING TO JOHN DEE, who was Queen Elizabeth I's Astrologer Royal, you can speak to angels in their own language. John Dee and a medium called Edward Kelley wrote down messages that they said they received from angels, and worked out a whole language. In this language you can call an angel down to Earth simply by saying, "*Ils dialprt, soba upaah chis nanba zixlay dodsih.*"

 SEE ALSO: DEMONS AND DEVILS P.79, HEAVEN AND HELL P.78, TREES PP.112-113

# ANGELS IN ART

ANGELS PLAY AN important part in Jewish and Muslim beliefs, but members of these faith systems aren't allowed to make images of religious figures. Christian art contains lots of angels. They've been popular for thousands of years with painters, carvers, songwriters, designers, stained-glass makers, and many others.

Over the centuries, people have used all sorts of materials and decorative styles, to try to show that angels don't have physical bodies like ours. The wings of angels in art often look like the feathers of exotic birds, such as parrots and peacocks. In medieval times, their halos, faces, and clothing were often made of gold leaf. More recently, artists have used mystical light and bright colors for their angelic special effects.

**ANCIENT ANGELS**
Angels in art are often shown in flight, like this marble carving, which was made thousands of years ago as part of a building in Ephesus, in what is now Turkey. Even today, pictures of angels often look very similar to this one.

**SERAPHIM AND OPHANIM**
Seraphim, like this one, usually have six wings and are often shown standing on top of one of the Ophanim, or Thrones, which look like wheels. Thrones are shown as fiery wheels because, according to the Bible, that's how Ezekiel described the four angels he saw in a vision in about the 6th century B.C.

## TYPES OF ANGELS

PEOPLE ARGUE about the order and importance of angels, and it has often changed. Archangels were once the most important, but today, the following order is mostly accepted.

● SERAPHIM  The Seraphim, or "burning ones," are said to be closest to God. They are red because they are burning with love for Him.

● CHERUBIM  The Cherubim work out how to carry out the Divine Plan, and they keep records of God's work.

● THRONES  Thrones, or Ophanim, consider how the decisions of God may be understood. They are shown as fiery wheels with many eyes.

● DOMINIONS  The Dominions give the orders as to how God's will is to be done. They are directed in their work by the Cherubim.

● VIRTUES  The Virtues direct miracles on Earth, and also help the Powers in their work with the Universal Laws.

● POWERS  These are responsible for keeping the laws of the Universe, such as the forces of Nature.

● PRINCIPALITIES  Princes, Princedoms, or Principalities govern the rise and fall of nations, and protect good spirits from evil spirits.

● ARCHANGELS  The Archangels watch over the World's worship of God. These are the angels that often bring God's messages to people.

● GUARDIAN ANGELS  Guardian Angels are responsible for areas such as music, art, love, teaching, and wisdom. These are the angels we are most likely to know personally, as they act as go-betweens for God and humans.

## CALLING YOUR ANGEL

ALL YOU NEED TO DO to call your Guardian Angel is to concentrate. First of all find a quiet space. Sit comfortably, close your eyes and take a few deep breaths so you can feel really relaxed.

Now imagine in your mind's eye that you are meeting your angel for the first time, and call out to it. You could start by asking its name. You might not hear an actual voice, but a name might pop into your head.

Welcome your angel in your mind, and you can start having a chat. You'll probably be amazed at what you hear. Also, if there's anything troubling you, tell your angel to take the worry away and it'll happen. Just believe it!

## DEVAS

A DEVA IS AN angel, or other divine being, who sends out light to help things to grow. Deva is the Sanskrit word for "shining one." It's said that you can pray to the Devas of plants to help them grow. The best way to see Devas is to walk in a forest, or even sit in your garden, and focus your eyes on the spaces in between the plants and trees.

# EXTRATERRESTRIALS AND UFOs

BEINGS FROM OUTER SPACE are sometimes called "aliens," but it's more accurate to call them "extraterrestrials," which means beings from somewhere other than Earth. People have been talking about beings from other planets for years and years. Some people say that UFOs (unidentified flying objects) and ETs (extraterrestrials) are simply figments of our imagination. Other people suggest that we can only see these beings when we're in a different state of consciousness.

Whatever we believe, it would be foolish of us to rule out the possibility of life existing on the planets of other stars in the Universe. The truth is nobody really knows!

## FAMOUS SIGHTINGS

IN 1947, ONE OF the most important cases in the history of UFOs began, called the Roswell incident. The U.S. air force is believed to have found a spaceship that crashed in the desert of New Mexico. The craft apparently contained beings that were about three feet tall! When the incident was first reported, it caused a sensation. It's become even more famous because it's probably the only time that a government has admitted that UFOs possibly exist. There's a copy of an FBI telegram that confirms the case, but only days after the discovery was made public, the United States authorities denied it.

UFO investigators believe that the whole story was then made secret.

In 1952, there were several incidents in the United States, which included lights circling above Washington's Capitol Building.

In 1976, in Iran, a near-collision between military jets and UFOs was reported.

In 1978 there were three sightings of UFOs over New Zealand by two pilots. The incident happened over the Pacific Ocean at Blenheim when a "mother ship" was spotted with two satellites. The pilots reported seeing glowing lights and they reckoned the spacecraft was travelling at approximately 900 miles per hour!

## EARLY VISITORS?

THERE MAY BE records of visits from outer space that were made back in 2000 B.C. There are huge designs of people and animals carved into the deserts of Peru. Some people think these may have been a way of helping spacecraft to find their way to the area where the Nazca Indians lived around 4000 years ago.

## UFOs

IT WAS IN THE 1940s in the United States that "flying saucers" were first reported. Since then there have been around forty million UFO sightings, and many of the accounts are similar. Most people who have had sightings reported glowing lights and saucer-shaped or cigar-shaped spacecrafts.

FLYING SAUCERS
In 1966, Stephen Pratt took this impressive photograph of what appear to be three saucer-shaped UFOs flying over the rooftops of Conisbrough, England.

# TYPES OF CLOSE ENCOUNTER

THERE ARE SPECIAL WAYS to describe the different kinds of close encounter that we can have with extraterrestrial beings.

- THE FIRST KIND is seeing a UFO close up.
- THE SECOND KIND is when there's physical evidence too.
- THE THIRD KIND is when someone meets an extraterrestrial being.
- THE FOURTH KIND is when a person is temporarily abducted by an extraterrestrial. The person may temporarily lose his or her memory.
- THE FIFTH KIND is when the same person is abducted several times. The person often only recalls what happened under hypnosis.

# ET ENCOUNTERS

IT'S SAID THAT ANGELS usually appear with wings and halos because that's what most of us imagine an angel to look like. It's possible that the myths about ETs are much the same. Our beliefs, upbringing, and culture can affect our judgment and our memory. There are certain recognized ETs, such as "The Greys," which are said to be small, skinny, greenish grey beings with pointed ears.

Some people who claim to have seen ETs say they've been approached by men in black, who question them about the encounter. These people are said to appear to anyone who's a bit too keen on investigating UFOs!

IMAGINE AN ALIEN
If we expect an ET, or alien from outer space, to be three feet tall with huge oval eyes, a strangely shaped head, and long skinny arms, then perhaps that's exactly how we would see one! What do you imagine an ET would look like if you ever met one?

# ALIEN ABDUCTIONS

SOME PEOPLE CLAIM that they've been abducted, or kidnapped by ETs. One of the most famous UFO abductions happened in New Hampshire, U.S.A., when Betty and Barney Hill claim they were abducted while driving through the White Mountains. The couple told their dramatic story under hypnosis, and it included ETs with huge eyes and strangely shaped heads. A film about the case was shown around the World. It led to many more reports of similar stories.

Another abduction case that's still raising questions to this day is what's become known as the "Ilkley Moor Entity." In the 1980s, a young police officer called Philip Spencer was walking in Yorkshire, England, when he claims to have seen a strange green creature with large eyes, long ears, skinny arms and legs, thick fingers, and a slit for a mouth. Philip hurried home, only to discover that two hours had passed unaccounted for. Under hypnosis he described being in a brightly lit room and being examined by ETs!

# THE BERMUDA TRIANGLE

THERE'S AN AREA in the Atlantic Ocean where a number of ships and planes have mysteriously disappeared, sometimes without trace. Some people say that strange magnetic forces make the airplanes and ships go off course, but others believe this is due to abductions by UFOs.

# GHOSTS AND HAUNTINGS

ALMOST EVERY CULTURE seems to believe in ghosts, although explanations for them differ. Most people agree that human beings have some kind of spirit as well as a physical body. Ghosts are usually said to be the detached spirit of someone who's died, and they may have good or bad intentions. Some early cave people used to bury their dead under stones and bind their hands and feet, so that their ghosts couldn't go on midnight walks! Some people, who don't believe that spirits can return to Earth, say that ghosts are demons pretending to be the souls of the dead. Whatever the truth, ghosts, hauntings, and other phenomena that are difficult to explain, continue to fascinate us, as we try to discover more about them.

## GHOULS

GHOULS ARE EVIL SPIRITS, phantoms, or ghosts. In Islamic folklore, a ghoul is a particular kind of demon that eats the flesh of human beings. Ghouls are said to wander around at night, in graveyards and other lonely places, feeding on both the living and the dead. Travellers and children are said to be especially in danger of attack from ghouls. The most feared of the ghouls is a female one that can appear in the form of a normal woman. It is said that this kind of ghoul often marries a living man, who then becomes one of her victims!

## WANDERING SOULS

PERHAPS WHEN WE DIE our souls go onto the astral level as a kind of stopping-off point before we reach our destination. Ghosts might be wandering souls who, for some reason, haven't moved on properly from this World to another. The Chinese believe there are two or three parts to the soul, so the dead can seem to be in more than one place at a time.

Some ghosts may even be the spirits of people who don't know that they're dead! They might have been killed in an unexpected way, such as in a car crash, and they find themselves wandering around unaware that their physical body is dead.

People say that if we don't grieve properly for someone who has died, they end up trapped between this World and the next. Apparently, there's a simple way of moving a trapped soul on. You have to tell it that it doesn't belong on Earth and it's time for it to go onto the next place.

A GHOSTLY SHAPE
Some people believe that when we die we leave some kind of energetic image behind. This photograph taken at Raynham Hall, Norfolk, England, in 1936, shows a ghostly figure on the stairs. The ghost has become known as "The Brown Lady of Raynham."

 SEE ALSO: AFTER LIFE P.77, SOULS AND SPIRITS P.76

# THE FLYING DUTCHMAN

THE LEGEND OF *The Flying Dutchman* is perhaps the best known story of a phantom ship. *The Flying Dutchman* and its crew are said to be condemned to sail around the Cape of Good Hope forever. Tales say that the ship was lost in a terrible storm, perhaps because the captain was cruel to his crew or offended a god. Some say it's because he lost a game of dice with Satan.

In 1881, a prince who later became King George V of England apparently saw *The Flying Dutchman* in the South Atlantic. In 1923, a ship believed to be *The Flying Dutchman* was seen by four seamen. It sailed toward them then disappeared only half a mile from their ship. Sailors believed that if they saw *The Flying Dutchman* it would bring them bad luck.

# POLTERGEISTS

THE WORD POLTERGEIST IS German for "ghost that knocks," but knocking is only one of their many activities. Poltergeists seem to enjoy making sounds, lights, and smells, opening doors and windows, and generally moving things around. There have even been occasions when people claim a poltergeist has pinched, punched, or spat at them! Apparently there are kind, mischievous poltergeists, and there are also grumpy ones that have a bit of a grudge and want to make someone's life uncomfortable.

According to research, poltergeists are said to become attached to an individual, rather than to a place, and they are more likely to appear in households where one of the people, usually female, is reaching puberty. It's said that these noisy ghosts need a particular kind of emotional energy to work with, and it may be possible to explain the activity by psychokinesis, which is a person's ability to move objects by the power of thought. The mischievous, or sometimes vicious, nature of the poltergeist could be an unconscious way for someone to express his or her anger or other emotions without being blamed for them.

# APPARITIONS

EXPERTS USE THE TERM "apparition" for an appearance of a dead person or animal, or a person who is living, but a long way away. The word "ghost" is used for a repeated apparition of a dead person, usually in the same place. Most of the recorded apparitions are of living people. Often, apparitions are not seen, but they may be sensed in other ways, such as strange noises and smells, a feeling of a presence nearby, and knocking or tapping sounds.

It's said that visual apparitions usually appear in a form that we can recognize. Many people say they've seen angels and, more often than not, these have wings and a halo. Most people imagine angels to be winged messengers, so that's how they're going to appear to us.

If you think all ghosts wear white sheets and float around with their heads tucked under their arms, then that's likely to be the way you'll have your ghostly encounter!

# HAUNTINGS

WHEN A GHOST, OR SPIRIT of the dead, keeps appearing in the same place, that place is said to be haunted. The place is often the home of the dead person, or a favorite place they used to visit, or the place where they died. Over the years there have been many reported sightings of phantom armies on the march. There are also reports of headless phantoms and a coach and horses being driven through a wall.

However, most hauntings are invisible. Stories about strange knockings, tappings, whispers, music, footsteps on the stairs, and other mysterious sounds are much more common than actual sightings.

## PARANORMAL AND SUPERNATURAL

ANYTHING THAT ISN'T easily explained in scientific or worldly terms is described as "paranormal," such as spooky events, ghosts, and hauntings. The "supernatural" is a term that's used to describe whatever we think is more powerful than Nature. Thunder and lightning were once thought of as warnings from the gods rather than physical events. In fact, Nature has a way of being able to explain everything – it's just that our brains can't always cope with the information! The more discoveries scientists make, and the more we learn about ourselves, the clearer our picture of the Universe will be.

# MAGIC

WE CAN DESCRIBE MAGIC as a way of using power. Magic can mean tricks done with cards, or witches and wizards casting spells, making potions, and bringing about extraordinary events. For many people, magic is the science of Nature's secrets, the harnessing of the power in the Earth and in ourselves.

Christianity divides magic into white and black, though most witches and magicians don't. White magic is said to come from God and black magic from Satan. White magic uses power to help others, never to harm or scare. Black magic is when people misuse power to cause harm. It usually rebounds on the person doing it.

**PENTAGRAMS**
Five-pointed stars like this are called pentagrams, or pentacles. They are said to protect people from witchcraft, and they are also used to draw magic circles.

## WITCHES AND WITCHCRAFT

LOTS OF US THINK of witches as old women flying on broomsticks, or gathering round a big, bubbling cauldron, casting wicked spells. In fact, men can be witches, too, although it's true that in earlier times most were women. The fact that they cleaned the house with a broom probably began the idea of a witch's magical broomstick! The idea of flying might come from early festivals where people leapt around in fields on various household tools, including shovels, sticks, and brooms.

The Anglo Saxon word *wicca* is the root of the word "witch," and it means "wise one." Witchcraft is different all over the World, and it can take many years to learn the skills. Modern witches use magic from Celtic and other pagan traditions, promoting spirituality and creativity, and most try to help, rather than harm others.

**WISE OR WICKED?**
In medieval Europe, many "wise ones" were punished because they practiced ancient pagan rituals, such as Earth magic.

**FAMILIARS**
An animal or spirit that helps a witch is called a familiar. In the trials of witches in earlier centuries, familiars were said to be demons or imps that assumed an animal form. Cats were often said to be familiars, perhaps because they look wiser than other animals, although they may have simply been household pets!

## MAGIC CIRCLE

A CIRCLE IS ONE OF THE MOST popular magic shapes, although any shape can be magical. Symbols get their power from the attention or energy that's directed at them. Circles can be made in many ways, including dancing, walking, and drawing. A magic circle represents the circle of life, the Universe, and the planets. Anything that goes inside the circle can bring in a spiritual element. A triangle can represent celestial, or heavenly, fire or the connecting points of God, humans, and creation. A rectangle can represent the four elements of earth, air, water, and fire.

 SEE ALSO: DEMONS AND DEVILS P.79, MYTHS AND LEGENDS PP.42-43, THE ELEMENTS P.123

# WARLOCKS AND WIZARDS

A MALE MAGICIAN CAN also be called witch, warlock, or wizard. The term "wizard" was first used in the 15th century, and comes from the English word *wis*, or "wise." There was a wizard in nearly every village and town, and they healed people, made charms and potions, and predicted the future. They usually didn't make much money, though, and had to have other jobs too! The word "warlock" means "deceiver," and was not really used by witches and wizards, but by other people. Warlocks were said to have a pact with Satan. People said a lot of negative things about witches, mostly out of ignorance and fear.

TRAPPED IN A TREE
According to legend, Merlin fell in love with Nimue, the Lady of the Lake, who persuaded him to teach her magic. When she had learned enough magic she used it to imprison Merlin in an oak tree.

## MERLIN THE MAGICIAN

MAGICIANS ARE SAID TO be wise people who use their will-power and work with the laws of Nature to make things happen. This sort of magic is really an advanced form of positive thinking. One of the most famous magicians is Merlin, from the legends of King Arthur and the Knights of the Round Table. He is believed to have been a member of the Druids, probably a priest or high priest, and was the driving force behind King Arthur's extraordinary life.

ALCHEMY
The Ancient Egyptians had a kind of early chemistry, called alchemy. Early alchemists believed that everything on Earth was made out of the four elements, so that any material could be changed into any other, if you knew how. Alchemy isn't really magic, although it may look like it. Today, trying to improve yourself spiritually is also known as alchemy.

## SORCERY

HIGH MAGIC IS A SET of beliefs, like witchcraft is today. Sorcery, on the other hand, is low magic. It's something you do to make something else happen. One example of sorcery is tying a knot in a piece of rope to store the wind for an ocean journey! Sorcery is also called "sympathetic magic." It often includes the chanting of spells and charms, which make it seem more powerful. Divination, or telling the future, is related to sorcery, and may be done by the same people.

## ILLUSIONS

STAGE MAGICIANS appear to be able to saw people in half and yet still keep them in one piece, or pull enormous objects out of a small hat. Some of them even seem to fly and do all sorts of other amazing magical things to entertain their audiences.

These are known as tricks or illusions. The magician has fooled the audience by doing something that looks like magic but is actually done by clever hand movements. A good magician never gives away a secret!

## THE OCCULT

THE WORD OCCULT MEANS "secret," or "hidden," and includes many types of knowledge, such as alchemy, demonology, astrology, and witchcraft. Often, texts written by occultists contain hidden meanings in a secret code, which most people would not see, but which other occultists would spot easily.

Certain numbers are very important in studies of occult knowledge. In the mysteries of Ancient Greece, number three represented masculine energy, and number four represented feminine energy. Together these two add up to seven, which is believed to be one of the most powerful numbers, even today.

# UNIVERSAL LAWS

PEOPLE HAVE INVENTED PLENTY of laws. Most of them are meant to help us to live in freedom, in a society, without interfering with other people's lives. But human laws and ways of behaving are not always in harmony with the Universe. This may be why there is disharmony on our Earth, such as war, poverty, and hunger. Many people believe in Universal Laws, which keep the World in balance. If people don't live by these laws, they cause an imbalance, which can have a terrible effect on our World.

## THE LAW OF ENERGY

EVERYTHING ON this planet, including us, is made up of particles of energy. Energy is the life force of the entire Universe. The fact that we're all made from the same material means that we're all linked to each other, and to everything else in the Universe. This is why it's important not to disturb the natural harmony of the system.

## THE LAW OF VIBRATION

ENERGY'S BEEN AROUND SINCE the beginning of creation, and particles of energy vibrate at different speeds. When energy vibrates very quickly it's invisible, which is why we can see some things and not others. For example, the energy particles in a cupboard are moving a great deal slower than the energy particles that make up radio waves, which is why you can see the first, but usually not the second.

## THE LAW OF ENVIRONMENT

THE CLOTHES YOU wear, the home you live in, and your friends are all extensions of your personality. They're like an image of your life and your beliefs. The way we choose to live shows on the outside what we think of ourselves, others, and the World around us.

## THE LAW OF FREE WILL

WE ALL HAVE THE right to choose in everything we do. It doesn't always feel like it, but in some way, everyone has the freedom to choose, for example, how to live, what career to follow, or whether or not to get married. In the same way, this means that we have to take responsibility for our actions. There's a saying that goes, "once you know, you have to take responsibility." In other words, if you've learned that stealing is wrong, you'll have to take the consequences if you decide to do it. But if you'd been brought up in a forest miles away from any stores, then suddenly found yourself in the middle of a shopping mall, you'd probably be forgiven for helping yourself to things, because you'd never have been taught not to!

SEE ALSO: EMOTIONS PP.24-25, LIFE FORCE AND ENERGY PP.90-91

# THE LAW OF GRACE

FORGIVING IS ONE OF the hardest things to do. But if you can forgive someone for doing wrong, or for hurting your feelings, you're probably abiding by the law of grace. It's important to be kind to ourselves, as well as others, and to forgive ourselves for our mistakes. We can do more damage by punishing ourselves emotionally for something than we did by doing it in the first place!

# THE LAW OF POLARITY

IN ORDER TO HAVE balance we have to have opposites, such as light and dark, joy and sadness, and good and bad. Polarity includes the idea of the Yin and Yang energies that work together to achieve harmony in the Universe. We need to know the darker, negative side of ourselves, as well as the positive side. If we try to be balanced, we can cope with the stresses of life. There's also more chance that our society will be balanced, too.

# THE LAW OF CYCLES

WHEN WE LOOK AT the seasons on Earth we can see how Nature responds to the law of cycles. People also have their own physical cycles of birth, life, and death. Even our spiritual patterns of behavior follow a cycle. Some people believe we're all here to learn spiritual lessons that we've brought with us for this lifetime. Once we've understood each lesson, the Universe will find something else for us to work on.

# THE LAW OF CAUSE AND EFFECT

WHATEVER WE DO HAS a consequence. If we cheat or steal, we'll either be found out and punished, or have to live with the inner guilt. If we help someone, even if they don't return the favor, you can bet that, by the law of cause and effect, someone will help us another time when we need it.

It's tempting only to do good things if they're likely to be noticed by other people. However, even if nobody thanks you for a worthwhile, kind, or caring deed, those angels and spirit guides in the invisible realm will notice, and they'll make sure you get your reward!

# THE LAW OF DIVINE LOVE

UNCONDITIONAL LOVE is love in the greatest sense of the word, with no strings attached. It's like the love of parents for children, no matter what they do. People say that divine love is so pure and bright it's impossible to describe. Those who've had "near death experiences," or who've achieved a higher spiritual level, talk about a wonderful love that is overwhelming and entirely positive.

# THE LAW OF ONENESS

SINCE WE ALL BELONG to the same Universe, taking care of others should be like taking care of ourselves, and equally important. We all have a place here and a job to do. It's not always easy to see that everyone on the planet is our family, and we sometimes push people away because we think they're different from us in some way. On a Universal level, we are all one.

# LIFE FORCE AND ENERGY

W<small>E SOMETIMES FORGET</small> that the most natural things in the World are powerful sources of energy, or life force. Sun, wind, and water power all carry the force of life. If you walk barefoot, you can even feel the energy of the Earth pulsating through your feet. We wouldn't function without it. When the body dies, its energy simply moves on. Life force is found in absolutely everything, from powerful waterfalls to immovable stones. It's a neutral energy, and it is the basis of all creation.

## NATURAL ENERGY

S<small>INCE THE MOMENT</small> that the Earth was created, it has been buzzing with energy. From the flaming heat of the Sun to the terrifying force of the ocean's tides, energy is all around us. The movement of the planets in space wouldn't happen without natural energy. It's difficult to imagine how it all began, but we're still feeling the effects of the Big Bang that scientists believe started the Universe. The Sun's light and heat makes plants grow, and the force of its gravity makes Earth and the other planets circle around it. Together, the Sun and the Moon produce the tides, and our weather. Rain, hail, and snow falls on the land, giving us rivers and streams for animals and plants to drink from. We can even harness the power of water or wind today to produce electricity – another kind of energy.

## YIN AND YANG

A<small>T THE HEART OF</small> Chinese philosophy is the idea of Yin and Yang. People believe that these positive and negative energies are the building blocks of our planet, human life, and the rest of the Universe. Both Yin and Yang contain elements of each other, shown as dots inside the two shapes, which help to provide balance in life, and make it more interesting.

The negative, passive force is called Yin. It is said to be feminine, and stands for dark, cold, inner energy.

The positive, active force is called Yang. It is said to be masculine, and stands for light, warm, outer energy.

 S<small>EE ALSO:</small> C<small>OLOR AND LIGHT</small> PP.54-55, F<small>AITH SYSTEMS</small> PP.130-133, F<small>ENG SHUI</small> PP.124-125

# AURAS

AROUND THE OUTSIDE of the physical body are invisible fields of etheric, astral, mental, and causal energy. Together, these are known as an aura. Some holistic medical practitioners believe that illness begins in the aura and works its way through to the denser physical body. People often say that serious illness can be caused by suppressing our feelings. Instead of being released from the body's cells and through the aura, they become trapped in the physical body and can make us ill. Some people can see the colors of other people's auras very clearly, and use the colors to diagnose and treat their illnesses. The colors mean different things, depending on the area. The right side of the body shows your outer self, the left side shows your emotional self, and the area over your head shows how you see yourself.

**AURAS**
This aura contains a lot of yellow. Other colors hardly show up at all. Yellow is the color of the intellect, and logic. A simple reading shows this person is intelligent and logical, with a bright, active mind.

# EARTH'S PULSE

THE EARTH HAS ITS own magnetic pulse, which we seem to need around us to stay in good health. Astronauts in space, for example, or people blocked from the pulse by electro-magnetic interference, can become ill.

In 1952, a German scientist called Schumann discovered this pulse, and accurately measured its frequency. The National Aeronautics and Space Administration, or NASA, now puts magnetic pulse generators, known as Schumann Simulators, into all spacecraft that carry astronauts, to prevent the astronauts becoming ill.

# KIRLIAN PHOTOGRAPHY

A KIRLIAN PHOTOGRAPH is usually a picture of the energy field around someone's hand. It's a way of capturing a person's aura on film. From the shapes and patterns around the hand on the photograph, you can read what's going on in your body, not only physically, but emotionally and mentally too. For example, gaps in the patterns around the edges of the fingers may mean you need more space, and might be feeling a bit trapped in your life.

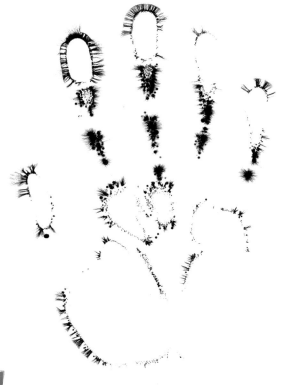

## FORCE FIELD

ENERGY IS THE LIFE FORCE in and around your body. Even though you can't see it, you can feel it. You might be sitting in a chair and someone quietly walks up behind you. You might not see them or hear them, but you can feel them, or sense them, once they've entered your energy field, or "auric space." Why not try this experiment with a friend or someone in your family? First, stand opposite each other with your hands held out in front of you, with your palms facing the other person's palms. Gradually walk toward the other person. Once you get close to each other your hands will start to feel warmer, or tingle slightly. This is the energy, or life force, travelling around inside his or her body, and causing vibrations in the space around it. Stand still for a few moments and sense the energy coming from his or her hands. Now move away again and notice how the energy levels from your partner gradually feel weaker.

# TYPES OF ENERGY

● PRANA For Hindus, Prana is the energy or life force that runs through the whole Universe. It enters us when we breathe, and leaves us in the last breath when we die.

● CH'I Chinese people believe in a positive energy, called Ch'i, that runs through the body in channels known as meridians, and also around the World. The opposite of Ch'i is Sha, which is negative energy.

● KUNDALINI Indian people say the kundalini is like a coiled snake at the bottom of our spines. When we move this energy up the spine, through our energy centers, it's said to change our consciousness and enlighten us.

# PRAYER

THE WORD "PRAYER" MIGHT conjure up a picture of somebody on bended knees in a church, synagogue, or temple praying to God, but there are dozens of ways of praying, and just as many places to do it. Prayer can be a way of getting in touch with God, the Universe, or even the spiritual side of ourselves.

We've probably all prayed at some time in our lives, even if we didn't know it. How often have you found yourself asking for help, not from your family or friends, but in a silent way to some unknown, unseen being or force? Even something as simple as this is a prayer. Over the centuries, people have made all sorts of rules about how and when to pray, but in fact you can pray anytime and anywhere.

## WAYS OF PRAYING

DIFFERENT PEOPLES have different ways of praying. Some Native American tribes have a special prayer stick, and sing their prayers to their gods. In Tibet, Buddhist monks use a prayer wheel, with symbols inside it, or written on it. Islamic people have special hand and body positions for different types of prayer.

Many people say that it doesn't matter how or where you pray. Prayer can be simply contacting a quiet place inside ourselves. That Universal Power or Light burns brightly wherever we are in the World and however we pray.

## WHAT DO I SAY?

MANY PEOPLE LIKE to say their prayers silently, but you can speak in a prayer just as you would speak to another person. You might want to admit to doing wrong, in a confession prayer, or say a thanksgiving prayer for a wonderful event. If you aren't sure what to say or how to say it, many faith systems have books full of special prayers, for almost every kind of situation.

## PILGRIMAGES

PEOPLE WHO GO ON a special journey to a sacred place to pray are called pilgrims. Their journey is called a pilgrimage. People have been making pilgrimages for centuries. For example, Hindus visit Tirthas, and Jews and Christians travel to Israel.

MECCA
During prayer, Muslims face toward Mecca, which is their holy city in Saudi Arabia. Each year, during the last month in the Islamic calendar, thousands of Muslims make a pilgrimage to Mecca. All those who are able to make the journey are expected to do so at least once in their adult life, to prove their faith.

### PRAYER POWER
IMAGINE HUNDREDS OR thousands of people praying to help someone to get better. Think of the amount of positive energy being focused on that person. There are many examples of people getting better when other people pray for them. Our prayers aren't always answered in the way that we expect. We may ask for the wrong sort of help for a problem, but then find that the right sort is sent! Sometimes just trusting that someone or some power cares about us, can really help.

## ANYONE CAN PRAY

EVEN PEOPLE WHO DON'T have a faith sometimes pray when something goes wrong. They plead to a force that they don't really believe in, and hope that it does exist and can help them get out of their trouble. There's nothing wrong with that. It can help just to speak about something, even if our prayers are not answered. A desperate situation can even be a starting point for some people, especially if their prayers are answered. They might then decide to start on an inner journey, in search of a God or power of their own understanding, to help them grow spiritually.

# MIRACLES

A MIRACLE IS AN amazing or wonderful event. It can be difficult to describe what makes something a miracle, and some events in history that were called miracles can now be explained fairly easily. Others are not easily explained, and most arguments about miracles are based on whether or not they actually happened. Perhaps miracles are really about the power of belief in overcoming something that seems impossible. They can happen anytime, even in the middle of a normal day.

1

2

3

THE MIRACLE OF LIFE
Some things that happen every day have miraculous qualities. If you've ever watched a plant or animal grow, you'll know how quickly it happens, and how amazing it is. The existence of life on Earth, and the variety within it, is as wonderful as any kind of miracle.

## STIGMATA

ST. FRANCIS of Assisi was one of the first people known to have stigmata. These are marks that have appeared on the hands and feet of many Christians, in sympathy with Jesus's being nailed to the cross. The positions of the marks match those on statues or other images of Jesus. In reality, anyone crucified would have had nails in their wrists and ankles, not their hands and feet. For this reason, one theory to explain what happens is that stigmatists are people who are highly open to suggestion. Seeing the holes on an image of Jesus makes a strong impression on them, and subconsciously they create similar marks, and sometimes even bleeding, on their own bodies. Whatever the truth may be, it's a miraculous thing to happen!

## PERSONAL MIRACLES

HAVE YOU EVER DONE something that's felt like a miracle, because you weren't sure you could do it? It doesn't matter a bit if nobody else notices. What matters is that you've gone beyond your normal limits.

Personal success, such as winning a race, or passing an exam, can bring joy, wonder, and a sense of miracle. It's great to appreciate our own personal miracles. They make us feel good, give us extra confidence, and they can spur us on to even greater things in the future!

## MIRACULOUS FEATS

THERE ARE LOTS OF miracles in the Bible, such as Moses parting the Red Sea and Jesus rising up after death. Many stories about the ancient gods and goddesses seem quite miraculous, and these deities were seen to possess superhuman powers.

Not all miracles involve divine beings, though. There are technological miracles, too. Who'd have thought a hundred years ago that we could ever fly to the Moon?

There was a time when airplanes, let alone spacecraft, would have seemed an impossible dream. Our technological ability is a miracle in itself.

SADHUS
There are Hindu people known as "sadhus" or "fakirs," who have developed amazing control over their bodies. They can perform miraculous feats, such as standing all the time, or holding one arm above their head for years on end. Some of them walk on hot coals, and sleep on a bed of nails!

# ORACLES AND DIVINATION

AN ORACLE IS A WISE ADVISOR. Oracles can be people or objects that bring messages from the spiritual world, to help us find out more about our lives. You might wonder why anybody would want messages from the invisible realms, but sometimes oracles can help us to see a situation in a different way. We may know the answer deep down, but the oracle helps us to see it. There are many ways to divine messages, from gazing into crystal balls to reading tea leaves. Of course, it's all open to interpretation, so we shouldn't take any message too seriously!

TEMPLE OF APOLLO, DELPHI
Ancient Greek gods were often linked with oracles, and great shrines were built to them in which holy women, such as priestesses, consulted the oracle on behalf of citizens. The Oracle at Delphi was one of the most famous. The name "Delphi" came from the snake of the Mother Goddess. The snake was said to live at the shrine until Apollo killed it. Then the shrine was rededicated to Apollo.

These are the eight trigrams used in I Ching.

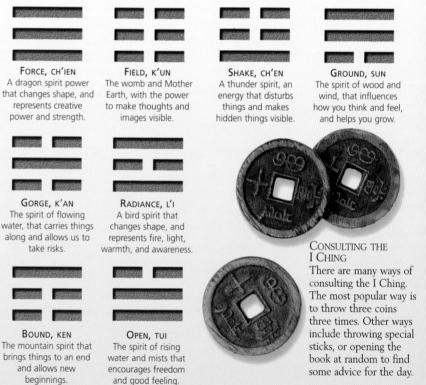

**FORCE, CH'IEN**
A dragon spirit power that changes shape, and represents creative power and strength.

**FIELD, K'UN**
The womb and Mother Earth, with the power to make thoughts and images visible.

**SHAKE, CH'EN**
A thunder spirit, an energy that disturbs things and makes hidden things visible.

**GROUND, SUN**
The spirit of wood and wind, that influences how you think and feel, and helps you grow.

**GORGE, K'AN**
The spirit of flowing water, that carries things along and allows us to take risks.

**RADIANCE, L'I**
A bird spirit that changes shape, and represents fire, light, warmth, and awareness.

**BOUND, KEN**
The mountain spirit that brings things to an end and allows new beginnings.

**OPEN, TUI**
The spirit of rising water and mists that encourages freedom and good feeling.

## CONSULTING THE ORACLE

THERE HAVE BEEN MANY different kinds of oracles throughout history. Some require sacrifices of food or animals, for example, before they can be consulted. Professional oracle readers, such as fortune-tellers, usually require payment of some kind. In most cases, oracles give an answer to a specific question. The answer is often in a sort of code language, and therefore difficult to understand.

The ancient cultures of the Middle East looked at natural elements for clues, such as patterns in the sky or on the land, or even the way their animals were behaving. Most things could be given a deeper meaning, or symbolism, and taken to be oracles.

Many cultures across the World still read oracles, for example, using bones or an animal sacrifice, before making important decisions such as when to sow and harvest their crops. Even the tea-leaf reader you might find at the local fair, uses the power of the oracle to help and advise us in our lives.

## THE I CHING

THE CHINESE BOOK of changes, or I Ching, is one of the oldest forms of oracles, and still one of the most popular. It was first used in about 2852 B.C. The idea is that we can read the Yin and Yang, male and female energies, through 64 hexagrams, made up of broken and unbroken lines. The hexagrams are combinations of the eight trigrams shown above. Depending on the way that people interpret the hexagrams they can give 4000 different meanings!

**CONSULTING THE I CHING**
There are many ways of consulting the I Ching. The most popular way is to throw three coins three times. Other ways include throwing special sticks, or opening the book at random to find some advice for the day.

## CRYSTAL GAZING

MANY PEOPLE WHO'VE seen crystal gazing at funfairs may find it difficult to take seriously. It takes place away from everyday distractions, and the person doing it gazes into the ball, or any other shiny surface such as a pool of ink, until a hazy mist appears. The mist's movement can be read in various ways. Gradually, a darker window appears in the mist. This represents the opening of the mind's eye, and in it can appear people, places, and symbols of emotions.

 SEE ALSO: LIFE FORCE AND ENERGY PP.90-91, THE ELEMENTS P.123, TREES PP.112-113

# RUNES

Characters called runes, meaning "secret," are said to have been created by the Norse god, Odin. According to legend, he hung upside down from the World Tree, Yggdrasil, for nine days in order to learn the wisdom of the runes. They are letters of the alphabet used by the earliest Gothic tribes of Northern Europe. Heroic deeds were recorded in runic writing, and rune stones were used for charms and divination. Rune stones are still very popular for divination, partly because they're simple to use.

## Ing
This means completion, protection, family, and the home.

## Odel
This is your inherited home, wealth, or characteristics.

## Peorth
This can mean a game of chance, or fate.

## Man
This stands for humans, their mental abilities, and communities.

## Ehwaz
This stands for loyalty, progress, and sometimes a journey.

## Ger
This means harvest, and may show the result of past actions.

## Ken
This stands for seeing, knowing, understanding, and new ideas.

## Beorc
This means the family and home, renewal, and recovery.

## Eoh
This rune means both death and rebirth.

## Ur
This stands for strength, courage, health, and the power of freedom.

## Thorn
This rune means protection, and also energy, which can be used for good or bad.

## The Blank Rune
Some sets of runes contain one that's completely blank. This is a recent addition known as Wyrd, and stands for fate and destiny, which are also contained in other runes. Many people think this rune is unnecessary.

## Nyd
This rune means need, and inner strength. It can also warn against taking a risky path.

## Gyfu
This represents a gift, and calls for a gift in return.

## Daeg
This rune means day, light, and life, especially dawn and the strength of the sun at its height.

## Rad
This means a wheel, ride, or travel. It can also be a spiritual journey, or quest.

## Sigel
This rune is a symbol of victory, and the triumph of good over evil.

## Tea Leaves
READING TEA leaves is an easy, fun way of using an oracle! You will need a teapot, fresh tea leaves, one cup, and one saucer. Make the tea in the pot, and pour it into the cup, without straining out the tea leaves. Drink the tea and think about a question you would like to have answered. Swirl the cup three times with your left hand and put the dregs onto a saucer or plate. The shape they make will be a symbolic answer to your question. For example, a horseshoe shape means good luck is on its way, and a heart shape means you could be about to find your true love.

## Lagu
This rune means water, which is both vital to life, and a danger to ships.

## Is
This means ice, which can be both beautiful and dangerous.

## Tyr
This rune means war, justice, and sacrifice for success.

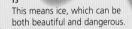

## Feoh
This means cattle, and the energy and hard work that leads to wealth.

## Eolh
This rune is highly protective, and symbolizes reaching up to the divine.

## Wyn
This is linked to reward, and is a feeling of harmony, joy, and success.

## Casting the Runes
The "inquirer" holds a bag or box of runes, while asking a question. He or she casts, or throws, the stones on the ground, or picks one at a time. The patterns of the letters, and the art of interpreting them, should result in an answer to the question.

## Hagal
This means hail, or something unexpected, and can also mean suffering or injury.

## Ansur
This rune represents divine power and creativity. It is also the rune of prophecy.

# NUMEROLOGY

NUMBERS ARE NOT just numbers! Each one holds a particular energy and quality. Every letter of the alphabet is linked to a number, from one to nine, starting with number one at A, and again at J, and so on. When all the letters of your name are added up and reduced to one digit it gives vital information about you! For example, if the total number of your forenames and surname came to 26 you would add the two digits to get 8.

Our name and date of birth alone can tell us a whole lot of information about what we're like and what direction our life may take.

## WRITING STYLES

In graphology, how quickly or slowly you write, and even the spacing and slant of your margins, are all open to interpretation.

One represents leadership and ambition. It's also the number for courage, independence, mental and physical activity, individuality, and achievement. One is often seen as a symbol for beginnings.

Someone whose personality has the number two is more likely to follow than lead. Twos can be sensitive, have great intuition, and bring balance into situations. They make good partners.

In spiritual terms Three is seen as the power of unity between the mind, body, and spirit. Three is adaptable, lively, sociable, good at communicating, and keen on harmony and balance in life.

Four is an earthy number and represents stability, loyalty, and practical thinking. It symbolizes the four seasons, elements, and points of the compass. A Four is usually honest and capable.

Five is the number of the senses, and represents freedom and adventure. Fives are usually cheery, optimistic types, with a love of travel that keeps them always on the move.

Six suggests a person who is imaginative and intellectual, and looks for perfection. Sixes are also very interested in family matters and relationships, and good at taking responsibility.

Seven is seen as a very spiritual number. It represents the seven days of the week and the seven colors of the rainbow. A Seven is wise, deep thinking, and interested in mystical things.

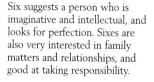

Eight is a practical number, often the number of people who are successful organizers, and good at business! Eights work hard in both the material and the spiritual worlds.

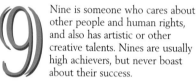

Nine is someone who cares about other people and human rights, and also has artistic or other creative talents. Nines are usually high achievers, but never boast about their success.

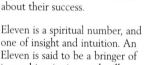

Eleven is a spiritual number, and one of insight and intuition. An Eleven is said to be a bringer of joy and inspiration, and will usually be sensible and down-to-earth, but often unconventional.

Twenty two is the number of completion and perfection. A Twenty Two can be a great visionary, and good at making things happen. People with this number like to be in control of their lives and their surroundings.

# GRAPHOLOGY

HANDWRITING IS NOT ONLY a way of communicating with other people, but can also tell us a lot about our personality and our likes and dislikes! These days large companies often employ graphologists to check the handwriting on a person's job application form to show up parts of their character. The police use graphology to help identify the sort of person they're looking for in connection with a crime.

A simple signature can tell a graphologist a lot about you. Whether your writing slopes forward or backward, whether it's round, square, or spiky, all these are signs of your personality. Large handwriting can be a sign of outgoing, generous behavior but it can also be a sign of selfishness or bossiness. Small handwriting might reveal patience, or a lack of self-confidence.

## WRITE IT OUT

WHY DON'T YOU HAVE a go at this? Get a sheet of paper, sign your name, and start to analyze it! Here are some basic guidelines:

- WRITING that leans to the right shows good communication skills.
- STRAIGHT, vertical writing shows independence and stability.
- WRITING that leans to the left may mean you find it difficult to communicate.
- SMALL writing can be a sign of modesty.
- LARGE writing indicates enthusiasm and generosity.
- WRITING that's a bit of a mixture of everything can show confusion!

 SEE ALSO: PERSONALITY P.22, THE ELEMENTS P.123

# DICE

ONE OF THE MOST ancient forms of consulting the dice is a method that's more likely to be found in gambling casinos today! The Chinese game of Mah-Jong works with the Earth's elements and the four compass directions, with symbols drawn onto special tiles.

A simpler version of Mah-Jong was made into an astrological game called the Part of Fortune. Dice, representing the planets, were thrown onto a board. Where they landed depended on what kind of luck you were going to have!

Traditional Tibetan methods of divination, called Mo, also use dice, together with texts that explain the meaning, to look at karma and help make decisions about spiritual things, and timings of events.

# DOWSING

THERE ARE MANY WAYS of dowsing. Most dowsers use wooden sticks of different shapes, depending on what they are looking for. The simplest and most popular way is to hold two sticks, one in each of your hands, and watch when and how they move.

People dowse to find different things, such as water, oil, or minerals, or powerful energy points on the land. A Y-shaped wooden rod is usually used for water, and L-shaped metal rods for the Earth's energy points. You can even use a pendulum over a map to get a rough idea of what you're looking for before you go outside. Dowsing can also help find lost objects, show you where you should place the furniture in your bedroom, or how to get answers to your most private, innermost secrets.

There are lots of theories as to how dowsing works but one of the most widely accepted views is that the movement of the rods or other object is caused by a combination of the energies from the Earth and the personal energies of the dowser.

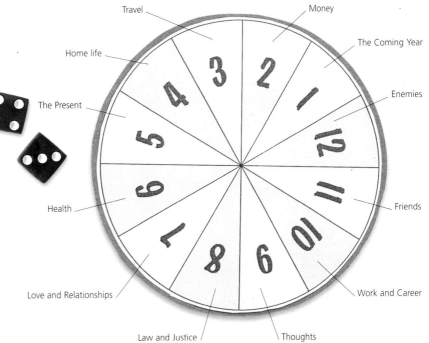

Labels around the wheel: Travel, Money, Home life, The Coming Year, The Present, Enemies, Health, Friends, Love and Relationships, Work and Career, Law and Justice, Thoughts

## THE FORTUNE-TELLER'S METHOD

THIS METHOD OF DIVINING uses three dice. You throw the dice onto the circular board, and depending where each one lands, it will affect that area of your life. The number shown on the top of each die shows its meaning:

1 This area looks good, but take care.
2 Concentrate on your relationships.
3 You will be successful in this area.
4 You may be disappointed or upset.
5 You'll find things are getting better.
6 The situation here is uncertain.

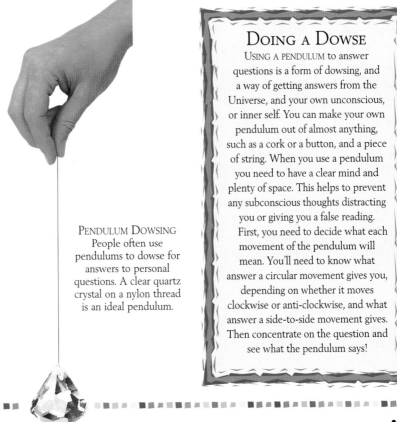

PENDULUM DOWSING
People often use pendulums to dowse for answers to personal questions. A clear quartz crystal on a nylon thread is an ideal pendulum.

### DOING A DOWSE

USING A PENDULUM to answer questions is a form of dowsing, and a way of getting answers from the Universe, and your own unconscious, or inner self. You can make your own pendulum out of almost anything, such as a cork or a button, and a piece of string. When you use a pendulum you need to have a clear mind and plenty of space. This helps to prevent any subconscious thoughts distracting you or giving you a false reading. First, you need to decide what each movement of the pendulum will mean. You'll need to know what answer a circular movement gives you, depending on whether it moves clockwise or anti-clockwise, and what answer a side-to-side movement gives. Then concentrate on the question and see what the pendulum says!

# TAROT

CARDS HAVE BEEN USED as a method of divination for hundreds of years, and their basic meaning has hardly changed. The first pack of tarot cards as we know them came from Italy in the 15th century, and the cards were used mostly as a game. The Church was against the use of cards to read the present and the future, and condemned it as a sure way to Hell. However, this does not appear to have put many people off. Like all forms of divination, tarot cards should be used responsibly, and never to scare others. All the interpretations can mean different things in different circumstances.

## CHOOSING A PACK

FOR MANY YEARS, THERE were just a couple of tarot packs. Then, in the 15th century, the Tarot de Marseille pack was designed. It's still thought of as the standard pack, but now there are many other kinds too. The cards in each pack look different, but they have the same meanings, and the same relationship to each other. It's best to use the same pack each time, so that the cards become familiar to you. A full pack contains 78 cards, made up of 22 Major Arcana and 56 Minor Arcana cards.

## THE MINOR ARCANA

THE CARDS OF THE MINOR ARCANA are split into four suits – Wands or Sceptres, Cups, Swords, and Pentacles. Each of these contains a King, Queen, Knight, and Page. Like the figures in the Major Arcana, we can think of them as

## HOW THE TAROT WORKS

MOST TAROT PACKS have a set of instructions with them. These tell you all about the Major Arcana and the Minor Arcana and give suggestions for spreads that you can use.

Most people lay out the cards in a pattern, and read the meaning of the card in each position. The suits help readers use their intuition, and the reading's accuracy often depends on skill and experience.

**TRUMP CARDS**
The Major Arcana are also known as Triumphs, or trumps. They were created in Italy in the 15th century.

**NUMBER CARDS**
The Minor Arcana, or Number cards, had reached Europe by the 13th century, probably from the Near Eastern countries.

representing aspects of ourselves or symbols that we can use in our lives. The rest of the cards are numbered 1–10, rather like those in a normal deck of playing cards, which are sometimes used for divination. The cards are also linked with astrological signs, and with numerology.

**WANDS**
The Wands represent the male, active forces in Nature, and the power of the magician's wand. They also mean hard work.

**CUPS**
The Cups represent the female, passive forces. They contain blessings, which are lost when the card is upside down.

**SWORDS**
The Swords symbolize the meeting of male and female forces, their struggle, and their union. Swords are very powerful.

**PENTACLES**
The Pentacles symbolize the result of the struggle between active and passive forces, and new beginnings.

# THE CELTIC CROSS

SOME OF THE CLASSIC spreads
you can use in tarot reading
are the Whole Person spread,
the Star spread, and the Celtic
Cross, which is probably the
best known. Each of the ten
card positions has its own
special meaning, which is
affected by the card that falls
there when you deal them,
and is linked to the question
the person is asking.

### POSITION 3
The third position is
called the Ground. It
symbolizes the roots of
the question, and the
conscious aim of the
person asking it.

### POSITION 10
The card in the
tenth position is
called Outcome,
and it shows what
is likely to happen
if the situation
remains just as
it is now.

### POSITION 5
The card in the fifth position
is the Possible Outcome. It
can show an alternative
outcome to the one in
position ten.

### POSITION 6
The card in the sixth
position is the Near
Future, and shows
something that will affect
the situation, although it
may not last long.

### POSITION 9
The card in the ninth
position is Hopes and
Fears, and summarizes
the cards in positions
seven and eight.

### POSITION 2
The card in the second
position is the Crossing
Card. It represents
something getting in the
way, creating a problem
related to the question.

### POSITION 1
The card in the first
position is the Central
Issue. It represents the
way that the enquirer
relates to the question.

### POSITION 8
The card in the eighth
position is called
Others. It symbolizes
the person's physical
and spiritual situation,
and the people around
him or her.

### POSITION 4
The card in the fourth
position is the Recent
Past, and shows recent
changes affecting the
question, or the person's
subconscious aims.

### POSITION 7
The card in the seventh
position is called Self.
It represents how the
person feels and thinks
about him- or herself, in
relation to the question.

# THE CROSS

THE SIX CARDS IN the cross shape, or positions
one to six, all relate to the relationship of the
person to the question. For example, the
Three of Swords in position one tells us that
the person has problems to sort out, which

may cause delays in resolving the question.
The Six of Cups in position two suggests
leaving the past behind and moving on, while
in position three, the Four of Wands shows
the person needs to focus on his or her aims.

# THE MAJOR ARCANA

THE CARDS OF THE Major Arcana are said to symbolize our mind, body, spirit, and emotions. The cards show our hopes, fears, strengths, and weaknesses, and our earthly desires. Most of the Major Arcana cards have an image of a character or object that represents many aspects of our lives and personality. The Sun, for example, can represent happiness, success, and partnerships, while the Moon can mean madness! Through the ages, many of the images and names of the cards have changed, often to reflect a change in people's religious or political beliefs.

Although each card has an individual meaning, when we read the tarot it's important to look at the cards in groups. The meaning of the cards changes depending on the other cards and how they are laid out. It's also important to remember that you're looking for an answer to a particular question, and not to get distracted from that question.

### THE MAGICIAN
The Magician symbolizes a maker. This card is linked to the will, creation, change, tricks, and bringing the dead back to life.

### THE HIGH PRIESTESS
The High Priestess symbolizes a silent, knowing person. This card is linked to the unconscious, intuition, secrets, and mystery.

### THE EMPRESS
The Empress symbolizes a mother. This card is connected with nature, sensuality, passion, and creation of material things.

### THE EMPEROR
The Emperor symbolizes a father. This card is connected with society, structure, order, peace, authority, and reason.

### THE HIGH PRIEST
The High Priest, shown here as Jupiter, symbolizes a teacher. This card is linked to wisdom, teaching, morality, and tradition.

### THE LOVERS
The Lovers are usually shown with an angel. This card is linked to choices, physical attraction, the soul, and relationships.

### THE CHARIOT
The Chariot symbolizes victory. This card is connected to willpower, strength, focus, progress, and control.

### JUSTICE
Justice symbolizes a judge. This card represents fairness, self-examination, punishment, balance, and law.

### THE HERMIT
The Hermit symbolizes a seeker. This card is connected with withdrawal, individual values, and an inner search.

### THE WHEEL OF FORTUNE
The Wheel of Fortune symbolizes a change of luck. This card is connected with chance, karma, irony, and fate.

**STRENGTH**
Strength symbolizes inner
strength. This card is connected
with bravery, force, openness,
endurance, and goodness.

**THE HANGED MAN**
The Hanged Man symbolizes
spiritual independence. This card
is connected with sacrifice,
surrender, and change.

**DEATH**
Death symbolizes great or
important change. This card is
connected with dying, endings,
and renewal.

**TEMPERANCE**
Temperance symbolizes balance
and art. This card is connected
with caution, balance,
and moderation.

**THE DEVIL**
The Devil symbolizes bondage.
This card is linked to control,
trickery, fate, temptation, and
worldly success.

**THE TOWER**
The Tower symbolizes upheaval.
This card is linked to breaking up
old structures, reversal, disaster,
and divine intervention.

**THE STAR**
The Star symbolizes hope and
return. This card is connected
with beauty, healing, hope,
promise, and peace.

**THE MOON**
The Moon symbolizes the dream
world. This card is linked to the
imagination, instinct, phobias,
psychic powers, and dreams.

**THE SUN**
The Sun symbolizes joy and
completion. This card is linked
to perfection, happiness,
and achievement.

**JUDGMENT**
Judgment symbolizes
awakening. This card is linked
to revelation, enlightenment,
rebirth, and reward.

**THE WORLD**
The World symbolizes the day
World. This card is linked with
growth, success, splendor,
freedom, and simplicity.

**THE FOOL**
The Fool symbolizes an
adventurer. This card is linked to
journeys, simplicity, chaos, and
spirit in the World.

# HAND-READING

OUR HANDS ARE AMAZING INSTRUMENTS. Not only can we eat, dress, and work with them, but they can also tell us about our characters and our lives. Hands contain so much information about who we are and our direction in life that they are almost like maps. You can find out lots about people simply by looking at their hands, and every palm tells a different story. Nobody knows exactly how palmistry, or hand-reading, began, but it probably started in the Far East about 4000 years ago, and it is mentioned in the Old Testament and in ancient Hindu scriptures. Hand-reading quickly spread to Greece and the Roman Empire, and it's been practiced in some form or other ever since.

**PALMISTS OF THE PAST**
Palmistry was practiced long ago by the Assyrians, Egyptians, and Hebrews. The Ancient Greeks and Romans studied and wrote about palmistry too.

## HAND SHAPES

HAVE YOU EVER noticed how everyone's hands are different? Looking at various hand shapes is a very good way to start reading palms. There are four main hand shapes, and each one is named after one of the four elements. Some people's hands are a mixture of all the elements. What type is your hand?

**EARTH HAND**
An earth hand has short fingers and a squarish palm. These people are practical, reliable, and down-to-earth. They can also be very creative with lots of energy.

**FIRE HAND**
A fire hand has a longish palm with short fingers. Fire has lots of energy, and so have people with fire hands. They are often sporty types who live life to the full.

**AIR HAND**
Long fingers are the sign of an air hand. These people are often artistic, and they are always looking for new, exciting things to do.

**WATER HAND**
A long palm with long, slim fingers is the sign of the water hand. These types are sensitive, caring, and sometimes rather dreamy.

**MOUNT OF SATURN**
This represents common sense and responsibility.

**MOUNT OF JUPITER**
This represents self-worth and ambition.

**MARS POSITIVE**
This represents energy levels.

**MOUNT OF APOLLO**
This represents artistic and creative talents.

**MOUNT OF MERCURY**
This represents communication and intelligence.

**MARS NEGATIVE**
This represents honesty and staying power.

**PLAIN OF MARS**
This represents emotions and passions.

**MOUNT OF LUNA**
This represents the imagination and intuition.

**MOUNT OF VENUS**
This represents health and happiness.

**MOUNT OF NEPTUNE**
This represents perception.

## THE MOUNTS

THE FLESHY PADS, OR MOUNTS, on the palm and at the base of each finger are full of information about us. Depending how big or small the pad is, each mount reveals details about our strengths and weaknesses.

### LEFT OR RIGHT?

THERE'S A BIG DIFFERENCE between the dominant hand and the passive hand. Your dominant hand is the one that you write with. All its lines and bumps reveal your personality and how other people see you. The dominant hand also shows your talents, health, and future successes in life. The passive hand contains information about your imagination, your instincts, and your potential. This hand reveals what you are given in life, whereas the dominant hand shows what you are doing with your life.

# LOOKING AT THE LINES

EACH OF THE FIVE main lines on our palms gives us information about our character and the events in our life. By studying the lines on someone's hands you can actually see at what stage of a person's life certain events might happen with his or her health, career, or love life.

All the crosses, stars, and other marks on the lines are signs of the events or turning points in a person's past, present, and future. Breaks in the lines are a stop in the flow of energy. Marks on these lines, such as crosses and stars, can also be a warning sign to take extra care at a particular time in our lives.

THE THUMB
If you want to find out about someone's personality, look at the position of their thumb. A thumb close to the fingers could be the sign of a shy person, whereas an open thumb belongs to a more relaxed kind of person. Even the shape of the thumb reveals more than you could imagine.

JUPITER is your index finger and is a sign of your leadership qualities.

THE HEART LINE
This line is about your feelings and relationships. Your heart line can show how you think about love, marriage, and sex. Even the way the heart line curves shows whether you're an extrovert or an introvert.

SATURN is your middle finger and it represents wisdom.

APOLLO is your "ring" finger and this shows how creative you are.

MERCURY is the little finger, which shows how good you are at communicating with others.

THE APOLLO LINE
Not everyone has an Apollo line but if you do, it's a mark of a sunny person who is likely to find success in life.

THE LIFE LINE
A life line is more about how you live your life than how long it's going to be. If this line is clear and strong it means you have lots of energy and are sociable. A weak line could mean you're not keen on sport, or you prefer your own company.

# FINGER FACTS

EVEN OUR FINGERS contain masses of information about who we are and where we're going in life. Every individual finger relates to a different area of our lives and even our fingertips can tell someone what kind of person we are. Pointed fingers often belong to a sensitive, artistic person, whereas square fingertips reveal a more practical, logical person.

THE HEAD LINE
This line is about how you view the World, and it can show whether you're easy-going or a worrier. A weak head line can be a sign of someone who's indecisive and emotional rather than rational and logical.

THE FATE LINE
A strong fate line is a sign of a person with leadership qualities. A weak fate line might suggest you could be a bit more buffeted around by life, and if there's no sign of a fate line at all it's a sign of someone who doesn't want any responsibilities. Your fame and fortune are marked out on this line.

# PSYCHICS AND CLAIRVOYANTS

THE THIRD EYE
Some people say the third eye was once a real eye in the middle of our foreheads. Those who've developed their psychic powers say they can open and shut this eye, so that they're not constantly exposed to psychic information.

THE PSYCHIC SENSE IS often thought of as our sixth sense. We may all have the ability to be psychic, but most of us don't know how to awaken the gift, although many people believe it can be trained. There are many forms of psychic ability, including precognition, or *déjà vu*, when people see something in their mind's eye, or "third eye," that's going to happen in the future.

Clairvoyants are psychic people who see something that appears to be real, but is in fact an inner vision. They can use the symbols, pictures, or words they receive to give information to other people. Another word for clairvoyants is "seers." Royal families and heads of state often employ seers to warn them of possible danger.

## MEDIUMS

A MEDIUM IS SOMEONE who claims to act as an instrument through which spirits from the etheric, or invisible world can speak. You might go to a medium and find that your great aunt, who died a few years ago, is suddenly talking to you through him or her!

Some mediums receive messages from "the other side" in pictures or symbols, and others through voices. They usually pass personal information from a spirit to an individual. Sometimes they even speak with the voice of the spirit who's contacting them. Some people don't believe in these powers because there have been numerous frauds.

## CHANNELING

A PERSON WHO RECEIVES messages from an invisible plane is said to be acting as a human channel. Some of the information that people believe is being channeled through them may really be messages from their unconscious.

Channelers are generally conscious when they are receiving information. They are alert and awake while the channeling is happening, and can ask questions of whoever is communicating with them. They may receive information in the form of spoken or written words. Channeled material often contains an important message for the human race in general.

## CLAIRAUDIENCE

HEARING A VOICE in your head that's not from this World is known as clairaudience. Information received in this way may come from the person's own personal spirit guides or from the spirits of people who've left this World and moved to another dimension.

If you walk into a room and can feel something in the atmosphere, you may be experiencing clairsentience. People who are clairsentient can instinctively feel, rather than see or hear, a spirit presence. It's said that many animals are clairsentient.

## PSYCHICS

THE WORD "PSYCHIC" comes from the Greek *psukhikos*, which means soul, breath, or life. A psychic person is said to be able to pick up messages from the spirit world and other worlds.

Children are often psychic because they're so open to new thoughts and ideas, but this can be a mixed blessing. Some people say that psychics can get messages from both bad and good sources. If we are psychic, we should take care to filter out any messages that come from bad sources, and allow only the good messages through.

## AUTOMATIC WRITING

IN AUTOMATIC WRITING, a spirit communicates through a living person by moving his or her hand, holding a pen or pencil, across paper. Often the person is in a trance while the image or words are coming through, and the results can be as much of a surprise to him or her as to anyone else!

The poet and artist William Blake claimed that a lot of his work came from dead poets, and his art from inspired or psychic visions. People who channel work like this are sometimes known as automists.

## PROPHECIES AND PREMONITIONS

THE WORD PROPHECY MEANS "speaking." It is the ability to predict events before they happen. Prophets are usually religious teachers, or people who receive messages from God. Most prophecies relate to World events, and many contain information about future states, wars, or inventions. Often the prophets write or speak in code, so they need other people to translate their prophecies. People are constantly finding new meanings in the prophecies of Nostradamus. Some famous ancient prophets include Moses, Isaiah, and Cassandra.

### SÉANCE

At a séance, a group of people form a circle and use their combined power to try to contact spirits, usually those of people they knew who have died. The spirits are said to speak through the medium leading the group, though the voices may come from the tension in the people themselves.

### OUIJA BOARDS

ANY SELF-RESPECTING psychic will tell you to leave the ouija board well alone. This old-fashioned parlor game was once very popular, and many people have been tempted to get together with friends to see if they can contact "the other side." However, if you do, you may not know what you're calling in. A trained medium has the ability to act as a "doorkeeper" and say which spirits can come in and which can't. People who don't have any experience of spirits may not be able to control them. They risk letting in dangerous spirits, or negative energy, instead of friendly, helpful spirits and positive energy. On the other hand, you might simply scare yourself and your friends!

# THE EARTH

## MOTHER EARTH

## CREATION

## EARTH MYSTERIES

## BELIEFS AND CUSTOMS

# NATURE

E VERYTHING THAT HAPPENS on and around the Earth is controlled by the forces of Nature. Natural cycles, such as the seasons, night and day, birth, growth, and death, have an effect on the lives of all plants and animals, including humans. Even rocks and minerals are affected by the movement of the Earth, the flow of rivers and streams, and the heat of the seasons. People and their technology seem to have found many ways of interfering with Nature, but it's difficult to control. In the battle for power over the Earth, the forces of Nature will almost certainly win.

## MOTHER EARTH

OUR PLANET IS OFTEN seen as a living, growing, and fertile being. Mother Earth got her name because she is the giver of life to all things. In some places, women lie down on the soil in the hope that it will help them to have babies themselves. Birth rituals sometimes include placing the new baby on the ground as a way of thanking the Earth for the continuing gift of life.

Mother Earth gives food and shelter to all living things. She nurtures us through life and reclaims our bodies after death to continue the cycles of Nature. Without the Earth's support, life would not exist.

## NATURE SPIRITS

EVERY PLANT AND FLOWER in the World is said to have an angel that carries its blueprint, or pattern of growth. The angel is sometimes known as a Deva, which means "shining one." Some people say there's a whole Devic kingdom which carries out the Earth's natural law. It's magical to imagine the spirits literally bringing a beautiful flower into existence.

When you think about the miracle of Nature's cycles and the wonder of how plants and flowers grow from seeds and blossom before going back into the ground, the idea that fairies and Nature spirits help it all to happen seems quite easy to believe. One Nature spirit that is found Worldwide in festivals celebrating the arrival of Spring is the Green Man. The earliest version is probably from India, and is known as the Green Thing, but the same spirit is also called Jack-in-the-Green, Wild Man, Robin Hood, Green Man, and even St. George, in the St. George and the Dragon tale.

**GREEN MAN**
The Green Man is a spirit of vegetation that appears in Spring festivals all over the World, in many different forms, and with many names.

**PAN**
The Ancient Greek god Pan was a symbol of Nature itself. He is usually pictured as having the legs, ears, and horns of a goat.

# NATURAL DIVINITIES

MANY OF THE GODS of the Ancient World were divinities of Nature. For example, the Greek god Pan was god of fields, woods, and animals, and Demeter was goddess of the cornfield. Poseidon was god of the ocean, and Gaia goddess of the Earth. Early people probably found the forces of Nature so amazing that the only way they could understand them was to believe that they were controlled by gods and goddesses.

# PLANTS AND FLOWERS

PLANTS PLAY AN ENORMOUS part in the cycles of Nature. Flowers not only make our planet look beautiful, but also provide food for creatures such as bees. The bees make honey for their young, and it's also one of humankind's favorite foods! People use the essences of flowers and herbs to heal their bodies and ease their souls. Plants make us feel good, because they are linked with love, light, and spirit. We grow them, eat them, cook them, grind them into medicines, and even make them into magical potions and charms that can help change people's lives.

# PLANTS AND THEIR MEANINGS

OVER THE CENTURIES, PEOPLE have given various meanings to plants. A bunch of flowers, for example, can mean quite a lot! Geraniums and yellow roses stand for friendship, and red roses for love. In heraldry, or coats of arms, a vine means joy, and the lily represents royalty, wisdom, truth, and loyalty. A sunflower is the sign of a good person.

# WATERS OF LIFE

WATER COVERS most of the Earth's surface, and is home to some extraordinary forms of life, many of which we have yet to discover. Many people believe that life on Earth began in the oceans, and only developed later into plants and animals that could live on land. The rivers and streams of the World are like highways between the oceans, transporting people and cargo all around the Earth. Water has the power to cut away stone, and it carves its own route across the countryside, sometimes forming fantastic underground caves, and huge canyons, such as the Grand Canyon in Arizona.

# NATURAL GARDENING

CENTURIES AGO, gardeners knew when to plant herbs and do other jobs in the garden by natural events, such as the waxing of the Moon. Some people believe that you can still work in harmony with Nature, including the pests and bugs, to keep your garden neat and tidy. One of the methods gardeners use to put off mice is to water plants with the water from a cat's drinking bowl! Garlic juice also puts off many unwanted visitors because of its pungent odor.

# ENVIRONMENT

EVERYTHING AROUND US makes up our environment, from the air we breathe to the ground we walk on. The places where we live and work are our immediate, or personal, environment. The natural environment is Nature in its truest and simplest form. Unfortunately, people try to control Nature, and have developed powerful ways of changing the environment. From building dams in rivers, and accidentally forming more deserts, to polluting the air, land, and oceans, we have managed to bring about so much change in the planet that some parts of it are hardly recognizable. If we ever were in control, we are not any longer.

## ECOLOGY

THE STUDY OF LIVING THINGS in relation to their environment is known as ecology. Ecologists try to find out how animals and plants are affected by each other, and by environmental factors. Environmental factors include the physical features of the land, weather, and human interference. Ecology also helps us find out what causes animals and plants to become extinct, and can help us to prevent extinctions from happening. Plants produce their own food, using the Sun's energy, and minerals from the soil. They are called producers. Animals consume, or eat, plants and other animals, and they are called consumers. A combination of producers and consumers can make up a complex system of survival, called a food chain or food web.

## ECOSYSTEMS

ALL LIVING THINGS DEPEND on others to survive. An ecosystem is an area where the conditions are particularly suited to certain plants and animals, and where they provide each other with food and shelter. Ecosystems are almost self-contained. The kind of food that we eat plays an important part in deciding where we can live. Over hundreds of years, animals and plants adapt to their environment, even if it is changing too. As long as there is no drastic change, such as flood or drought, the system stays in balance.

## THE GAIA THEORY

THE TERM "GAIA THEORY" was first used in the 1970s by James Lovelock. The word "Gaia" comes from Ancient Greek mythology, in which the Earth goddess, Gaia, was a Mother figure for all living things. Lovelock linked human evolution with the evolution of the Earth. He said that unless we treat the planet as a living being and work in harmony with Nature, we may have to face the consequences, in the form of natural destruction, such as floods. Today, many people believe that Earth is not only living, but also sacred and special. They're trying to limit the damage humans do to the Earth, such as cutting down forests and causing pollution, and want to save animals and plants from extinction.

 SEE ALSO: COMMUNITIES PP.136-137, NATURE PP.108-109

# RECYCLING

As people become more aware of the damage we're doing to our planet, many have begun to use renewable sources such as wind, solar, and water power to make electricity rather than using oil-fired power stations, or nuclear plants, which produce dangerous waste. There are millions of recycling schemes which help us to reuse products, such as paper, glass, plastics, and aluminum.

### IT'S IN THE CAN
In some countries, recycling is a way of life. People in poorer countries have to recycle as much as possible to save money. This usually means they cause less damage to the environment, too. This colorful photograph shows an enclosure that's made entirely from reused drinks cans.

# GLOBAL ISSUES

It's important to be aware of global issues – things that affect our environment, such as pollution and deforestation. Many pesticides sprayed onto crops are ruining the land and the air we breathe. Acid rain, which is the result of polluted air from toxic fumes, harms crops, fish, and other animals. CFCs, or chlorofluorocarbons, found in some aerosols and old refrigerators, destroy the protective ozone layer above the Earth. Cutting down rainforests has ruined the natural home of millions of animals and plants. The rainforests help control the Earth's atmosphere. Their destruction is having a serious, Worldwide effect.

# POLLUTION

It's difficult to think of something we do that doesn't pollute the Earth. You name it, we do it, from polluting the air with cigarette smoke to dumping waste at sea. Most of the cars, buses, and trucks we drive poison the atmosphere with lead from their fuel. All of these bad habits damage our habitat and destroy the wildlife.

# THE GREEN MOVEMENT

It's easy to forget how important it is to care for our Earth. In order to preserve Earth for future generations, we must look ahead. If we returned in a future life it would be shocking to see how much we have contributed to destroying our natural habitat. The "Green Movement" is a term used to describe campaign groups which were set up to fight for the rights of the Earth. They look at ways to combat pollution, including acid rain and global warming.

### SAVE THE EARTH
If you want to help save your Earth, you can start by finding out where your local recycling bank is. Separate the glass, clothes, and cans from your other rubbish and take it to be recycled. Try not to waste paper, and save old newspapers to put in a recycling bin. Give comics and magazines to somebody else to read, or recycle them together with your other paper, and encourage your family and friends to do the same.

# TREES

W HEN YOU THINK how long trees have been growing on Earth, and how many changes they must have seen, you can understand why people look upon them as a source of wisdom. Trees play a huge part in our lives. Over the centuries, we've worshiped them, climbed them, fed and clothed ourselves from them, and used them for medicine and fuel. Many types of trees have special significance and particular powers. Deciduous trees represent the cycle of life, death, and rebirth, and evergreen trees symbolize everlasting life.

## MYTH AND MAGIC

FOR A VERY LONG TIME forests and woods have been thought of as the home of fairies and powerful spirits. According to folklore, fairies are found where oak, ash, and hawthorn trees grow together.

Hawthorn trees are easy to spot because of their strange, gnarled branches, and they were often used as meeting places in the past. These trees are often connected with witchcraft, perhaps because witches would agree to meet under a particularly remarkable hawthorn tree.

The elder is said to protect against witchcraft. If you rub a wart with a stick of elder cut in the waning Moon, then bury the stick where it won't be disturbed, the wart will disappear as the stick rots. But you must ask the tree spirits living in the branches before you cut a piece of wood.

Apple trees also have a strong magical meaning and appear in many myths and legends. Some legends say that visitors from other worlds will appear on Earth carrying a branch of the apple tree with bells on it.

In classical mythology, woods were full of tree nymphs called dryads. These spirits were friendly to humans, and they lived for as long as the tree that they lived in did, which could be for thousands of years.

In Norse mythology, Yggdrasil is the World Tree. It's an evergreen, honey-dripping ash tree that links Heaven, Earth, and Hell. The branches support the world, and in the tree are an eagle, a squirrel, and four stags. Among its roots are the sources of the rivers, or waters of wisdom.

### ACORNS FOR LUCK
Despite its tiny size, an acorn contains the essence of the mighty oak tree, and is said to have the power of health and vitality. Some people carry acorns with them to help them stay youthful and to protect against sickness.

## TREES AS SYMBOLS

IN CHINA, THE mulberry tree symbolizes the cycles of life. Its berries change color three times while they are ripening – white, which represents youth, red for the active years, and black for the wisdom of old age and death.

The yew tree's poisonous needles link it with death, but the Celts believed that the yew tree protected them against evil spirits.

Laurel was a symbol of immortality and victory to the Ancient Greeks and Romans. The laurel wreath was given to brave soldiers and those who excelled in the sciences or arts.

The willow tree, with its drooping branches, represents death and grief in Western countries. But in Eastern countries this same tree is a sign of strength, beauty, and grace.

### THE TREE OF KNOWLEDGE

To Christians and Jewish people, the Tree of Knowledge symbolizes the temptation of Adam and Eve in the Garden of Eden. The fruit on the tree represented the fruit of knowledge, and God warned Adam and Eve not to eat it. But the Serpent tempted Eve to taste the fruit, so God banished them from Paradise and sent them to live on Earth.

Eve

Adam

The Serpent in the center of the tree represents the Devil.

# TREE WORSHIP

PEOPLE HAVE BEEN WORSHIPING TREES since ancient times, probably because they are so tall and strong and they can withstand the forces of nature, such as storms, gales, and freezing temperatures.

For the Ancient Egyptians, the sycamore was the earthly form of the sky goddess, Nut. The leaves represented peace on Earth and in the next world.

According to the Buddhist faith, Buddha sat under the bodhi tree, which is a kind of fig tree, while he meditated and became enlightened. This is why bodhi trees are sacred, and are grown near Buddhist monasteries.

To Celtic peoples, the oak tree was sacred. The old British word for oak is *derw*. The Druids of early Britain worshiped the sturdy oak tree, which they regarded as the king of the forest. The Druids probably got their name from the word *derwydd*, which means "oak-seer." Even today oak trees are seen as a symbol of strength and everlasting life in many parts of the World.

## YEW, HOLLY, AND MISTLETOE

TODAY, THE Christmas tree is a symbol of Christ, but people were decorating trees and branches way before Christianity began. During the "raw nights" of December 25 to January 6, people brought branches of yew or other evergreen trees into their homes and lit candles to keep away evil spirits. Holly was also supposed to ward off spirits, and mistletoe was sacred because it was often found growing on oak trees. In Norse mythology

Yew trees can live for over 1000 years, and are a symbol of eternal life.

Balder, the Sun god, was killed by a mistletoe arrow. The other gods loved him so much that they brought him back to life, and the mistletoe promised never to hurt anyone again. This is why mistletoe is a symbol of love, and it may be why we kiss under the mistletoe at Christmas.

TOUCHING THE SKIES
With their roots buried deep in the ground and their branches stretching up toward the sky, tall, straight trees like these seem to form a link between Heaven and Earth.

# ANIMALS

THE ANIMAL KINGDOM IS MADE UP of millions of different species, or kinds, from ants to antelopes. Some animals, such as dogs and horses, have a close, friendly working relationship with humans. Every animal, whether a fish, bird, or insect, has its place on Earth. Like us, animals have feelings and intelligence, and they deserve our respect and kindness. They all have senses too, though not always the same senses as ours.

PEGASUS
According to Greek myth, when Perseus killed the gorgon Medusa, a winged horse named Pegasus came out of her body. Bellerophon tamed Pegasus using a golden bridle given to him by the goddess Athena. Bellerophon was successful in many quests, and became so big-headed that he rode Pegasus up to Heaven, but Zeus made a fly bite the horse, and Bellerophon was thrown down to Earth. From then on, Pegasus carried Zeus's thunderbolts.

This colorful totem pole was made in Vancouver, Canada.

## ANIMAL SPIRITS

FOR THOUSANDS OF YEARS people have been discussing whether or not animals other than humans have souls. Many people claim they have seen, heard, and felt the spirits of dead animals, in the same way as they have met the spirits of humans. Animal spirits are often said to appear to people when they need help or support, although some can be mischievous, too. The spirit of an animal may be more advanced than us, if it has had more lives and more chances to learn its lessons. Animals and humans have different ways of knowing, and their spirits can help each other in different ways.

## TOTEMS

ANIMAL TOTEMS ARE animals that represent a tribe or an individual, and may be seen as an outward symbol of an invisible relationship. Some Native American people make carved or brightly painted totem poles, often displaying the animal or animals closely related to a tribe. Animals, for example a bear, symbolize the tribe in the same way as a flag symbolizes a nation.

## ANIMALS AS SYMBOLS

USED IN A SYMBOLIC WAY all over the World, animals often represent a nation of people. The American Eagle and the Russian Bear both symbolize the strength and power of their nations.

Native American peoples believe that life should be lived by the body, mind, and spirit. Mother Earth, Father Sky, and all the animals that walk upon the land are connected, and can help each other. They believe that animals are our healers and that when you call upon the power of a creature you can ask it to teach you a particular lesson.

## TYPES OF SYMBOLS

Here are some well known animal symbols.
- DOGS are a symbol of loyalty.
- HUMMINGBIRDS represent joy.
- DEER represent gentleness.
- HAWKS represent messengers.
- BUFFALO represent prayer and plenty.
- SNAKES are a symbol of change.
- DOLPHINS represent the breath of life.
- EAGLES are a symbol of the spirit.
- WHALES represent the record keepers.

 SEE ALSO: FAITH SYSTEMS PP.130-133, GODS AND GODDESSES PP.44-45, SIGNS AND SYMBOLS PP.138-139

# SACRED ANIMALS

MANY RELIGIONS and faith systems have animals that are sacred, often because they are said to have helped someone, such as a god or a prophet. In Ancient Egypt the domestic cat was sacred to the goddess Bast. Anyone who killed a cat could be put to death. To Hindu people, the cow is sacred, and must not be killed. In Hindu towns, cows are often allowed to wander wherever they like.

# ANIMAL SPEECH

MOST ANIMALS CAN communicate using some kind of language, but it's not always one we can hear. Elephants use subsonic sounds, and dolphins use clicks and squeaks that are beyond our range of hearing. Some psychics claim to have conversations with animals, and we can often understand what our pets are trying to tell us even if they're not using words.

# SHAMANISM

THE PRACTICE OF shamanism is a way of getting in touch with the spirits of good and evil which some people believe rule the World. A shaman is a kind of priest who enters a trance-like state in order to talk to these spirits on behalf of a person or group of people. Animals are often very important in shamanistic ceremonies, as they can help the shaman to communicate with the spirit world. An animal spirit might be invoked, or called up, to help heal the sick, or to foresee the future. The shaman would use "props," such as carved figures of animals, in his work. Afterward these would be buried or hidden away from the rest of the village because they were considered to be so powerful.

SHAMANS
Shamans often wear masks, headdresses, and cloaks made of animal skins and feathers. These are said to help give them the same powers as their animal helpers.

SWIMMING WITH DOLPHINS
Some people believe that whales and dolphins are the most highly evolved creatures on Earth, with enormous healing powers. Perhaps they carry powerful messages for us, and are here to help us learn how to take care of each other and the planet. There certainly seems to be a strong rapport between humans and these magnificent creatures. Swimming with dolphins is becoming a popular healing and spiritual exercise.

# ANIMALS AS PETS

KEEPING A PET IS one way of teaching us to care for others. For children, having a pet is the first step toward taking responsibility for others as well as themselves. Every time it feels like a chore to clean out the guinea pig's hutch we should remind ourselves what our beds would be like if nobody ever bothered to change the sheets! What would we do if there was no food on the table, and no clean clothes to wear? Just as we depend on our parents to take care of us, so our pets rely on us to take care of them.

# HELPING AND HEALING

SOME PEOPLE SAY THE spiritual importance of animals is that they're here to guide us. If we're kind to animals, we open the channels of communication with them and are able to receive the messages they're trying to give us.

Some animals appear to be psychic, able to sense an event before it happens. There are many tales of people's pets somehow warning their owners about imminent disasters, from earthquakes to hurricanes. Some will even risk their own life to save a person's life.

There are remarkable stories about the ability of animals to heal humans, too. Animals are often taken into hospitals on visits, because people get better more quickly when they spend some time stroking and touching an animal.

## CAT CHAT

WHEN YOU'RE in a happy mood with few distractions, sit down quietly with your cat, dog, or other pet. Try speaking to him or her and see what you get back. Look into your pet's eyes, and try to make contact with his or her thoughts. You'll be amazed at how much you can communicate.

# NATURAL WONDERS

SOME PEOPLE SAY natural disasters are Earth's reaction to human interference. They believe there's a natural law of order in the Universe, and that when people get in the way things start to go wrong, including landslides, fires, and pollution. But earthquakes, ice ages, and deserts all existed way before people did. The Earth is still cooling and changing, and volcanic eruptions, earthquakes, and floods are part of Nature. The most amazing things that happen on the planet are called natural wonders, and they are almost all caused by one or more of the four elements – earth, air, fire, and water.

## WIND

JAPANESE MYTHOLOGY mentions several gods of the Wind, including the Whirlwind god. Some winds are very powerful. Hurricanes begin at sea in warm conditions, and gradually build up strength until they travel into cooler temperatures or over land. Tornadoes form over hot ground, and a narrow core of air rises. If a tornado forms over water, it can suck up a column of water, like a huge jet. This may explain the stories of enormous sea monsters!

## EARTH

THE EARLIEST GREEKS worshiped Earth, as a goddess called Gaia. They believed she was the Universal mother. The North American Indians regarded Mother Earth as the provider of food, and life itself. Even today, many spiritualists like to walk barefoot on the dewy grass each morning to feel the Earth's energizing powers.

Earthquakes are a sign of the Earth under stress. They're caused when plates under the Earth's surface develop cracks, called faults. These sometimes move, causing an earthquake. Los Angeles and San Francisco, California, U.S.A., lie on the San Andreas Fault.

## FIRE

FIRE IS A SYMBOL OF DESTRUCTION, and people who lived close to volcanoes believed that its eruption was great anger in response to their bad behavior. The extinct volcano of Mount Fujiyama in Japan is the most revered, and pilgrims climb it to worship the Sun. Most volcanoes are found in an area called the Ring of Fire, around the Pacific Ocean. Volcanoes are similar to earthquakes, because they're caused by pressure inside the Earth. Increased pressure blasts hot, molten rock, called lava, up through the top of the volcano. One of the most famous volcanoes, Mount Vesuvius in Italy, erupted in A.D. 79. It buried the city of Pompeii and buildings and bodies were discovered beneath the rock many hundreds of years later.

# THUNDER AND LIGHTNING

FLASHES OF LIGHT AND CRASHES of thunder were once thought to be caused by an angry god. In Assyro-Babylonian mythology, Adad was the god of lightning and tempests, and sometimes arrived clothed in black clouds. He was responsible for the growl of the thunder, the fury of the winds, and the deluge of the rain. In Norse mythology Thor was said to be the god who hurled thunderbolts from the sky.

Today, we know more about how storms are caused, but the modern explanation is just as amazing as the myths! On hot, humid days, thunder clouds form. Inside the cloud, currents of air make drops of rain or hail collide, or bump into each other, and produce an electric charge. Lightning flashes between the charges, and can streak down to the ground. The lightning makes the air around it heat up very quickly, to as much as five times the heat on the surface of the Sun, and the air expands suddenly, with a clap of thunder.

# THE AURORAS

TWO OF THE MOST MAGICAL sights on Earth are the Aurora borealis, or northern lights, and the Aurora australis, or southern lights. The Serbs believed that the Sun was a handsome king, and that at his side stood Aurora of the Morning, and Aurora of the Evening.

The North and South Poles attract electrically charged particles sent out by the Sun. When the particles collide with gas particles in the atmosphere, they cause bursts of bright light. This photograph shows how dramatic the effect of such an occurrence can be.

# WATER

FLOODING IS SAID TO BE A SIGN of natural forces being out of control. It symbolizes passion, but is also said to show death and downfall. Many cultures have stories about God, or a creator, sending a flood to punish wicked people in the early days of the Earth. Flooding is usually the result of freakish or unexpected weather patterns. Heavy rain can cause rivers to overflow onto what is normally dry land.

A geyser occurs when water heated below the Earth's surface builds up pressure. A tall column of hot water suddenly erupts, or gushes out. This reduces the pressure, and the geyser may not erupt again for some time. In some places, hot water trickles out more slowly and forms warm lakes and streams, or beds of bubbling, hot mud.

Enormous downpours of rain happen in tropical places, such as India and Southeast Asia, when the wet southwesterly wind meets with the dry northeasterly wind. These are called monsoons, and can be dangerous, but they are also welcomed because in certain areas, without them, crops will not grow.

# CRYSTALS

THE MINERALS THAT crystals are made of were created at the same time as the Universe! So, next time you hold one of these stones, remember that you're holding an ancient and most extraordinary part of our history. Crystals come in a multitude of shapes, sizes, and beautiful colors. Since early civilizations, people have believed that each type of stone has particular spiritual qualities. In the past they were sometimes used as talismans, or lucky charms, to help people feel safe and protected. Today, more and more people are using crystals for their special properties. You can even program a crystal, and give it your own special message. Crystals are said to be sensitive, so look after them! The rewards will be well worth it.

## CRYSTAL TIPS

IT'S IMPORTANT TO remove the energies of other people who have handled your crystal. Experts say you need to blow on it three times. You can also cleanse crystals in salt water. Putting them in the Sun gives them more energy and power.

You can ask a crystal to be your guide. After you've cleansed it, ask it in a quiet way to hold a quality for you, such as peace or happiness.

## HOW CRYSTALS FORM

ALL CRYSTALS ARE MINERALS. They consist of either organic or non-living materials. Different types of crystals are made by different conditions, such as heat and pressure in the Earth. When they're in their natural state, you can usually see a pattern in their structure. This pattern is often lost when the crystals are polished and cut. Some crystals, such as obsidian, have no clear pattern. Obsidian is made from volcanic lava, which cooled too quickly to form a crystalline structure.

CLEAR QUARTZ CRYSTAL
Quartz crystal may be clear or milky, and doesn't always have the same shape. It amplifies energy, so it can give you more vitality and strength.

ROSE QUARTZ
The pink color of rose quartz symbolizes love. It's great for helping you to release any tension or stress, and can also help you if you're feeling sad or lonely.

ROUGH OR SMOOTH?
Almost all gemstones are cut out of rock. Amethyst is described as crystalline because its atoms are arranged in regular patterns. This piece is in its rough state. It may be cut further, or highly polished to enhance the color.

## GEMSTONES

BEAUTY IS THE ONLY QUALIFICATION for a mineral to be called a gemstone, or gem. There are over 3000 minerals, but only about 50 are commonly worn as gems. Some people wear gems because they believe they bring them luck. Gems include diamonds, emeralds, sapphires, and rubies. Diamonds are said to symbolize purity, emeralds to have healing power, and sapphires to stand for truth and luck. Rubies are said to protect the wearer. Some organic materials are also worn as gemstones, including amber and jet. Amber is fossilized tree resin, and is supposed to help the memory. Jet, which is fossilized wood, was once thought to have healing power.

AMETHYST
A beautiful purple stone from Mexico and Brazil, amethyst is said to bring spiritual and healing qualities to the person using it. It's very calming, and can help you to sleep at night. The Ancient Greeks used to drink from amethyst goblets to prevent hangovers! Amethyst is said to disperse blood clots and can be used to treat some cancers.

### AMAZONITE

Essence of amazonite is said to be the pure energy of Universal love, and it's often used for sending love to people. It's also used for soothing the nerves and to help balance the body's energy field.

### RED JASPER

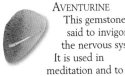

This gem was said to bring rain and to extract the venom from snake bites. Today it is used mostly as a comfort for bereavement and fear.

### LAPIS LAZULI

Vision, clarity, and connection to the heavens are said to be some of the properties of lapis lazuli.

### SODALITE

An ingredient of lapis lazuli, this stone comes in many shades of blue, and is found in lava rock. It is said to relieve depression and to give vitality to its owner.

### AVENTURINE

This gemstone is said to invigorate the nervous system. It is used in meditation and to encourage mental powers.

### SNOWFLAKE OBSIDIAN

In the 16th century, John Dee and Edward Kelley claimed to receive messages from angels through a disk made of polished obsidian, a black volcanic glass.

### JADE

Chinese people see jade as a stone of perfection and immortality, and often carve statues out of it. In New Zealand the Maori tribes make amulets and lucky charms from jade.

### TIGER'S EYE

This was once used as a talisman to protect against the Evil Eye. It also has fire-retardant properties, and is used in fireproof fabrics, boiler coverings, and insulation.

### CARNELIAN

This gemstone promotes wisdom and concentration. It can combat depression and lethargy, and helps the bloodstream.

### TURQUOISE

Aztec people used turquoise in their jewelry, and decorated objects. Turquoise is also popular with the Native Americans, and said to be a sign of success and courage.

### MOONSTONE

This stone is sacred in India and is a lucky charm from a groom to his bride. It is used as an aid against obesity and also selfishness.

### BLOODSTONE

This gemstone is so powerful that it is usually used in conjunction with rose quartz or crystal to treat obsession, aggression, and over-indulgence.

## BIRTHSTONES

EVERY astrological sign has a particular birthstone, which is said to bring luck.

- ARIES  Red jasper
- TAURUS  Rose quartz
- GEMINI  Amethyst
- CANCER  Moonstone
- LEO  Tiger's eye
- VIRGO  Carnelian
- LIBRA  Aventurine
- SCORPIO  Citrine
- SAGITTARIUS  Sodalite
- AQUARIUS  Clear quartz
- CAPRICORN  Obsidian
- PISCES  Bloodstone

## CRYSTAL POWER

IN LEMURIA AND ATLANTIS, civilizations that no longer exist, people used crystals to attract the Universal energies. They also used them for creating energy, such as light. Even today crystals are used in lots of things, including watches and radios. The use of crystals to treat illness was common to many Ancient peoples, including the Egyptians and Mayans, and it's now popular all over the World. Native American shamanic healers believe that the mineral kingdom can help us on our spiritual journey.

### CITRINE

Mostly from Brazil and Spain, the yellow citrine is often used for healing and the release of fear.

### YOUR OWN CRYSTAL

STRANGELY, CRYSTALS tend to find us. If you need a particular stone for a while, then it'll almost certainly end up in your hands. Either somebody will give the crystal to you, or you might walk into a shop and be attracted to one that you feel you just have to have! If that happens, it's probably because the crystal has special power in an area that you need help with. Don't be too distressed if you lose a crystal, though, because that can often be a sign that you no longer need its particular power. It might have moved on to help somebody else who needs it more.

# CREATION

CREATION GODS
To the Babylonians, Marduk was the creator of all things and the greatest of all gods.

IT'S SAID THAT THE Earth is more than four and a half billion years old, yet it was one of the last planets to be created in this Universe. There are many theories about how our planet began. Some are based on religious beliefs, and some on scientific observation. For many people, trying to understand scientific theory and hold onto their religious beliefs can be difficult, because one often contradicts the other. Whatever happened at the beginning of time, it's important to make the most of the planet we live on, and to care for it as well as we care for ourselves.

## CREATORS

THERE ARE SO many beliefs about who or what the Creator of the planet might be that it's not surprising many people give up wondering. Some people say it simply doesn't matter what you believe as long as you can have faith in something bigger and more powerful than yourself, which will act as a guiding light for you in this lifetime.

If it's hard to imagine a God or even a Creator, try thinking of each person having a soul, or higher self. This is the invisible part of yourself, the light or the good part that watches over you. You could call it your conscience, or your inner voice. Some people believe that the higher self is the superconscious self, an invisible energy field where we can receive information from the Universe.

## EARLY DAYS OF THE EARTH

AFTER MILLIONS OF YEARS travelling through space, then slowly cooling down, Earth became a planet that could support life. After millions more years, simple plants, like algae, began to appear in the waters on the Earth's surface. Eventually, Earth had a huge variety of animals as fins, legs, and wings developed. Nature took so long to develop that, in comparison, people have only just arrived! When you think of that, consider how much we have changed the Earth, and how much we have harmed it. There was a time in Earth's history, not so long ago, when people lived in harmony with Nature, instead of trying to conquer it.

ONCE UPON A TIME
Once, long before humans caused such harm on Earth, the land was free from roads, traffic, factories, and pollution. The seas were clear, the skies were blue, and the forests were green and lush. In some remote parts of the World there are still a few untouched, unspoilt places like these.

## BIG BANG THEORY

MOST SCIENTISTS NOW BELIEVE that millions of years ago there was a "Big Bang," or explosion at the beginning of the Universe, and all the dust and tiny bits of matter went on to form the planets and stars. There are still meteorites, or pieces of rocks, and dust spinning in outer space. Quite a lot of the matter has formed into galaxies, or clusters of stars, planets, and other matter. Recent observations have proved that the Universe is still expanding, and that it

# CREATION MYTHS

THE FIRST MYTHS OF ANY CIVILIZATION tried to answer the questions about how the Earth was made, and how the first men and women arrived. Most of us know at least one creation myth. Every culture and civilization has its own version of where the World came from. People who have studied and collected these stories have noticed that many of them are similar – even those from civilizations on opposite sides of the World, whose people never had any contact with each other! One of the common themes in creation myths, from those of North America to those of the South Pacific, is the idea of the gods arriving as a result of a marriage between the Earth and the Sky or the Sun and the Ocean.

is moving away from the center where the Big Bang happened.

The interesting thing about the Big Bang Theory is that it is does have a connection to the spiritual belief that we all come from the one source. Whatever the differences between us as humans, our origins are the same. It helps us to be able to recognize our spiritual connection with each other, to put aside the differences, and to know that at the deepest core level we all come from one place.

**GODDESS OF THE SUN**
According to one ancient Japanese myth, the Sun goddess, Amaterasu, hid inside a cave in Heaven because she was frightened by her brother's bad behavior. She blocked the entrance to her cave with a rock, and the whole World was plunged into darkness. All the other gods gathered together to try to force her out of her hiding place. Eventually they succeeded in making her come out, and the Sun shone once more. The goddess Amaterasu was worshiped as a heavenly body and also as a spiritual deity.

## STARDUST

THE REASON THAT SCIENCE and spirit are beginning to agree is partly because scientists now think that everything in the Universe, including us, is made up of atoms. Atoms are made of even smaller particles, which are energy. In other words, all things begin as invisible energy, and some of it becomes visible and solid. This means that people are made of the same materials as the stars. You could say we're all stardust! The fact that scientists recognize that some particles can't be measured in the visible realm makes it easier to believe in the idea of spiritual, or invisible, power.

## THE END OF THE UNIVERSE?

IF THE Big Bang Theory is correct, there are three possibilities for what will happen to the Universe in the far distant future. There may come a point where the forces balance, and all the planets, stars, and other contents stop moving away from the center and stay still. Alternatively, once they've stopped, the gravitational force may be strong enough to pull the stars back in toward the center, and the whole Universe may shrink, and even start all over again. The third possibility is that it will never reach a point of balance, and all the contents of the Universe will keep on moving further away from the center, without stopping. Scientists are working hard to find out what they think is most likely to happen, but we've got a few million years before it does!

# PLANETS AND STARS

SCIENTISTS ARE ALWAYS coming up with new information about the Universe and how it was created. Early people didn't have much knowledge of science, so they tried to understand planets and stars through myths. They had gods to represent the Sun, Earth, and Moon and many other stars and planets. People have worshiped the planets for thousands of years and, according to astrology, they have a strong influence on our lives. Even the tides are affected by the movement of the Sun and Moon and their gravity, so it's not surprising that they can affect us!

## THE MOON

THE MOON IS A CONSTANT source of fascination, as it influences our calendars and our ocean tides. Its changing shape, from a thin crescent to a full Moon and back again, symbolizes death and rebirth. The Greeks called the Moon goddess Artemis, and the Egyptians called her Isis. Even today we have lots of stories about the Moon, one of the more popular being "the man in the moon," who was said to have been sent there as a punishment.

## THE SUN

THE SUN BRINGS heat and light to all the plants and animals on Earth. Without it, there would be no life. The rising and setting of the Sun symbolizes death and rebirth, as does the changing shape of the Moon. For the Greeks, the Sun was a god named Apollo, who drove a flaming chariot across the sky each day.

## THE EARTH

OUR EARTH IS ONE of the nine planets that orbit the Sun. As far as we can tell, it's the only planet to support life as we know it, because it has oxygen and water. There may be life on other planets that need different substances.

Many people now think of Earth as a living organism, so that whatever happens to its plants, water, land, or animals has an effect on the whole planet. We are beginning to realize that if we look after our planet, we are also looking after ourselves.

## THE PLANETS

MANY OF THE PLANETS were given their names by the Ancient Greeks and Romans. Venus is named after the Roman goddess of Beauty, and Jupiter after the ruler of the gods. The Chinese called these planets Gold Star and Wood Star. In recent times, astronomers have discovered more planets, including Saturn, Neptune, and Pluto. Saturn is the sixth planet from the Sun. Its rings are storm clouds.

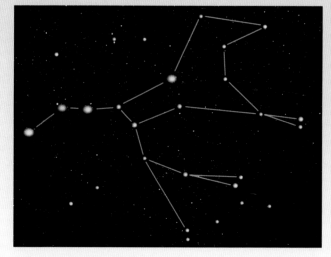

## THE STARS

SOME ANCIENT CIVILIZATIONS thought that our galaxy, the Milky Way, was a bridge between Earth and the sky. Groups of stars in the Milky Way form patterns called constellations. People named them after gods, heroes, and animals. This picture shows the constellation of Ursa Major, or the Great Bear, which is said to be a beautiful girl called Callisto who was turned into the Bear by a jealous god.

Saturn's rings

# THE ELEMENTS

THE ELEMENTS OF EARTH, fire, water, and air are the building blocks of our planet. We couldn't exist without them. For thousands of years people lived much closer to Nature than we do. They believed that the elements were the key to the Universe and all its mysteries. There's still a sense of magic about them today. It seems the more we realize how much harm we've done to our planet, the more we appreciate the importance of getting back in touch with the vital elements of Nature.

The Ancient Greek, Empedocles, invented the term "elements." He believed that people, as well as the Earth, were made up of them. In astrology, each sign of the Zodiac is said to be connected to one of the four elements.

## WHICH ELEMENT ARE YOU?

- A FIRE person can be career minded and quick to get angry. Aries, Leo, and Sagittarius are fire signs.
- AN AIR person is cheery and creative. Gemini, Libra, and Aquarius are air signs.
- AN EARTH person is sensible and reliable. Taurus, Virgo, and Capricorn are earth signs.
- A WATER person is sensitive and deep thinking. Cancer, Scorpio, and Pisces are water signs.

## EARTH

THE EARTH IS FAR OLDER than humans, and is seen as the ultimate life-giver and mother of all living things. Our food grows in the soil, as trees and plants. Minerals and metals come from the Earth, and for thousands of years people have mined it for fuel, gems, and metals. Many living creatures also make their home in the Earth. Many of us bury our dead underground because according to tradition, the dead will one day spring to life again, in the same way that new plants grow from underground bulbs.

## FIRE

FIRE GIVES US ENERGY, as heat and light. We burn candles to give us light, and logs or coal to keep us warm. Fire is said to ward off evil, but it can be very dangerous if it gets out of control. Early people worshiped and feared their fire gods. The mythical dragon symbolizes the power and danger of the fire. The flame from a candle is said to symbolize our soul, which is one of the reasons why candles and fires play such an important part in our rituals of life and death. Fire is often used to purify people and objects, and many people prefer their bodies to be cremated when they die.

## AIR

WE NEED AIR to breathe, so it's vital to our existence. Some Native American people believe in a place high up in the air where the "star people" live. They say there are four great spirits of the north, south, east, and west winds and that because all living things breathe the same air we're all connected. Angels and creatures that fly through the air are considered powerful and mystical. The butterfly is said to be a sign of everlasting life.

## WATER

MOST OF THE PLANET is covered in water, and the body is 75 percent water, so it's easy to see how vital water is to life. Water is thought of as a female element, and often used in fertility and birth rituals. These days more and more babies are born in water, because of its quiet, calming qualities. Water is said to be cleansing and purifying, and there are many rituals in which water is used. Like all the elements, water can heal, but it has great power, and can also harm.

SEE ALSO: ASTROLOGY PP.32-33, GODS AND GODDESSES PP.44-45, NATURAL WONDERS PP.116-117

# FENG SHUI

IF YOUR LIFE'S NOT working out quite as you planned, it could be because you live in a house with bad Feng Shui. Feng Shui, or the art of placement as it's sometimes known, means "wind and water." The idea is that we need to balance these two elements and live in harmony with them, if we are to attract happiness and contentment. This is fundamental to the Eastern way of living. Today, Feng Shui is practiced the World over. People have discovered that if there's chaos where there should be order, and untidiness instead of neatness, the simple action of moving the furniture can bring incredible results!

## FENG SHUI SYSTEMS

THERE ARE TWO POPULAR systems, or schools, of Feng Shui. The Form School looks at the shape of the land and determines the best site for a home or office. Green Dragons and White Tigers play a very important part in this practice. The Dragon is probably the most important luck-bringing symbol in China, and is said to live in the hills. Apparently, wherever you find a Green Dragon you're likely to find a White Tiger. The Compass School is more concerned with an individual's direction in life, and looks at where objects are placed in the home or workplace. It uses the Pa Che compass to find out which direction is best for each individual.

## CH'I

TO BE HAPPY and in harmony with the World, we need to have plenty of Ch'i, which is Chinese for "energy" or "life force." Feng Shui looks at finding the best way to bring Ch'i into our lives, which in turn will help to make us contented and successful.

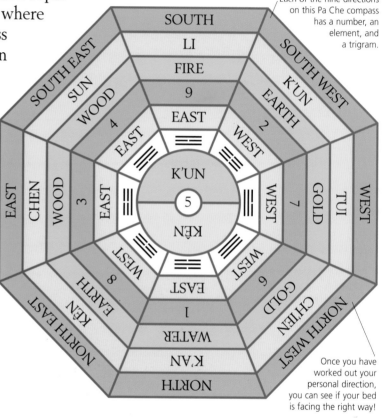

Each of the nine directions on this Pa Che compass has a number, an element, and a trigram.

Once you have worked out your personal direction, you can see if your bed is facing the right way!

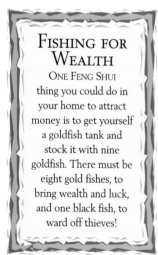

## FISHING FOR WEALTH

ONE FENG SHUI thing you could do in your home to attract money is to get yourself a goldfish tank and stock it with nine goldfish. There must be eight gold fishes, to bring wealth and luck, and one black fish, to ward off thieves!

## PA CHE FENG SHUI

TO FIND OUT YOUR own direction, you need to work out your Pa Che number. There are two ways of doing this – one for males and one for females. A male subtracts his year of birth from 100, then divides the result by nine. If he was born in 1984, it's 100 minus 84, divided by 9. The amount left over is his number. A female takes 4 from her year of birth, then divides the result by 9. The remainder is her number. If there's no remainder, the number is 9.

Number five has no directional force, so a male whose number is five should follow the reading for two, and a female should follow that of eight.

## SHA

THE OPPOSITE OF CH'I is Sha, the life-taking breath that can take over if the Ch'i is weak. Sha only travels along straight lines, and is said to be like a cold wind that can stop us achieving what we want. Luckily, if you think you have Sha in your home you can reduce or eliminate it by blocking its path with other objects, such as trees, mirrors, or lights. Wind chimes are the ultimate good luck symbol because they're good at getting rid of Sha, and the musical sounds attract Ch'i.

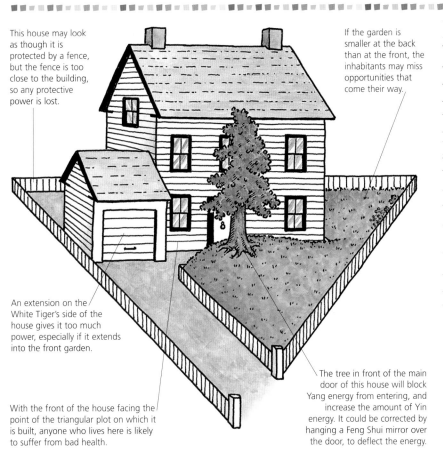

This house may look as though it is protected by a fence, but the fence is too close to the building, so any protective power is lost.

If the garden is smaller at the back than at the front, the inhabitants may miss opportunities that come their way.

An extension on the White Tiger's side of the house gives it too much power, especially if it extends into the front garden.

With the front of the house facing the point of the triangular plot on which it is built, anyone who lives here is likely to suffer from bad health.

The tree in front of the main door of this house will block Yang energy from entering, and increase the amount of Yin energy. It could be corrected by hanging a Feng Shui mirror over the door, to deflect the energy.

# BAD FENG SHUI

WHEN BUYING, or building, a house, the most important thing to check is the position of the main door. This is the door that protects the house, and both Sha and Ch'i can enter through here. If the door is on the right hand side of the house, it will allow the White Tiger on that side to overpower the Green Dragon on the other side, which can cause disharmony in the house.

The same thing can happen if the house has an extension or a garage on the side of the White Tiger. A tree in front of the main door can be very bad luck, as it blocks the Yang and sends too much Yin into the house, causing an imbalance. If the door is opposite a narrow opening in a fence or faces another building, it may cause money to ebb away. A sharp corner is also unlucky because it is like a dagger pointing at the house.

# GOOD FENG SHUI

IN FENG SHUI, THE Green Dragon on the left side of the house, and the White Tiger on the right side, are said to be like guards that must work together to keep everything in harmony. In order for a house to bring good fortune to its occupants, the main door should be either in the center, or to the left, so that it gives more power to the Green Dragon than to the White Tiger. A flat site is best, preferably with protective hills at the back, and open space at the front, which allows the Ch'i to flow naturally.

Hills behind the house represent the Somber Warrior, and protect the house. High land also gives the inhabitants support from family and friends.

A back garden that is larger than the front garden is a sign of support and protection.

Houses that are wider than they are deep encourage happiness and stability inside the home.

The crescent-shaped fishpond in the front garden symbolizes the Red Bird, who looks after that area of the house, and brings wealth and perhaps a financial windfall.

These fences are at the right distance from the house, and will provide protective Feng Shui.

# SACRED SITES

THERE ARE MANY SACRED sites all over the World, each with meaning for different cultures and faith systems. Some sites are natural, and others were made by people. Most are permanent, but some appear and disappear suddenly. Many people who visit sacred sites believe their power can be passed on. People worship at impressive sites because they seem to be the work of a god, and the more people visit and worship a place, the more special it seems to get. It's as though the energy of the people adds to the energy of the site itself.

ULURU (AYERS ROCK)
The Aboriginal Australians say that this piece of sandstone was made in the Creation or Dreamtime, when the spirit ancestors created the landscape. Uluru is said to be the point where all the sacred places connect.

## LEY LINES

ANCIENT TRACKS OR PATHS that criss-cross the countryside in straight lines are often found to link ancient burial grounds, temples, stone circles, and other sacred sites. These lines are called ley lines. They are to the Earth what the meridian system is to the human body, and are thought to make up a system of energy that runs along the Earth's surface. Ancient people, who may have been more sensitive to the energies of the Earth, built their temples, sacred wells, and shrines along the paths of the ley lines.

Hauntings, psychic people, and other examples of supernatural power also appear more often along ley lines. Some people think the lines are above an underground rock fault.

The lines themselves are not always easy to find, but they send out a lot of powerful energy. Some people say they're connected across the whole Earth and form a planetary grid.

The Chinese call their ley lines "dragon paths," and they're of great importance when it comes to Feng Shui, the art of positioning buildings and objects in harmony with Nature.

SHIPTON HILL
Thousands of years ago, people made their mark on the hilltop just above the village of Shipton Gorge, changing its shape and making it steeper.

## CHALK SIGNS AND SYMBOLS

IN EARLY CIVILIZATIONS, it was common to make enormous pictures on the ground. These were often carved into the ground, to expose the layer of rock underneath the soil or sand. Many of the drawings were made on hillsides, so lots of people could see them. Some of the most famous lines and figures are in the Nazca desert of Peru, where there are about a hundred pictures, including animals, plants, and mazes. They're so big that you can only really see them clearly from the air, and some people believe that the people who drew them may have been able to fly in hot air balloons. Some believe that the figures were drawn as landmarks for visitors from space.

CASTLE DITCHES
The first hill fort on the Castle Ditches site was probably built in about 200 B.C. It was destroyed by the Romans, then built again in about A.D. 1000.

CERNE ABBAS GIANT
This huge chalk man, cut into the chalk in Dorset, England, stands 180 ft (55 m) high. It may have first been made in Roman times, or possibly even earlier.

### MAZES AND LABYRINTHS

IN ANCIENT CULTURES the maze or labyrinth was seen as a symbol of the soul on its way to salvation. Stone mazes and maze-like spiral carvings were once very popular in Christian churches. In fact, some of the carved mazes were known as the road to Jerusalem, because they helped pilgrims to meditate on their religious beliefs and ideals, and achieve salvation.

 SEE ALSO: CHAKRAS AND MERIDIANS PP.52-53, FENG SHUI PP.124-125, SACRED STRUCTURES PP.128-129

# MOUNDS

THERE ARE MORE THAN a hundred thousand Earth mounds in the United States, and many in the U.K. and other parts of the World too. They come in all shapes and sizes, including pyramids, snakes, and bears.

Many people believe that early Native American peoples made their mounds as tombs. The most famous mound is in Ohio, U.S.A., and it's called the Great Serpent Mound. Traditional myths say it represents the vital link between the Earth and water, which results in fertile land.

North

### SIDBURY HILL FORT
The ley line from Stonehenge leads on to the Iron Age hill fort at Sidbury. The line passes through the southeastern ramparts that once surrounded the fort.

### GROVELY CASTLE
The line for the midwinter setting Sun at Stonehenge points directly at Grovely Castle, another ancient site, to the west.

### STONEHENGE
This ancient stone circle is at the point where two ley lines cross each other, which is a particularly powerful place to build. People have been coming here to worship for thousands of years.

### OLD SARUM MOUND
A large mound at Old Sarum is mostly visited for its Norman castle and the foundations of the old Salisbury cathedral. There was also a hill fort here in prehistoric times.

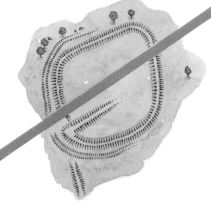

# THE SEVEN CHAKRAS

SOME PEOPLE BELIEVE THAT the Earth has chakras just like the human body, and that there is a sacred site on each one of them.

● THE FIRST (ROOT) CHAKRA is said to be Mount Shasta in the U.S.A. Legend says people hundreds of years old live inside it!

● THE SECOND CHAKRA is Lake Titicaca, in South America. The Island of the Sun, in the lake, is where the Incas believed the gods taught humans how to behave properly.

● THE THIRD CHAKRA is said to be Uluru, a huge rock in the Australian desert.

● THE FOURTH CHAKRA is Glastonbury, in England. The chalice used at the Last Supper is believed to lie in the Chalice Well.

● THE FIFTH CHAKRA is the site of the Great Pyramid in Egypt. It's also linked to Mount Sinai in Egypt and the Mount of Olives in Jerusalem.

● THE SIXTH CHAKRA shifts with each new Age.

● THE SEVENTH CHAKRA is Mount Kailas, in Tibet. It's a site of forgiveness for Hindus, Buddhists, and Jains.

### SALISBURY CATHEDRAL
This is a complete medieval cathedral. Building started in 1220, when the old cathedral was pulled down and moved from Old Sarum. It took 50 years to complete the work.

# CROP CIRCLES

GEOMETRIC SYMBOLS that appear in cornfields are called crop circles. Some people claim to have seen them forming. The patterns and sizes vary, but over the years they've become bigger and more complicated. Some say they contain messages from the Universe for humans. Others believe them to be the work of extraterrestrials, people playing tricks, or simply the wind. Whatever or whoever makes them, they've caused a great deal of debate.

To Clearbury Ring

# SACRED STRUCTURES

CERTAIN SHAPES AND STRUCTURES hold a special kind of energy. Early people went to great lengths to honor their gods, or their dead. Some structures remain fascinating to us even today, such as pyramids, ziggurats, and stone circles. Imagine how difficult it would have been for early people, with no cranes to help them, to lift a huge stone onto its end. Somehow, the effort, time, and money spent in making something seem to add to the energy of the finished object.

STONEHENGE
One of the most famous stone circles in the World is Stonehenge in England. It's said to represent a star, and some say it was used as a calendar because the position of the stones indicates the movements of the Sun and the Moon.

## ZIGGURATS

THE ANCIENT BABYLONIANS built stepped temple towers called ziggurats. The word itself means "pinnacle," or a mountain top. During their worship, people in the small temple on top of a ziggurat would have felt closer to God, just as they would on a mountain top.

A ziggurat's four corners are thought to relate to the four points of the compass, and the general design appears to represent a staircase or ladder. Some say these stepped towers symbolize the upward journey of human spiritual development. Interestingly, very similar shapes can be found in temples of early American civilizations, such as the Mayans.

The wide base of the ziggurat makes the building strong. Each level gets smaller, as you climb to the tiny temple at the top.

## STONE CIRCLES

SOME PEOPLES BELIEVE stone to be a particularly sacred material, perhaps because it is so ancient and strong. Stone circles are found all over the World. The Aboriginal Australians and Native Americans believe stones have magical qualities. In Africa there are hundreds of stone circles made out of huge single stones called megaliths. At many of them you can feel a powerful energy field. Many circles are still used today in pagan, or traditional ceremonies.

## PLACES OF WORSHIP

TEMPLES AND OTHER places of worship are often built in a particular way because it is important to the people who worship there. Most Christian churches are cross-shaped, to remind the worshipers of Christ's crucifixion. Muslim temples are always built to face Mecca.

# PYRAMIDS

THE GREAT PYRAMID at Giza in Egypt is believed to have taken 400,000 people 20 years to build. It's said to contain the mystical secrets of the Egyptians and to be a sign of great wealth. Pyramids are full of hidden tunnels and passages. Some people believe these could teach us about the Universe, if we could only unlock the secret. Mythology like this makes the pyramids fascinating and mysterious.

Some people believe that the shape of a pyramid alone can create all kinds of miracles. The more people understand about pyramids, the more they seem to be featuring in our lives, from pyramid-shaped buildings to a healing therapy called pyramid power, where people meditate and seek cures for physical ailments by sitting inside a pyramid shape.

STANDING STATUES
Some of the huge statues found inside the volcano on Easter Island have been stood up, and now these huge giants stare out to sea.

# CARNAC

THE STONE MONUMENT at Carnac, in Brittany, France, contains about three thousand stones, standing in straight lines. Many people believe that, like Stonehenge, they were used in astronomy. There's no doubt the stones had some kind of ritual or religious significance, but there are so many theories about their purpose that it's still a mystery to this day!

# THE LONG EARS

THERE ARE SOME very unusual standing stones on Easter Island, in the Pacific Ocean. They are said to be funeral monuments that were carved by a tribe known as the Long Ears. The Long Ear tribe was killed off in a battle with other islanders known as the Short Ears.

Many years later, hundreds of carved stone figures were discovered lying abandoned inside the crater of an extinct volcano. It's possible that they were put there to appease a god of the volcano.

## PYRAMID POWERS

WHY NOT MAKE a pyramid? It doesn't matter what it's made from. Make sure that one side of the pyramid faces North. Then put a piece of fruit, such as a banana, under the pyramid, and put another one next to it. If you go back the next morning, you should find that the fruit inside the pyramid has ripened less than the fruit outside. It's said that a pyramid can even bring a dying house plant back to life!

The Tower of Babel mentioned in the Bible was probably a ziggurat, and may have looked something like this one.

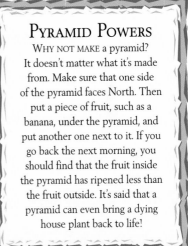

# FAITH SYSTEMS

PEOPLE HAVE DIFFERENT VIEWS about the Universe and its source, which some of us call God. At the heart of all religions is a belief in something bigger and more powerful than humans, an invisible being who takes care of us. Sadly, religious enthusiasm has caused the death of millions of people who have fought on the side of one religion, or faith system, against another. These days, most faiths encourage their members to try to understand and accept other people's beliefs. Many see their spiritual journey as a search to learn to forgive, to love unconditionally, and to be compassionate toward others.

JESUS
According to Christianity, Jesus was the Earthly embodiment of God in his Heaven. Jesus taught simplicity, gentleness, humility, tolerance, honesty, and self-sacrifice. Like many great leaders, he suffered ridicule.

## BELIEVE IT OR NOT

NOT EVERYBODY has a religion, or a God. Those who only believe in what they can see, and understand what's going on in the World around them, are called agnostics. Agnostics do not deny that there may be a God, or gods, but they believe that if there is, people on Earth couldn't possibly know anything about it. An atheist doesn't believe in a God or gods of any kind.

## SPIRITUALISM

A SPIRITUALIST BELIEVES that every living thing in the Universe is connected in some way to a powerful center outside the planet. Spiritualists believe that there is a part of us that lives on after death and that we can communicate with people after they've died, through a psychic or medium. Spiritualists hold services where mediums receive messages from the dead and pass them onto members of the congregation. Spiritualists also heal sick people, often by laying their hands on them.

## CHRISTIANITY

CHRISTIANS BELIEVE that Jesus Christ was the Son of God. He was born in Bethlehem in Judea and he began his teachings after he was baptized in the River Jordan. He travelled with twelve disciples, or followers, and was said to have performed many miracles, including healing the sick. Eventually Jesus was crucified, or put to death on a cross, by people who feared the power of his supporters. Three days after Jesus's death, he is said to have risen from the grave, appeared to his followers, and ascended into Heaven. Many of the stories about God and his son Jesus are to be found in the book of teachings called the Bible.

## BUDDHISM

BUDDHISTS BELIEVE IN TRUTH and a way of life, rather than a God or gods. They say that the root of all problems in life is suffering, which is caused by materialism – the desire to own objects. Buddhism teaches that when we lose this desire to own things, such as a new computer, bike, or toy, there'll be no more hardship. To avoid the suffering caused by materialism, Buddhists follow eight laws known as the Eightfold Path. These laws are: Right Understanding, Right Thought, Right Speech, Right Action, Right Livelihood, Right Effort, Right Mindfulness, and Right Concentration.

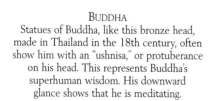

BUDDHA
Statues of Buddha, like this bronze head, made in Thailand in the 18th century, often show him with an "ushnisa," or protuberance on his head. This represents Buddha's superhuman wisdom. His downward glance shows that he is meditating.

# ISLAM

THE MUSLIM RELIGION IS BASED on human beings having a connection with Allah, the Arabic name for God. Allah chose the prophet Mohammed to lead the Islamic faith, and his teaching is very popular in the Arab world. Mohammed was a successful businessman until he turned his life to meditation, prayer, and fasting. During a pilgrimage, the Archangel Jibriel, also known as Gabriel, visited Mohammed and gave him divine messages, which he wrote in a holy book called the Koran. Over the centuries, Islamic teaching has spread, and has developed into several different Muslim traditions of worship, such as the Sunni, Sufi, and Shi'ite forms.

### THE KORAN

The authorized version of the Koran is written in classical Arabic. Muslims believe that it should be read in its original form. The Koran was compiled in about A.D. 650 after the death of Mohammed, the prophet. It is the last in a series of the revelations that Allah sent to the World. The Koran is highly treasured, as its teaching is said to reveal the character of God, and it contains a code of conduct for humankind.

# JUDAISM

THE JEWISH religion, called Judaism, comes from the Middle East. Most of its teachings are contained in the Torah, which is a book about the everlasting truths of life. Jewish people believe that in the beginning God created the World and they predict that a Messiah will come again to restore it and save humanity. Family is an important part of this religion and its believers say all parts of our lives are holy. Men and women often pray separately, and women are expected to bring up their children and keep their home in a traditional Jewish way.

# SIKHISM

A SIKH BELIEVES there is only one God and that all people are equal in His eyes. Sikhs, Hindus, and Buddhists believe that every soul has more than one Earthly life, and is reborn after death. Sikhism once had ten great leaders, known as gurus, and each had a particular quality. The first leader was Guru Nanak. He taught people to find happiness and peace through repeating the name of God. The last leader, Guru Gobind Singh, helped to finalize the modern version of the Granth – the book of song and prayer sung everyday by devout Sikhs.

# HINDUISM

ONE OF THE oldest religions in the World is Hinduism. Hindu teachings are found in a book called the Bhagavad-Gita, which tells of a conversation between a person and God.

Hindus believe we have many different lives, so that we can learn spiritual lessons through our experiences on Earth. They believe in karma, which is a system that takes account of people's actions in the past and reflects them in their future lives. A person's good or bad deed may not immediately appear to have any result, but in a future life it may lead to a lesson for the person to learn.

### SACRED COWS

In India, Hindu people regard the cow as being sacred, and a symbol of the Earth. The great god Shiva the Destroyer and Reproducer was said to be carried by a bull.

# VOUDOU

A COMBINATION of Roman Catholic and African beliefs makes up a faith called Voudou, which is most popular in Haiti. People who practice it prefer to spell it Voudou, Vodoun, or Voudoun, rather than "Voodoo," because in the past, the word Voodoo was associated with strange rituals.

Millions of followers around the World believe that the work of the gods appears in every part of life, and that pleasing the gods leads to health, wealth, and contentment. Voudounists believe that a Supreme Being, called Gran Met, made the World, but that he has long since returned to other worlds.

# KABBALAH

THIS IS A PHILOSOPHY and a way of life that is based on the mystical Jewish teachings. The idea is that humans can express the divine in their everyday life. Some people thought these teachings were revealed to Adam, while others believe they were the secret teachings spoken to Moses on Mount Sinai, when he received the Torah, and the Ten Commandments.

The meaning of the word kabbalah is "tradition," and the Tree of Life provides a kind of map for humans to work from and experience different levels of consciousness. These teachings were originally passed on by word of mouth. The mystical aim of the Kabbalah is to unravel the mystery of God's relationship with the World through prayer, meditation, ritual, and learning.

# ZOROASTRIANISM

THE FOLLOWERS OF a prophet called Zoroaster, or Zarathustra, are known as Zoroastrians. In the 10th century, Zoroastrians called Parsees fled from persecution by Muslims to India. They believe the most important thing in life is to take responsibility for our actions. They say that after we die, our conscience takes us to the Bridge of Judgment. From there, we are sent to Paradise or the House of the Lie.

# JAINISM

LIKE BUDDHISM, Jainism is a code for living rather than a religion. Jains say that we are all divine, and we can get in touch with our spiritual side by releasing the soul. The Great Vows, or Mahavratas, that Jains take include telling the truth, avoiding violence, not taking anything unless it's given, and being detached from people, places, and things. They are not supposed to eat after dark.

AHURA MAZDA
Zoroastrian forces for good and evil are the life creator, Ahura Mazda, who has an angel army, and the destroyer, Angra Mainyu, who has a devil army. A symbol of this faith is the Ahura Mazda, attached to a disk with wings.

# TAOISM

 AT THE HEART of Chinese Taoism is the balance between Yin and Yang, the negative and positive forces of creation. A Taoist seeks to feel peaceful and calm on the inside, whatever is going on in his or her life.

The *I Ching*, or *Book of Changes*, teaches Taoists how everything in the World is connected.

# CONFUCIANISM

THIS FAITH IS BASED on the beliefs and teachings of Confucius, a Chinese sage who died in 479 B.C., aged 72. He believed that the young should respect their elders and ancestors, and that we should behave toward others as we would like them to behave toward us. He believed in self-discipline and education, and stressed the importance of hard work and harmony in the home.

# SHINTOISM

THE TRADITIONAL faith of the Japanese people is called Shintoism, and it is based on the elements of Nature. Shintoists believe that there is healing power in the mountains, streams, wind, and trees. In Shintoism there are four kinds of worship – cleansing, offering, prayer, and feasting. Shinto people believe the mirror is very important because when a person looks into it he or she can hide nothing.

In Japan, almost every mountain has a god. Sengen-Sama is the goddess of Mount Fuji. Pilgrims climb Mount Fuji to worship at sunrise.

 SEE ALSO: CONSCIOUSNESS P.31, GODS AND GODDESSES PP.44-45, PROPHETS AND GURUS PP.134-135

## MAORI

THE BELIEFS OF THE MAORI people in New Zealand are steeped in legends and myths. Maori legends say that Mother Earth and Father Sky were the creator gods, and were separated by their sons, who in turn created the human race. They believe that the life force that's in all of creation is a gift from the gods. The Maori word *tika* means doing the right thing, or following the moral laws of the gods and the tribe. The opposite is *he*, which means doing the wrong thing, or going astray.

### HEITIKI
Heitiki, like this one, are neck ornaments that Maori people often wear. They are believed to represent a human embryo, probably a still-born child. Maoris consider the spirits of still-born children to be very powerful and pure, because they were cheated of life.

## AUSTRALIAN SPIRITUALITY

ABORIGINAL AUSTRALIANS communicate with their gods through art and dance. They attach great importance to their dreams, and much of their prayer and ritual is done through Nature. Many Aboriginal Australians go "walkabout," which means that they go wandering through the outback of Australia for periods of time, to help them to connect with the Universe and its source. They believe that the ancient paths still sing a song about the creation of the land.

## KWANZA

THIS AFRICAN RELIGION is based on seven laws, which teach living in the community with family and friends, working, creativity, and faith in God. In the traditional religions of Africa, God is seen as the mother and father of the Universe. People believe that God is in everything, so they have a great interest in Nature. The ancestors are guardians of the spirit and pass on to everyone the energy of the Divine.

## BAHA'I

BAHA'U'ULAH, which means "Glory of God," is the chosen name of the person who established the Baha'i faith. After several spiritual experiences, Baha'u'Ulah believed he was a messenger of God. His followers believe that Heaven and Hell are states of mind rather than places we go to when we're dead. Bah'ai people don't have public ceremonies, but they fast and meditate, and read the writings of the Baha'u'Ulah.

## NATIVE AMERICAN BELIEFS

EVERYTHING IN LIFE is sacred for the Native Americans, who live amongst Nature and spend much of their time in silence. They have a very strong connection to the elements and to the animal world. Native Americans believe that life is a spiritual journey which involves one's mind, body, and spirit, and they call it an Earth Walk. A Native American works hard to be an honorable and useful member of his or her tribe. Their spiritual activities include using tools such as herbs, sacred pipes, and feathers, and they perform powerful chants and dances.

## THE NEW AGE

THE TERM "NEW AGE" covers a wide range of beliefs. Most New Age believers agree that we are all connected to the same source, and we should try to look at the Universe mystically, rather than just scientifically. New Age people take a holistic approach to life. They try to achieve global consciousness, or an awareness of the World and everything that lives in it. New Age spiritualists believe that each individual has a right to choose his or her own path. Much New Age thinking concerns the Millennium in the year 2000, and the predictions for the next century.

### TEN NATIVE AMERICAN COMMANDMENTS

THESE TEN COMMANDMENTS from Native American cultures contain such profound truths they can be found on posters and inscribed on various objects throughout the World.

- TREAT the Earth and all that dwell thereon with respect.
- REMAIN close to the Great Spirit.
- SHOW great respect for your fellow beings.
- WORK together for the benefit of all mankind.
- GIVE assistance and kindness wherever needed.
- DO what you know to be right.
- LOOK after the well-being of mind and body.
- DEDICATE a share of your efforts to the greater good.
- BE truthful and honest at all times.
- TAKE full responsibility for your actions.

# PROPHETS AND GURUS

A PROPHET OR GURU is someone important in a religion or faith. Prophets are said to be people who speak through divine inspiration, or get messages from a higher place. They may be able to prophesy, or see, future events, and help and inspire people. Of course, not all people who call themselves prophets or gurus really are.

Prophets usually have many followers, and belong to a religion. Gurus give spiritual guidance to a smaller number of disciples, and may not be linked with a particular religion, other than one that they set up themselves.

## MOSES

THE GREAT LEADER and prophet Moses helped the Jewish people to escape from Egyptian slavery. He parted the waters of the Red Sea so that they could walk through it to freedom. People of the Jewish faith regard Moses with some awe, as he was the prophet that God knew face to face. It's said that God handed over the Ten Commandments to Moses on Mount Sinai, on tablets of stone.

MOSES BRINGS WATER OUT OF THE ROCK
This painting shows a scene from the Old Testament in the Bible. After Moses had led the Israelites out of Egypt, they were in need of some water. At God's command, Moses struck a rock with his rod, and out flowed some water!

On the right-hand side of this painting you can see Moses leading the Jewish people out of Egypt. In the foreground the elders are holding up their hands in astonishment as Moses brings water out of the rock.

## FAITH FOUNDERS

● MOHAMMED was leader of the Islam religion. While sitting in a cave on Mount Hirae, he received messages from an angel. He was told to tell the people that there was one God, who became known to Muslims as Allah.
● GURU NANAK was the first teacher of Sikhism. He believed that all people were united in God's eyes, and he gave this message to the Hindus and Muslims who lived in what is

now Pakistan. Nine more Sikh gurus followed him. The last was Guru Gobind Singh, who was said to have founded the Brotherhood of Sikhs, which was called Khalsa.
● SIDDHARTHA GAUTAMA, later known as Buddha, was an Indian prince brought up in great wealth. However, when he saw the suffering of his people, he gave up his riches and went on a journey around India, and eventually founded Buddhism, a

philosophy based on "the truth."
● JESUS was born to the Virgin Mary. He and his disciples travelled around healing, performing miracles, and telling parables. Christianity was founded on the teachings of Jesus.
● JACOB, son of Isaac, and grandson of the prophet Abraham was given the name of Israel by God, and the people of Israel named their nation after him. Jewish people believe that they are all descended from Abraham.

# MOTHER MEERA

SOMETIMES KNOWN as The Divine Mother, Mother Meera is revered by followers across the globe. Many people believe that she is an avatar, or a supreme being who has come to live on Earth to help people during a time of crisis on the planet. It's said that avatars bring us messages from God.

Mother Meera is said to have a wonderful healing light, which she uses to help the Earth and its people. She believes that our connection with God, or the Divine, is most important for our transformation or growth into more spiritually aware beings.

# SAI BABA

LIKE MOTHER MEERA, Sai Baba is known as an avatar, or supreme being. He says that he was incarnated in the World at this time of stress to help people rediscover the ancient wisdom of Vedic (ancient Hindu) teachings.

Sai Baba believes that we are all part of God, and his most important teaching is that we should all recognize this and learn to love one another. People who've met Sai Baba say he sends out love to everybody he meets. Hindus predicted that he would be a kind of savior for the planet, and would return three times.

# CHARLES TAZE RUSSELL

THE FOUNDER OF THE JEHOVAH'S WITNESSES movement was called Charles Taze Russell. He believed strongly that people should prepare themselves for the apocalypse, or end of the World, and Armageddon, a day of judgment. By Russell's calculations, the end of the World would have been in 1914. This turned out to be the year of the beginning of World War I. This terrible World event was so close to Russell's prediction about the end of the World that it gained him and the Jehovah's Witnesses movement many new followers.

# RAJNEESH

BHAGWAN SHREE RAJNEESH set up a center for religious meditation. This ashram, or retreat, in India is as popular as ever with visitors today, even though he died some years ago. Rajneesh believed that meditation was the answer to everything, although unfortunately for him he was accused of enjoying great wealth and other excesses. At one time there were said to be about 600 different centers around the World.

# MAHARISHI YOGI

MAHARISHI MAJESH YOGI was an Indian monk who introduced a very popular method of meditation, known as transcendental meditation. People who use his method aim to reach an altered state of consciousness. His techniques included using a mantra, which is the same word repeated over and over again to help quieten the mind.

# THE DALAI LAMA

FOR TIBETAN BUDDHISTS, the Dalai, or leader, is an all-important part of their faith, and a living example for others to follow. The name Dalai means "ocean of wisdom." The Dalai Lama usually earns his position during his childhood, through remembering past incarnations. At a very young age, a potential Dalai can recall objects, places, and people he knew in a past life. The wisdom of the Dalai Lama inspires people all over the World and across all cultures.

The present Dalai Lama is a monk called Tenzin Gyatso (shown above). Born in 1935, he was awarded the Nobel Peace Prize in 1989. Since the Chinese invasion of Tibet, he has been living in exile in the Himalayas.

# CULT LEADERS

THE WORD "CULT," WHICH IS a term for a group of people with similar beliefs and behavior, is often associated with a guru. Recently people have criticized cults because some gurus have been filmed or photographed on expensive holidays, driving fast cars, and generally spending a great deal of money, while preaching that their followers should live a simple life and give up their wealth! However, most of today's major religions were once small cults. The difference between a cult and a religion is often nothing more than the number of members it has, and whether it is of international importance.

## SCIENTOLOGY

THE CHURCH OF SCIENTOLOGY is a 20th-century church, which has millions of members around the World. Some call Scientology a religion, while others argue that it is simply a philosophy of life. It was founded by Ron Hubbard, whose teachings include religion, physics, and science fiction. Ron Hubbard became most famous for writing a book about Scientology called *Dianetics, The Modern Science of Mental Health*. He believed that unhappy events in our lives can weaken us. But once we understand their root, the memory no longer has power over us.

# COMMUNITIES

COMMUNAL LIVING
In traditional communities, like this one in Indonesia, even the youngsters help with preparing the food and other domestic tasks.

P EOPLE HAVE LIVED IN communities for thousands of years, probably since very early people evolved. We may live in tribes, families, villages, bands of travellers, or in "intentional" communities, where people choose to live together for a shared purpose.

In some countries, people live in extended families. An extended family includes not only parents and their children, but also grandparents, uncles, aunts, and cousins all living in the same house, or very nearby.

There's something about the word "community" that makes us think of pulling together, sharing, caring, and loving one another. That can happen in any kind of group. Equally, being in a community can cause arguments and conflict if we don't respect other people's rights.

## OUR TRIBAL ROOTS

IT'S THOUGHT THAT humans first appeared about two million years ago in Africa, and gradually spread around the World. Early people were born into a tribe, which they belonged to for life. Tribal members lived by a code of practice or set of rules which were decided by the tribe's leaders. Often, life revolved around hunting, farming, or herding, and everyone had to work as part of the team. Teamwork also helped when they needed to defend their territory against other nearby tribes.

## TRIBAL LIFE TODAY

MANY PEOPLE STILL LIVE together in small tribes, although it's becoming less common. Today, many tribes live in or near towns and cities, and some members may have office jobs. Their way of life is very different from the traditional one, but the leaders still try to keep the other members of the tribe loyal to their roots and sense of community. Sadly, the old ways often become lost or forgotten, along with the traditional stories and songs.

> *You will truly have good lives if you help each other. That is the way you could make each other happy ... always feel willing to do for each other ... this you are to do as long as the people's earth remains.*
>
> WHITE BUFFALO DANCE, FOX TRIBE

## NUCLEAR LIVING

THESE DAYS, IT'S NOT uncommon for people to live with just their immediate family, sometimes hundreds or even thousands of miles away from other members of the family. This is called nuclear living. Sadly, it seems that the more technologically advanced we become, the more we lose our sense of tribal values and community. Most families can no longer rely on the natural cycle of extended family living, in which all members of the family lived close together and helped each other out, depending on what was needed. Grandmothers and grandfathers may not be close enough now to help bring up their grandchildren, and aging parents cannot be sure that their children will be able to take care of them when they become old or ill.

## FAMILY AND FRIENDS

SOMETIMES IT CAN BE frustrating to live with the same people all the time, even if there's plenty of space. But our families are important to us. They teach us about life in the wider community, and give us support when we need it. In return, they may need our support from time to time. In a small group like a family, we learn tolerance, forgiveness, and sympathy with other people's difficulties. People who live with friends sometimes think of themselves as a family, and we can sometimes be closer to friends than we are to our real family.

## NOMADIC LIVING

YOU DON'T HAVE TO live in a house to be part of a community! Travellers or gypsies are people who've chosen to move around together. They tend to go to places they're drawn to, or where they can find work. For instance, they might visit sacred sites, or festivals and fairs in different parts of the country. Being in a community of any kind, whether it's a village or a group of people who share a belief or interest, creates a sense of belonging, simply because people are working together for a common purpose.

## COMMUNITY AND ONENESS

LIVING IN A COMMUNITY is a great way of learning about yourself and how to live with other people. Some people talk about being able to learn about our "boundaries." Knowing your boundaries means knowing who you are – where you start and where you end. It's also knowing how far you can push other people, and when to stop.

We are all individual souls. The shape of our body and the color of our skin depends on where we come from. If your family is from somewhere near the Equator, such as Africa, you'll have dark skin. People who live in colder climates have lighter skin.

We all have a mixture of the same hopes and dreams, concerns, and fears. Unfortunately, not everyone sees it like that, and some people dislike others because they are different from themselves. Living in a community, especially one as multi-racial as most of today's cities, teaches us to accept and appreciate the differences between people, as well as the similarities.

An ideal community is about being free to be who you are, to live in a safe place where you can express your beliefs, and, perhaps more importantly, to be able to live out your beliefs in reality.

## INTENTIONAL COMMUNITIES

THE WORD "INTENTIONAL" is sometimes used to describe a community which a group of people has set up together because they have shared interests. They live in the same home and share duties like the cooking and cleaning. People living in intentional communities often have something in common, such as organic gardening, or religious beliefs. Those who feel they want to share resources and care for our Earth might form a community that's self-sufficient, growing their own food and rearing animals according to their own beliefs. Many communities believe that they are setting an example and are creating a positive vision that will inspire others.

## THE GLOBAL VIEW

WE ARE ALL PART OF A HUGE global community. With modern technology, communication with people in other parts of the World is an everyday occurrence. We are all learning more about other nations and peoples, and beginning to understand cultures that are different from our own. In today's World, we must accept the differences between people across the globe, and enjoy the variety of our cultures. Lots of different peoples live in different countries, so modern society is often multi-racial and multi-cultural. We all need to feel connected to each other, and also to the Universe. Feeling we are part of a global community gives us a sense of worth and belonging.

# SIGNS AND SYMBOLS

SYMBOLS AND SIGNS can be found in all areas of our lives. They hold a special meaning or significance for us, and are used in all walks of life as a way of giving out information. Symbols have been used for centuries and can hold deep meaning or truths. Signs tend to have a more practical, Earthly purpose, such as showing us where to go.

The same symbol can have different meanings for different cultures. Equally, something may be symbolic to an individual, but mean nothing to anyone else. In a sense, any image can become powerful for you because of the emotional energy you put into it.

The thumbs up sign means "O.K."

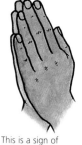
This is a sign of greeting and prayer.

This is a sign that something is good.

This is to protect from bad luck.

## CULTURAL SYMBOLS

ALL CULTURES USE signs and symbols. People fly the flag and wear the national costume of their country or region to show that they're proud of it. The totem pole of a Native American tribe works like a flag. It often shows all the animals and other figures that are important to the tribe.

Many members of religions and faith systems have symbols to show others that they follow its laws. A Sikh displays five special signs of his faith. The most obvious sign is the turban. Rastafarians are recognizable by the dreadlocks that they wear.

## HAND SIGNALS

SOME HAND SIGNALS are the same all over the World. Waving the hand can be a greeting or a farewell. Other hand gestures could be a polite sign in one country, but an insult in another. Signing, the language invented for people whose speech or hearing is limited, is a complete language that is just as good as speaking.

WAVING THE FLAG
People wave their flag to show national pride. At this music concert in the U.K., people from all over the World are waving their flags in appreciation of the musicians.

## TYPES OF SYMBOLS

 THE DOVE is an international symbol of peace. It also represents deliverance and forgiveness to Jews and Christians, renewal of life to the Ancient Greeks, and long life and love to Chinese people. Two doves represent faithfulness in marriage.

THE EAGLE is associated with might, fearlessness, and strength. To many Native Americans, it symbolizes Universal Spirit, and to the Aztecs the rising Sun and Heavenly power. To the Ancient Romans and the people of the U.S.A., eagles represent the State and strength.

THE ELEPHANT symbolizes wisdom and power. Its massive size also represents greatness, in the areas of strength, lifespan, wisdom, patience, and memory. The Elephant and Castle shown in Christian heraldry represents the strength of a church built on faith.

THE FISH represents life, death, and fertility. Ancient Egyptians often wore jewelry with a fish on it, as an amulet against drowning. To Buddhists fish symbolize freedom from all restraint. A fish is the emblem of the two Christian fishermen saints, St. Andrew and St. Peter.

THE FLEUR DE LYS, or lily, symbolizes wisdom, fidelity, and honesty. This symbol was used by the French royalty in heraldry, or coats of arms. According to legend, a lily was given to Clovis, the king of the Franks, in 5th-century France, when he decided to become a Christian.

THE GRIFFIN is a symbol of wisdom, vengeance, and alertness to danger, and it is said to be good at finding and guarding treasure. It has the head, wings, and talons of an eagle, but a lion's body. In Ancient Greek myth, the griffin was said to pull the Sun's chariot across the sky.

 SEE ALSO: ANIMALS PP.114-115, DREAMS AND VISIONS PP.16-17, SUPERSTITIONS PP.14-15

# SHAPES

**CIRCLE** This represents the never-ending cycles of life, the Sun, Earth, and gold. Some Native Americans describe a Circle of Life, with all the tribes living in harmony within the circle.

**CROSS** This shape has been used to symbolize the compass, the four elements, health, fertility, life, immortality, Heaven and Earth, body and soul, the Sun, and the stars.

**HEART** An emblem of unconditional love the World over, the heart was believed to be the organ which generated emotion – the spiritual center of the body.

**TRIANGLE** This is used in alchemy to denote water, fire, air, and earth, in various forms. In a mandala, the triangle symbolizes the female and male principles.

**SQUARE** The square is solid, and may symbolize Earth. A square inside a square represents our unconscious, surrounded by the physical World, or our conscious mind.

**STAR** This is a symbol of light, hope, and goals. For Jewish people, the Star of David's six points are the six days of Creation, and the hexagon in the center is the seventh day, or Sabbath.

**SWASTIKA** This was a symbol of good fortune throughout much of the World, until it was adopted by Nazi Germany. The Chinese regard it as a sign of infinity.

**WHEEL** In Buddhism, the Wheel of Law represents the teachings of Buddha, and its eight spokes are the paths to Enlightenment. Fate is sometimes described as the Wheel of Fortune.

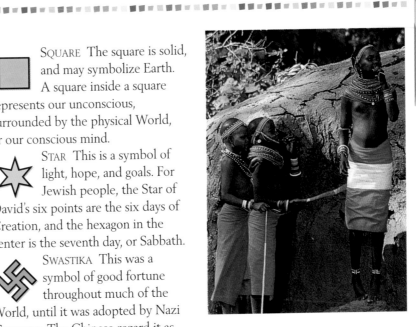

# SYMBOLS IN ART

IMAGINE TRYING TO PAINT something as complicated as the triumph of goodness over evil. You wouldn't know where to start. Many painters use well-known symbols to help them paint what they want to show, so that other people can understand their paintings. Over time, however, the meaning of a symbol may change. A lion in Ancient Greek art often represented royalty, but in Christian art a lion's victory over a dragon often symbolizes goodness's victory over evil.

# SIGNS OF BELONGING

THERE ARE SEVERAL ways of showing other people that you belong to a particular group. The clothes that you wear, or even a school uniform, tell people something about you, whether you like it or not.

There are many other signs of belonging, such as the hairstyle and colors that people choose to wear. A facial expression or the way you laugh may also show others that you are related to the rest of your family or tribe. These are signals that you can't do much about!

**THE LION** is a symbol of power, strength, and bravery. As king of the beasts, the lion can also represent royalty, and is often seen on coats of arms. Stone lions are also found on the gateways and doorways of houses, and are said to guard the people inside the building.

**THE LOTUS FLOWER** is a symbol of creation, purity, and resurrection – returning from death to life. It was the emblem of Ancient Egypt and India, and is often seen in paintings and on buildings. The Buddha seated on a lotus flower symbolizes a jewel resting on perfection.

**THE ROSE** means spiritual truth, love, and beauty. It was the flower of the Ancient Greek and Roman goddesses of love, which is why it is often given as a gift from one lover to another. The Tudor Rose is a mixture of the symbols of the Houses of York and Lancaster during Tudor England.

**THE SNAKE** is a symbol of healing and the emblem of the medical profession. It formed the "staff of Aesculapius." Aesculapius was the Roman god of medicine. As well as being a symbol of healing, the snake represents fertility, sexuality, renewal, and temptation.

**THE SUN** is a powerful symbol of male energy, divinity, the gods, light, warmth, and life. Images of golden Suns appear in many French buildings as the emblem of Louis XIV, who was also known as "the Sun King." The Sun is also the central force in the Zodiac, and rules the sign of Leo.

**THE TRIDENT** is a symbol of the divine. Poseidon, or Neptune, the ancient god of the ocean for the Greeks and Romans, is often shown with a trident, which he used to protect ocean travellers. The Hindu god, Shiva, also carries a trident to represent his three roles of creator, preserver, and destroyer.

# CELEBRATIONS

IF THERE'S ONE THING that cultures across the World share it's a love of rituals, festivals, and celebrations. Parties and other celebrations are essential for our spirit and sense of joy, happiness, and well-being. As we all know, life can be pretty routine and full of chores, such as cooking, cleaning, washing, learning, and working. We need to have a balance in our lives, though, and that comes from being able to set our souls free, have fun, and experience a sense of lightness and freedom. That doesn't mean to say we don't have to put a lot of work into our celebrations, but in the end the effort itself can make the results even more enjoyable.

THANKSGIVING
During Thanksgiving, many American people eat turkey, pumpkins, corn, and cranberries. The Native Americans taught the newly arrived European settlers about these foods.

## RITUALS AND RITES

MANY CELEBRATIONS have rituals and rites from way back in history. Dancing to encourage rain, or burning the fields after harvest, were rituals that people did every year at the same time, and they built up traditions around them. Halloween is the day before All Souls' Day, which is a Christian festival in memory of those who have died, said to be the day when souls walked the Earth. Trick or Treat is based on the Native American belief that if you don't respect your dead ancestors they'll return to Earth and play tricks on you.

On Guy Fawkes' night, at the beginning of November, English people have fires and fireworks to celebrate the burning of Guy Fawkes, who tried to blow up the English Parliament. Centuries ago, Celtic peoples lit fires to drive away witches and evil spirits, then put them out to symbolize the end of the Celtic year.

## COMING OF AGE

MANY SOCIETIES HAVE special rituals that children go through when they reach a certain age. These are often called "rites of passage," and prove that someone is ready to take on adult responsibilities. In some hunting communities, for example, a child who is tall and strong enough to hunt a wild animal might go through a rite of "first blood." The adults take the child on a hunt, and allow him or her to kill the animal. This becomes the main part of a feast to celebrate the achievement. Sometimes the child is anointed, or dabbed, with the blood of the animal, as a mark of newly-attained adulthood. Other societies have much simpler rites, such as giving the new adult the door key!

## CARNIVALS AND PROCESSIONS

ONE WAY OF CELEBRATING is to have everyone dress up in costumes and colorful clothes, parade around, and dance to music in the streets. This way, large numbers of people can enjoy themselves in one enormous party. Outdoor celebrations like these are usually held at times when good weather is usual.

# HARVEST FESTIVALS

ALL THE WORLD OVER, people celebrate harvest festivals. The celebrations may be different in different cultures, but the intention is generally the same. They celebrate the fruits of the Earth and give thanks to God, Mother Earth, or the Universe for the abundance of food and drink in our lives. Thanksgiving Day, celebrated in the U.S.A. in Fall, is a typical harvest festival during which the people eat seasonal foods. In Israel, there are three harvest seasons, so the people there have three harvest festivals.

# ST. VALENTINE'S DAY

IT'S SAID THAT St. Valentine left a final message for his loved one on the walls of his cell before he died. His Saint's day is February 14, and people all over the World send cards, notes, or flowers to each other in memory of his romantic gesture. The Valentine's card has been popular ever since its invention in the 19th century.

# BIRTHDAYS

THE DAY THAT WE come into this life is a date for celebrating both the beginning of our Earthly existence, and the caring and nurturing that we get from our parents. Most societies have special birthdays, such as when we reach our teenage years, our coming of age, and the birthdays that celebrate a decade or a number of decades of life. In many modern societies, it's important to know how old we are, so that we can qualify to vote in our country's elections, for example, or learn to drive. For this reason, we count the years carefully.

# BAR MITZVAH

IN THE JEWISH FAITH, a boy becomes Bar Mitzvah when he reaches the age of 13, and a girl becomes Bat Mitzvah at the age of 12. When they reach this age, they are expected to take on adult responsibilities, declare their belief in the Jewish faith, and follow all its religious commandments. Boys celebrate their coming of age by attending the synagogue, and reading in public from the Law and the Prophets' texts. In recent years, some synagogues have also begun to celebrate a girl's Bat Mitzvah with similar rituals.

# SPRING FESTIVALS

SPRING BRINGS NEW LIFE, in the form of young animals and new plants. Lots of countries celebrate the arrival of Spring, and many use the symbol of a green man to represent this time of rebirth and renewal. At the Hindu festival of Holi in India, people celebrate the end of Winter and the coming of Spring by throwing or spraying each other with colored water or powder. In England, on a Spring festival called May Day, children dance around a maypole with colored ribbons, weaving in and out of each other in a complicated pattern. This is a very old tradition, linked with fertility rites.

# GETTING MARRIED

ON A SPIRITUAL LEVEL getting married means publicly and personally linking yourself to another human being for the rest of your Earthly life. The members of some faith systems even believe that marriage lasts into the after life. For them, marriage is not only a romantic connection, but an eternal connection between souls.

Getting married means two people are formally, and often legally, joined together, sometimes with a divine blessing. These days, however, you can get married anywhere, and anyhow. All that really matters is that the setting is special and sacred for the people getting married. It can be a church, a stone circle, a desert island, or a forest. More and more people are choosing to have their own special ceremony, in their favorite place.

Colorful costumes and headgear like these are typical of a street carnival.

## FESTIVALS OF LIGHT

LIGHT IS INCLUDED IN all kinds of festivals. It often signifies the light of God, and the enlightenment of His followers. Like many others, Hindus and Sikhs have a festival of light and fire. It heralds the beginning of the year, among other things. The people pray to Lakshmi, goddess of wealth and fortune, candles or lanterns are lit in the houses, and children run around the streets with torches and fireworks. Jewish people celebrate Hanukkah, which is a recreation of the miracle in which a small bottle of lamp oil lasted for eight days instead of one. People light a candle or oil wick each day for eight days. On the final day, they sing a traditional hymn.

LIGHTING CANDLES
During Festivals of Light people light candles in churches, temples, and their homes, to celebrate their love of God or gods, or to show respect for the dead.

## WINTER FESTIVALS

WHEN MANY ANIMALS go into hibernation for the Winter, people's lives change too. In Northern countries, Winter is a time for rest, and nights spent around the fire, looking forward to the coming of Spring. Many cultures, including some Native American peoples, celebrate the end of Summer and the beginning of Winter with ceremonies to keep away the spirits of the dead, or to keep them happy by showing them the respect they deserve.

## CHINESE NEW YEAR

NEW YEAR FOR CHINESE people is at the time of the Winter solstice, when the days are at their shortest. The festival lasts for several days, and is very colorful and spectacular. At this time of year people try to be polite and kind to each other, and promise that they will continue to be all year round. At the end of the festival, beautiful paper lanterns are hung everywhere, and there is a great parade featuring a huge dragon made of paper and cane, with lots of people dancing along underneath it.

## SUMMER FESTIVALS

THE SUMMER SOLSTICE is when the Sun is at its highest. After this the days get shorter. The power of fairies, magic, and divination are important aspects of Summer festivals. In many traditional festivals, people light fires to help the Sun to shine. Both fire and water are important in midsummer festivals, and wells and springs are often blessed, while people may bathe in dew, which is sacred, on Midsummer's night or at dawn. The best time to gather magic plants is on Midsummer's Day before dawn, while the dew is still on them.

DANCING DRAGON
The Chinese dragon symbolizes the supernatural powers of air, fire, and water.

# MILLENNIUM

WE ARE APPROACHING the third Millennium, or thousand-year cycle, of the Christian era. Many people are very excited about this, and some well-known prophets have predicted that great events will happen around this time. It is said that the turn of a century, or 100 years, usually signals a change in the way people think and act, so imagine the way things have changed in 1000 years! The last Christian Millennium began when the Vikings were travelling around Europe and parts of North America, 500 years before Columbus!

## THE YEAR 2000

MOST PEOPLE AROUND the globe use the Gregorian calendar for everyday business, so they will be joining in the Millennium celebrations in the year 2000, according to that calendar. However, many people use another calendar for important dates in their faith system or religion. These people will mostly celebrate their own Millennium at the right time according to their own calendars.

Christianity is a very widespread religion, and its calendar is so widely used, that most of the World will see some kind of celebration on the evening of January 31, 1999. Parties have been planned years in advance, and special buildings have been built in many cities! Other people don't believe the Millennium is important, so some won't celebrate at all!

*In the year 1999 and seven months,*
*From the skies shall come a great king of terror.*
*To bring back to life the Great King of Angolmois,*
*Before and after Mars reigns happily.*
NOSTRADAMUS

## MILLENARIAN PROPHECIES

NOBODY REALLY KNOWS what the future holds, but many people have made predictions about the new Millennium. Some people suggest there will be an apocalypse, which is a time of visions and revelations, or a battle between the forces of good and evil, often called Armageddon. This may be followed by peace. Others say that we will learn to live in other dimensions, and Earth will look quite different from the way it looks today.

## AGE OF AQUARIUS

IT'S SAID THAT WE ARE moving from the Piscean Age, which is one of materialism and conflict, to the Aquarian Age. In the Aquarian Age love, peace, abundance, and harmony should form the basis of our lives.

The Age of Aquarius should be a time in which we improve our understanding of who we are, and discover our purpose and personal path to freedom and happiness.

The Millennium has been described as a time of spiritual transformation for individual human beings and the planet as a whole, and a good time to find the way to inner truth.

Many people are trying to predict where the Sun will rise on the first day of the new Millennium, so that they can be among the first to see it, but nobody is quite sure where to go!

SEE ALSO: FAITH SYSTEMS PP.130-133, PROPHETS AND GURUS PP. 134-135, STORY-TELLING PP.40-41

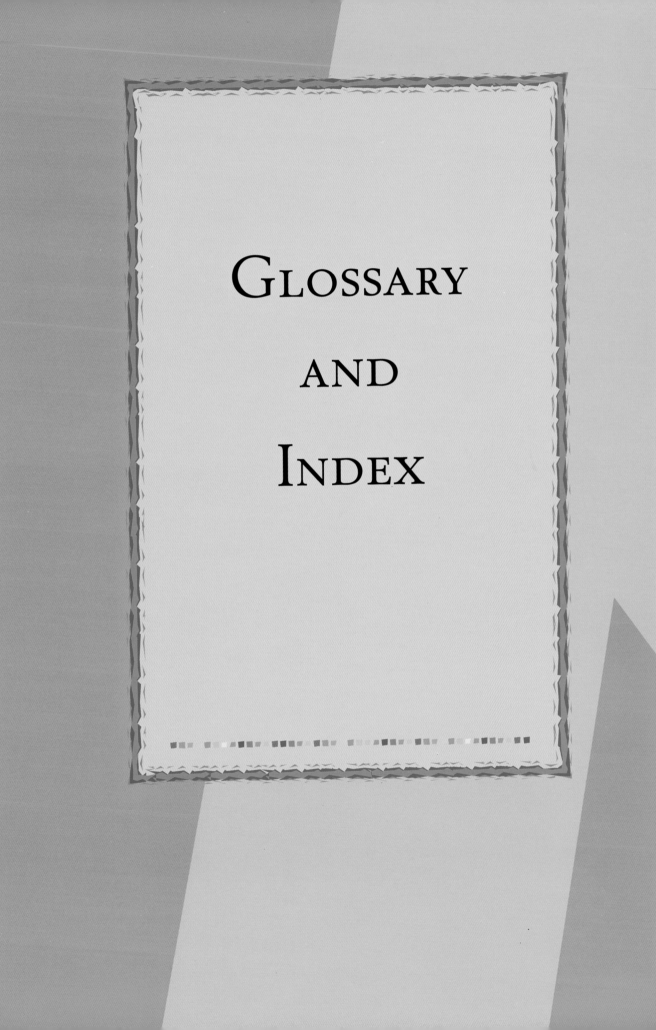

# GLOSSARY

# AND

# INDEX

# GLOSSARY

**Acupressure** A healing method, similar to acupuncture, using thumb pressure on the pressure points instead of needles

**Acupuncture** A Chinese healing method that works with the meridian system, by putting fine needles into certain points to relieve various conditions

**Addiction** A strong need for particular people, foods, drinks, or other things, which is very hard to resist

**Affirmation** A positive statement that you repeat to yourself to help you work toward a goal

**Akashic Record** The record of each soul's thoughts, feelings, and actions during all its lifetimes on Earth

**Alchemy** Changing one thing into another, especially turning base metals into gold

**Alexander Technique** A physical technique used to align the head, neck, and spine correctly

**Amulet** Something people wear or carry to protect them from evil

**Angel** A spiritual being close to God, who may bring messages to Earth

**Aromatherapy** Massage using essential plant oils to affect the mood positively

**Astral body** The part of you that exists in the astral plane

**Astral plane** The spiritual level nearest to the physical Earth

**Astrology** The study of the Sun, Moon, and planets, and how they relate to our lives, according to Western thought

**Atlantis** A lost city, said to exist before the Ancient Greeks and after the Lemurians, inhabited by highly intelligent people who knew about atomic energy, the principles of flight, and the power of crystals

**Aura** The energy surrounding a person's body, which some people can see and use to diagnose and treat disease

**Avalon** A place said to have existed in ancient times in England, and where King Arthur may be buried

**Automatic writing** Hearing messages from the spirit world and writing them down for others to read

**Avatar** A supreme being, or spirit in human or animal form, that brings messages from God

**Ayurvedic Healing** An Indian method of healing, which involves working with the Earth's elements and the body's five physical senses

**Bible** The sacred book of the Christian religion, consisting of the Old Testament, which is also sacred to Jewish people, and the New Testament

**Bioenergetics** A system for releasing feelings and blocked energy in the body through movement

**Biorhythms** Regular physical, emotional, and mental cycles that everyone experiences, either consciously or unconsciously

**Birth Rite** Words and actions that people use as a ritual, or as a tradition, to celebrate the birth of a baby

**Buddhism** The teaching of Buddha and his followers

**Chakra** One of seven energy centers found in the human body, and connected by the meridians

**Ch'i** A positive energy said to flow through the human body, and throughout the World

**Chinese astrology** The Ancient Chinese study of the Sun, Moon, and planets, and how they relate to our lives

**Chiropractic** A way of working with the spine to help heal the body

**Christian** A member of the Christian faith, or religion

**Christianity** The faith system, based on the New Testament, of people who believe that Jesus was the Son of God

**Church** A building for worship and prayer, mostly used by Christians

**Clairaudience** Hearing messages or voices from the "spirit world"

**Clairsentience** Having a physical sense of the presence of spirits or other supernatural forces

**Clairvoyance** Seeing in your mind's eye events or objects from the spirit world

**Consciousness** Our state of awareness. We use our conscious mind when we are thinking logically or carefully

**Counseling** A therapy in which a trained person listens to our problems and anxieties, and advises without judging, to help us find our own answers

**Coven** A group of witches who meet regularly to practice their craft

**Cranial Osteopathy** A method of massaging the bones of the skull to help cure illness in the body

**Crop circles** Circles and other shapes that appear in cornfields inexplicably

**Crystal Healing** Working with crystal energies to heal body, mind, and spirit

**Déjà Vu** When something seems oddly familiar, as though you've experienced it or seen it before

**Demonology** The study of demons

**Dependency** Reliance on another person, substance, or object, so that it is difficult to manage without him, her, or it

**Divination** Receiving information from the spirits, or the Universe, often using physical objects, such as tarot cards

**Dowsing** Finding water, oil, or other substances by holding a rod or pendulum, and noting how it moves

**Drama** The acting out of ideas from the imagination, or creative mind

**Dreams** Pictures and events, often vivid and dramatic, which we experience in our mind whilst asleep

**Dreamtime** A time and place closely linked to this World, in which Aboriginal Australians believe their ancestors live

**Drug** A natural or artificial substance which affects the body in various ways, and can sometimes be used for healing

**Ecology** The study of life and how it relates to its surroundings

**Encounter** An unplanned meeting with, or sighting of, two or more beings, such as ghosts and extraterrestrials

**Enneagram** One of nine different personality types that we can use to describe people

**Environment** Everything around us, in water, in air, and on land, including animals and other people

**ESP** Extrasensory Perception, or receiving information using one's intuition, or sixth sense rather than physical senses.

**ET** Extraterrestrial, a being from a planet other than Earth

**Feldenkrais Therapy** A method of healing using gentle movement to help people become more aware of their body and posture

**Feng Shui** The Chinese system of living in harmony with the natural elements and forces of the Earth

**Flower Remedies** Healing essences made from various flowering plants

**Gaia Theory** The idea that the Earth is a living being that we should care for

**Ghost** The spirit of a dead person, seen or felt in some way by a living person

**God** A divine and revered being, believed by many to be the creator and ruler of the Universe. Some believe there is one God, and others believe there are many

**Graphology** The study of handwriting and how it reflects our personality

**Green Dragon** A luck-bringing animal spirit, said to live in the hills of China, whose energies should be balanced with those of the White Tiger

**Guru** Someone with a strong influence over people, possibly a leader of a cult or particular belief system

**Hades** The Underworld, and home of dead souls, in Greek mythology

**Hallucination** Seeing imaginary things that other people don't see

**Herbalism** Medicine in the form of drinks, ointments, tablets, or poultices, made from herbs or plants

**Higher Self** The spiritual part of a human being, also called the soul

**Hindu** A member of the Hindu faith

**Hinduism** A faith system in which Brahma is seen as the supreme being and people have many lives on Earth

**Holistic treatment** A form of healing that treats the whole body

**Homeopathy** The idea that something that causes a disease, can also cure it

**Hydrotherapy** Various forms of medical treatment using water

**Hypnosis** A trance state in which you are receptive to suggestions that may help you to heal yourself

**Imagination** The ability to picture something in your mind

**Immortal** A being who lives forever

**Incarnation** A life on Earth. To incarnate is to be born

**Intelligence** The ability to understand, usually thought of as a mental ability

**Intuition** Instinct, or "gut feeling," that can act as a warning system. Sometimes called the sixth sense

**Iridology** The diagnosis and treatment of illness achieved by studying the patterns and marks in the eyes

**Islam** The faith of Muslim people, based on the Koran, and the area in which it is practiced

**Jew** A believer in Judaism

**Judaism** The faith of Jewish people, based on the Old Testament and the teachings of the Torah

**Karma** The idea that the way you live in this life will affect your next life

**Kinesiology** The diagnosis and treatment of illness through muscle responses

**Kirlian Photography** A way of showing a person's aura, or the energy surrounding their body, on film

**Knowledge** Wisdom, which we gain throughout our lives

**Koran** The sacred book of the Islamic people, or Muslims

**Legend** Stories told by many generations of people, usually about ordinary people and extraordinary events

**Lemuria** The legendary home of the first humans, who were immortal, which sank under the Indian Ocean

**Levitation** Raising the body, or an object, off the ground, using mind power alone

**Ley Lines** Paths of energy said to run across the Earth's surface

**Life Force** The energy of all living things

**Lyonesse** A lost land, near Cornwall in England, said to have been the site of King Arthur's last battle

**Magic** The use of supernatural power to influence events, people, and objects

**Magnetic Healing** Using magnets on the body to heal the muscles

**Mandala** A symbol used in meditation

**Mantra** A special word or chant used in meditation or prayer

**Martial Arts** Methods of fighting, mostly developed in Eastern countries, and often practiced as a sport

**Massage** releasing stress and tension by kneading and rubbing parts of the body

**Meditation** A way of getting into an altered state of awareness, through quiet concentration

**Medium** a person who acts as a messenger between the spirits and living people

**Meridians** the network of channels in the human body through which the life force, or Ch'i, flows

**Metabolism** The body's process of producing energy from food

**Metaphysics** The study of life beyond the physical World

**Mind Power** Using mental determination to control our thoughts and behavior

**Miracle** An extraordinary event that is inexplicable and welcome

**Mormon** A member of the Church of Jesus Christ of Latter-Day Saints

**Mosque** A building used by Muslims for worship and prayer

**Muslim** A member of the Islamic faith

**Myth** Stories about gods or other superhuman beings

**Naturopathy** A type of healing with four main principles – clean water, clean air, healthy food, and lots of exercise

**Numerology** The study of numbers, such as those in a person's date of birth, and the way they influence our lives

**Occult** Knowledge that is often kept secret, or hidden, such as magical or supernatural abilities

**Omen** A sign or symbol that tells or warns about something in the future

**Oracle** A wise advisor, in the form of a person or an object

**Osteopathy** Treating the whole body through massage and movement of the bones and other parts of the body

**Ouija Board** A tool that groups of people use for communicating with spirits

**Pagan** A religion other than Islam, Judaism, or Christianity, especially one in which many gods are worshiped, or a person or practice relating to such a religion

**Paranormal** *see* **Supernatural**

**Pendulum** A weight hung from a cord, often used in dowsing

**Personality** The characteristics of human beings, such as their emotions, that make them individuals

**Philosophy** The study of the meaning of nature, science, and belief systems

**Phobia** An irrational fear

**Polarity Therapy** A combination of counseling, body work, and improvements in diet to clear energy blocks in the body

**Poltergeist** A mischievous ghost that throws things or makes noises

**Positive Thinking** Concentrating on success rather than failure, which helps you to succeed

**Poultice** A mixture of healing ingredients placed on the skin, often used to help swelling or improve circulation

**Practitioner** A person who practices a profession or art of some kind

**Prayer** A way of asking for help or giving thanks to God or the Universe

**Precognition** Knowing about, or sensing something before it happens

**Prediction** The telling of an event in the future before it happens

**Prophecy** A message or warning from God or the Universe, about something due to occur in the future

**Prophet** Someone who prophesies, or passes on messages from God or the Universe to other people

**Psychic** Someone who is able to receive messages and emotions from the Universe and from people who aren't physically present

**Psychic Healing** A way of healing using personal or external energies

**Psychokinesis** The use of mental determination to move or change physical objects without touching them

**Psychology** The study of human and animal behavior and thoughts

**Psychometry** The reading of thoughts, feelings, or facts by touching an object. Also measuring states of the mind, or thought processes

**Quantum Theory** The belief that everything in the Universe is made up of energy in various forms

**Rebirthing** A therapy in which someone recalls the experience of their birth to help them understand their problems

**Reflexology** A therapeutic method of massaging certain areas of the feet that represent other parts of the body

**Regression** Going into a trancelike state, in which you remember your childhood, or past lives

**Reiki** A Japanese form of healing by touch, using various types of energies

**Reincarnation** Having more than one life, in diffferent times and different bodies

**Rolfing** Deep massage of the muscles and connective tissues

**Sha** A negative energy, the opposite of Ch'i, said to flow into places and people when the Ch'i is weak

**Shaman** A priest who can control good and bad spirits to affect what happens in the World

**Shangri-La** A Paradise said to exist in the Himalayas, the Mongolian mountains, or the Kun Lun mountains of China

**Shiatsu** A Japanese form of healing using massage

**Silver Cord** The cord that is said to link the physical body to the astral body, especially during sleep

**Sixth Sense** *see* **Intuition**

**Solstice** The shortest day of the year, which is in Winter, and the longest day, which is in Summer

**Soul** The essence of the Universe, which is part of every living creature

**Spirit** The infinite, constantly flowing energy of the Universe, or of a person

**Subconscious** The part of our mind that we use without being completely aware of it, such as when we dream

**Supernatural** Extraordinary events that can't be explained in physical terms

**Superstition** A belief that a ritual or object can bring good or bad luck

**Synchronicity** Timing that seems like coincidence, or chance, but which may be a result of the connection between people and the Universe

**Talmud** The sacred book of Jewish religious laws

**Talisman** A symbol that's used to attract good fortune, such as a lucky charm

**Telepathy** Communicating with the mind, without using speech

**Temple** A building made for worship and prayer, and dedicated to a god or gods

**Therapeutic Touch** A form of healing that uses touch to rebalance the energy fields in the body

**Therapy** The treatment of mental, emotional, or physical disorders

**Third Eye** An invisible eye, said to be in the middle of the forehead, where we receive information from other worlds

**Torah** The traditional Jewish teachings, and the scroll on which they are written

**Trance** A state of mind in which we are less aware of physical things than we are normally

**Transcendence** To overcome or work through a current situation or problem, and get to a higher level of learning

**UFOs** Unidentified Flying Objects, often thought to be extraterrestrial spaceships

**Unconscious** The part of our brain that we use without being aware of it. Also the state of someone who has fainted

**Universal Laws** The natural laws of order in the Universe

**Vision** The physical sense of sight, and also a picture in the mind that seems to be a message from God or the Universe

**Visualize** To picture something happening in your mind, in order to help make it happen in reality

**Warlock** *see* **Witch**

**White Tiger** A luck-bringing animal spirit, said to live in the hills of China, whose energies should be balanced with those of the Green Dragon

**Yang** The Chinese name for the positive energy in the Universe

**Yin** The Chinese name for the negative energy in the Universe

**Yoga** A type of physical exercise that benefits the mind, body, and soul

# INDEX

# BIBLIOGRAPHY

*An ABC of Witchcraft Past and Present*, Doreen Valiente,
Robert Hale Ltd., 1973

*Ancient Art*, Jillian Powell, Wayland, 1994

*Art of Hand Reading*, Lori Read, DK, 1996

*Atlas of Holy Places & Sacred Sites*, Colin Wilson, DK, 1996

*Atlas of the Supernatural*, Derek & Julia Parker,
Prentice Hall Press, 1990

*Celtic Tree Mysteries*, Steve Blamires, Llewellyn, 1997

*Circle of Angels Workbook*, Leia A. Green, Crystal Journey Publishing, 1993

*Complete Book of UFOs*, Peter Hough & Jenny Randles, Piatkus, 1994

*Creating Affluence*, Deepak Chopra, Amber Allen Publishing
& New World Library, 1993

*Creative Mythology*, vol. 4 of *The Masks of God*,
Joseph Campbell, Penguin, 1992

*Dates and Meanings of Religious and Other Festivals*,
John G. Walshe & Shriala Warrier, Foulsham, 1993

*Divine Magic*, André & Lynett Singer, Boxtree, 1995

*Donning International Encyclopedic Psychic Dictionary*,
June G. Bletzer, Whitford Press/Schiffer Publishing, 1986

*Emotional Intelligence*, Daniel Goleman, Bloomsbury, 1996

*Enneagrams Made Easy*, Renée Baron & Elizabeth Wagele,
HarperCollins, 1994

*Feng Shui for Beginners*, Richard Webster, Llewellyn, 1997

*Festivals*, Meryl Doney, Watts Books, 1996

*Flower Remedies*, Stefan Ball, Blitz Editions, 1996

*How Trees Help*, Bobbie Kalman & Janine Schaub,
Crabtree Publishing Co., 1992

*Iron John*, Robert Bly, Element Books, 1990

*Isaac Asimov's Mythology and the Universe*,
Gareth Stevens Children's Books, 1990

*Karate*, Karl Oldgate, Cassell, 1991

*Learn about the Body*, Steve Parker, Lorenz Books, 1996

*Looking at Totem Poles*, Hilary Stewart,
Douglas & McIntyre, 1993

*Love is in the Earth*, A. Melody, Earth Love Publishing, 1995

*Meditation – A Treasury of Technique*, Pam & Gordon Smith,
The C.W. Daniel Co. Ltd., 1989

*Mind, Body & Spirit: A Dictionary of Ideas, People & Places*, Eileen
Campbell & J.H. Brennan, Aquarian Press, 1994

*Mysteries of the Supernatural*, Jillian Powell, Aladdin Books,
Watts Books, 1996

*Parkers' Astrology*, Julia & Derek Parker, DK, 1991

*Peoples of the World*, Andrew Langley,
Wayland, 1985

*Philosophy Made Simple*, Richard H. Popkin,
Heinemann, 1986

*Power of Gemstones*, Raymond J.L. Walters,
Carlton, 1996

*Predictions Library Series (Dreams, Graphology,
Numerology, Runes, Tarot)*, David V. Barrett,
DK, 1995

*Primal Myths*, Barbara C. Sproul, Harper
San Francisco, 1992

*Principles of Native American Spirituality*,
Wa'Na'Nee'Che' & Timothy Freke,
Thorsons, 1996

*Quantum Healing*, Deepak Chopra,
Bantam Books, 1989

*Revelations: Wisdom of the Ages*, Paul Roland, Bloomsbury, 1995

*Science in our World: Time*, Brian Knapp & Peter D. Riley,
Atlantic Europe Publishing Co., 1993

*Signs and Symbols*, Miranda Bruce-Mitford, DK, 1996

*Song of the Earth*, Mary Hoffman & Jane Ray, Orion Children's Books, 1995

*Superstitions, The Book of Ancient Lore*, Peter Lorie,
Simon and Schuster, 1992

*World Religions*, John Bowker, DK, 1997

*12 Universal Laws*, Leia Stinnett, Light Tech. Comns. Servs., 1996

*Talking about Drugs*, Fiona Foster & Alexander McCall Smith,
Macdonald Publishers

*The Book of Ogham, The Celtic Tree Oracle*, Edred Thorsson,
Llewellyn Publications, 1992

*The Complete Book of Chinese Horoscopes*, Lori Reid, Element, 1997

*The Complete Book of Dreams*, Julia & Derek Parker, DK, 1995

*The Complete Book of T'ai Chi*, Stewart McFarlane, DK, 1997

*The Complete Book of UFOs*, Peter Hough & Jenny Randles,
Piatkus Books, 1997

*The Complete Family Guide to Alternative Medicine*,
C. Norman Shealy, Element Books, 1997

*The Complete Illustrated Guide to Chinese Medicine*,
Tom Williams, Element Books, 1996

*The Dorling Kindersley Children's Illustrated Encyclopedia*, DK, 1996

*The Encyclopedia of Mind, Magic, and Mysteries*,
Francie X. King, DK, 1991

*The Encyclopedia of Secret Knowledge*, Charles Walker, Rider, 1995

*The Element Encyclopedia of Symbols*, Element Books, 1996

*The Illustrated Book of Myths*, Neil Philip, DK, 1995

*The Illustrated Encyclopedia of Divination*, Stephen Karcher, Element, 1997

*The Psychic Workbook*, Craig & Jane Hamilton-Parker, Vermilion, 1995

*The Secret Life of the Unborn Child*, Dr Thomas Verny & John Kelley,
Warner, 1993

*The Seeker's Guide*, Thorsons 1992

*The White Goddess*, Robert Graves, Carcanet, 1997

*The Whole Person Catalogue*, Mike Considine, Brainwave, 1992

*The Encyclopedia of Witches and Witchcraft*, Rosemary Ellen Guiley,
Facts On File, Inc., 1989

*The Young Martial Arts Enthusiast*, David Mitchell, DK, 1997

*The Young Person's Guide to Music*, Neil Ardley, DK, 1995

*Trees*, Joy Richardson, Watts Books, 1993

*Trees for Healing*, Pamela Louise Chase & Jonathan Pawlik,
Newcastle Publishing Co. U.S., 1991

*Usborne Book of the Earth*, Corinne
Stockley, Usborne, 1992

*What's My Type?*, Kathleen V. Hurley &
Theodore E. Dobson, HarperCollins,
Harper San Francisco, 1992

*Witches*, Stewart Ross, Aladdin Books/
Watts Books, 1996

*World of Festivals*, Philip Steel, Macdonald
Young Books, 1996

*World Religions*, David Self,
Lion Publishing, 1996

*Your Psychic World A-Z*, Ann Petrie,
Arrow, 1984

# ACKNOWLEDGMENTS

**From Joanna Crosse:**

"This is the part I've looked forward to writing most because I'm bursting with gratitude for all the help I've received – both worldly and spiritually – in being able to help put together such an exciting encyclopedia! The subject matter is very close to my heart and I am delighted that this information is going to be read by such a valuable and important part of our society – children! So I'll start my 'thank you' list with special gratitude to my own three – Skye, Merrick, and Sedona, who were truly the inspiration behind this book. My deep thanks and love to my husband Jim Ferguson for his support and encouragement, and to my late father Nicholas Crosse who introduced me to the invisible worlds. Thanks to my mother Jennifer Shennan for all her help and back-up, and to my sister and brother-in-law Pen and Richard Wall for their constant support. My heartfelt thanks also go to Bruce Gyngell, without whose help I might not have taken such a big step forward on my own spiritual journey, and to Jayne Irving for helping in that process.

Thanks to Element Children's Publisher, Barry Cunningham for having the courage to publish this book, and to Christiane Gunzi and the team at Picthall & Gunzi for all the laborious hours that they put in.

Thanks to Sandra Bird, childcarer extraordinaire and to Kate Bird for her great feedback and positive encouragement. Thanks to travelling companion and booklender Pamela Barton, and to fellow bookworm Meg Sanders for believing it could happen. Thanks to Suzzi Tayara and my Stratford friends, all at Mickleton House, and anyone else I have inadvertently left out. Last, but not least, I have to say 'cheers' to my cappucino macchine, which was a constant ally during the writing of this book!"

Chez Picthall and Christiane Gunzi would like to thank everyone who has helped with the production of this book, especially the following organizations and individuals:

**Illustrators:** Dominic Zwemmer, Eric Thomas, William Donohoe, Nicholas Hewetson, Karen Cochrane, Gillie Newman, Yahya El-Droubie, Andrew Waddington, Amanda Ward.
**Studio photography:** Andrew Crawford, Geoff Brightling
**Technical support:** Belinda Ellington
**Editorial assistance:** Jill Somerscales
**Design assistance:** Carol Ann Davis
**US editor:** George Pitcher
**Index:** Lynn Bresler
**Photographic props:** Thanks to Bite Communications Limited for the photograph of the Apple Computer; to Oscar Dahling Antiques; Riadh El-Droubie; and Dominic Zwemmer for the loan of objects; and to Betty Gunzi, for kind permission to use her personal photographs.
**Models:** Thanks to Skye, Merrick, and Sedona Ferguson; Freya Gunzi; Phillippa Sayers; and "Holly," the cat, for their help with modelling. Thanks also to Mark O'Shea, the Curator of Reptiles at the West Midlands Safari Park, for allowing us to photograph him at work.
**General assistance:** Thanks to Geoff Brightling; Duncan & Christine Brown; Belinda Ellington; Steven Goodridge; and Donald Kerr, of Middlesex University Students' Tai Chi Association for help with research; and to Jennifer May for production advice.

Special thanks go to Annie Frankland, and everyone at Picthall & Gunzi for all their hard work.

PICTURE SOURCES:
**Bruce Coleman Collection:** 56bl, 136tl
**Dominic Zwemmer:** 25bl, 38cr, 54cl, 81tr, 109tr, 111tr, 113br, 120bl
**Element Books Ltd:** 65c, 65tcr, 65tr, 118tr, 124tl
**Empics Sports Photo Agency:** 51bl
**E.T. Archive:** 121tr

**Fine Art Photographs:** 41tr and 8tr, 58b
**Fortean Picture Library:** 21bl, 82br, 84br, 93c
**The Hutchinson Library:** 19cr, 24c, 31cr, 49tl, 66tl, 70b, 115tr, 139 tr
**The Kobal Collection:** 104
**Image Bank:** 50bl, 62c, 112c
**Robert Harding Picture Library:** 55cl, 59tl, 78cl, 92cr, 94tl, 114c, 128tr, 129tl, 132b, 135tr, 137c, 138c
**Science Photo Library:** 23cl, 68b
**Spectrum Colour Library:** 54tr, 61br, 117tr, 126tr
**The National Gallery Picture Library:** 134b
**The Savoy Group:** 15tr

l = left; r = right; c = center; b = bottom; a = above; br = bottom right; bl = bottom left; cr = center right; cl = center left; tr = top right; tl = top left; tcr = top center right.

QUOTATION SOURCES:
*Encyclopedia of Mind, Magic, and Mysteries,* Francis X. King, DK, 1991: 80
*Little Book of Zen Wisdom,* John Baldock, Element, 1994: 13
*Oxford Dictionary of Quotations,* Oxford, 1981: 30
*Tao of Jeet Kune Do,* Bruce Lee, Ohara, 1975: 72

*Please note that every effort has been made to trace the copyright holders. Element Children's Books apologizes for any unintentional omissions, and would be happy to include an acknowledgment in subsequent editions of this book.*